D1029681

TO

WALK

—— *in* ——

GOD'S WAYS

TO
WALK
— *in* —
GOD'S WAYS

Jewish Pastoral Perspectives on Illness and Bereavement

ספר והלכת בדרכיו

Joseph S. Ozarowski

JASON ARONSON INC.
Northvale, New Jersey
London

This book was set in 11 pt. Berkeley Oldstyle by Alpha Graphics in Pittsfield, N.H., and printed by Haddon Craftsmen in Scranton, Pennsylvania.

Library of Congress Cataloging-in-Publication Data

Ozarowski, Joseph S.
    To walk in God's ways : Jewish pastoral perspectives on illness
and bereavement / by Joseph S. Ozarowski.
        p. cm.
    Includes bibliographical references and index.
    ISBN 1-56821-388-3
    1. Pastoral counseling (Judaism)   2. Pastoral theology (Judaism)
3. Sick–Pastoral counseling of.   4. Visiting the sick (Judaism)
5. Bereavement–Religious aspects–Judaism.   6. Judaism–Customs and
practices.   7. Mourning customs, Jewish.   I. Title.
BM652.5.095 1995
296.6'1–dc20   94-40782

Manufactured in the United States of America. Jason Aronson Inc. offers books and cassettes. For information and catalog write to Jason Aronson Inc., 230 Livingston Street, Northvale, New Jersey 07647.

Dedicated to the eternal memory
of my *Chavruta* and best friend
Rabbi Stanley F. Greenberg

who taught me how to walk in God's ways
through *hesed*—acts of kindness
and who was taken from us in a car accident
during his youthful years

Contents

III DEATH, GRIEF, AND BEREAVEMENT

Acknowledgments

The genesis of this work began with my doctoral dissertation entitled, "Jewish Pastoral Perspectives at Life's Crisis Points: Illness and Bereavement," finished at Lancaster (Pennsylvania) Theological Seminary in early 1992. My very deep thanks go to Professor Emeritus Paul Irion, distinguished Protestant scholar and theologian, who guided me through the early parts of the project, and Dr. Frank Stalfa, professor of Pastoral Theology at the Seminary, who shepherded me through much of my research and writing and also gave me a great deal of his time and encouragement. I am also grateful to the members of my committee: Rabbi Jacob Goldberg, founder and director of the Mourner's After-Care Institute, Rabbi Dr. Charles Spirn, chief chaplain at Mount Sinai Hospital in New York, and Ms. Mary Roufa, friend and former staff member at Groff Funeral Home in Lancaster, Pennsylvania, all of whom read the original manuscript and offered helpful suggestions and comments. My *hakarat hatov* (deep appreciation) goes to Rabbi Yitchak Knobel, *shlita, rosh yeshivah* of Yeshiva Gedola Ateres Yaakov (South Shore Yeshiva), Hewlett and Elmont, New York, who checked the manuscript for halakhic accuracy. I also thank others whose helpful suggestions have been incorporated into the final draft, including Rabbi Jack Riemer and Rabbi Dr. Emanuel Feldman, editor-in-chief of *Tradition*. I owe a great debt of gratitude to my sister-in-law, Gitelle Rapoport, who did a great deal of editing on the final manuscript and who gave many helpful suggestions on writing style.

I also acknowledge the help of my publisher, Arthur Kurzweil, and the staff at Jason Aronson Inc. Their encouragement and help have been invaluable.

My very special thanks go to the members and leaders of my congregation, the Elmont Jewish Center, Elmont, New York, who graciously allowed me to conduct my studies, research, and writing while serving as their rabbi. Their kindness and support has sustained me throughout the entire project. Besides using them as a sounding board while teaching much of this material, they have helped me develop the pastoral-lay relationship and bond that I describe in the book. A rabbi could not ask for a sweeter, lovelier, and finer group of congregants to serve.

I offer my thanks to my wife, Ashira, and my children, Eli, Shalom, Chani, and Raphi, for their patience and tolerance during the time I spent writing and researching this book. I pray that they also be privileged to walk in God's ways of kindness and *hesed*. I also appreciate the encouragement and support I received from my dear parents, Oscar and Eva Ozarowski of St. Louis, and from my dear in-laws, Rabbi Dr. Shlomo and Hilda Rapoport of Chicago.

Finally, I humbly thank *Hashem Yitbarakh*, the Almighty, Who has guided me on this particular path of Torah learning and practice. By learning to walk in God's ways, I hope and pray that I can guide others on those ways as well.

Introduction

THE NEED FOR THIS BOOK

The importance of pastoral care has grown dramatically as more people seek out clergy assistance when in trouble and more clergy are taking the requisite training. Yet very little has been written on this subject from a Jewish perspective, specifically in the areas of illness and bereavement. This is true even though illness and grief are experiences all people must encounter at some point in their lives. The goal of this book is to examine and present material on pastoral theology and care regarding sickness and grief from a Jewish outlook. Jewish tradition has much to say on these topics, and yet this material has never been fully explored or offered in a manner accessible to the English-reading public.

While I refer in the text to earlier works in the field, this book is a pioneering effort in several ways. First, there is a paucity of sources in English regarding the *mitzvah* of visiting the ill, and this is therefore one of the first major works on *bikur holim* written in English. This book uses a wide array of classic Hebrew texts to develop a Jewish approach to visiting the patient and dealing with illness. Second, this book combines halakhic, theological, and clinical perspectives regarding illness and grief, unlike many other works that deal with only one of these perspectives. Third, the footnotes provide extensive background and reference material, allowing readers of differing Jewish educational levels to further study the sources. Finally, my book discusses tasks for both rabbis and laity, thus helping to better define the important role of both the rabbi and of every Jew in the pastoral care of the ill and the mourner.

Besides helping rabbis and Jewish laity understand their pastoral responsibilities to the ill and grieving, this material may serve as reference reading and guidance for non-Jews interested in the Torah's approach to illness and bereavement.

HOW TO USE THIS BOOK

The reader will find most value in using this book as a resource for study and thought before tragedy strikes, or as a source for further reflection afterward, in order to better understand what he or she has endured. The perspective I am attempting to offer will be helpful in explaining why Jews practice what they do at these times, as well as the therapeutic value of Jewish tradition. It is also possible to use this book at times of crisis. I have included the important halakhic highlights within the text, and the book can be used as a practical guide during illness and bereavement.

There is a great deal of original Torah source material within these pages. While some might consider this an overuse of proof texts, my desire is for the reader to actually study this material. I have attempted to render classic Hebrew and Aramaic sources into an English understandable to most readers. As a result, all translations within this work are mine, except as noted. I take full responsibility for them. In addition, I have attempted to use gender-neutral language in the text, except for the translations where this would render the material awkward and inauthentic. Nevertheless, it should be noted that referring to the Deity in the masculine does not mean that God is a human male.

One final note: I write this book as an Orthodox rabbi, a believer in the Torah as God's gift to us and in the halakhic process as the means by which we make the Torah come alive in our lives. Yet my book is not meant for an exclusively Orthodox or observant clientele. I aim to show that the Torah's wisdom is meant for all Jews and that the framework of *halakhah* and Jewish theology related to illness and bereavement can offer emotional and therapeutic benefit, facilitating healing for all those in need. The more I have studied this material, the more I am humbled by the wisdom of the Torah and our Sages of blessed memory in these matters of life and death. We need to reclaim this wisdom without denominational labels. The principles and goodness of our tradition have much to teach those who wish to bring healing to a world with more than its share of sickness and grief.

I

PASTORAL THEOLOGY AND JUDAISM

1

The Basis for a Jewish Pastoral Theology

RABBINIC SOURCES

The crisis points of life—illness and death—are an integral part of our existence. We cannot escape them. We constantly face the suffering of our own illnesses and those of our loved ones. We also will face the reality of death—of our loved ones and ourselves—at some point in our lives. Pondering this, one might be led to adopt a rather morbid conception of life, and indeed, there are many thinkers who opine in this direction. Judaism, however, teaches that we affirm life even while facing pain and death. A major way in which we do this is by imitating our Creator, or walking in God's paths.

This idea is beautifully illustrated in rabbinic sources:

> R. Hama said in the name of R. Hanina: What does it mean, "You shall walk after the Lord your God"? (Deuteronomy 13:5). Is it possible for a person to walk and follow God's presence? Does not [the Torah] also say "For the Lord your God is a consuming fire"? (Deuteronomy 4:24). But it means to walk after the attributes of the Holy One,[1] Blessed be He. Just as He clothed the naked, so you too clothe the naked, as it says "And the Lord made the man and his wife leather coverings and clothed them" (Genesis 3:21). The Holy One, Blessed be He, visits the ill, as it says,

"And God visited him [Abraham] in Elonei Mamreh" (Genesis 18:1); so you too shall visit the ill. The Holy One, Blessed be He, comforts the bereaved, as it says, "And it was after Abraham died and that God blessed his son Isaac . . . " (Genesis 25:11), so too shall you comfort the bereaved. The Holy One, Blessed be He, buries the dead, as it says, "And He buried him [Moses] in the valley" (Deuteronomy 34:6), so you too bury the dead.[2]

A similar excerpt is found elsewhere in the Talmud. R. Yosef understood a particular biblical passage (Exodus 18:20), "And you shall show them the way that they shall walk on it and the act that they shall do . . ." as follows:

"You shall show" refers to the house of their lives. "The way"— this is the practice of loving-kindness [Heb. *gemilut hasadim*]. "That they shall walk"—this refers to visiting the sick. "On it" refers to burial. "And the act" refers to the Law. "That they shall do" refers to acting[3] beyond the requirement of the Law.[4]

Thus in Jewish eyes, we can deduce from the above passages that one who truly wishes to walk in the path of God must imitate God. Specifically, this refers to *hesed*, loving-kindness, at the crisis points of life such as illness and death. By comforting the bereaved and cheering the ill, we follow "God's path," acting as God does. We are bidden to act even beyond the call of duty, beyond the specifics of the Law. This is illustrated in a famous passage that has been incorporated into the daily liturgy, recited at the beginning of each morning service.

These are the things of which one enjoys the fruits in this world, while the principal remains in the hereafter; namely: Honoring father and mother, the practice of kindness, early attendance at the house of study morning and evening, hospitality to strangers, visiting the sick, dowering the bride, attending the dead, devotion in prayer, making peace between people, but the study of Torah is equal to them all.[5]

Traditional belief holds that there are 613 *mitzvot* or commandments given by God in the Torah. The Rabbis could have used many other *mitzvot* to show how we can walk in God's ways, such as eating kosher meat, observing the Sabbath or Holidays, participating in the sacrificial system of Temple times, abiding by the civil laws of the Torah regarding murder or thievery, or perhaps by following the various moral laws such as those regarding adultery.[6] Indeed, Jews who have observed these laws and continue to observe them generally believe they are following God's ways. Yet all of the above passages refer to the aspects of Torah tradition that deal with human kindness. They show us a loving, caring God whom we can imitate and in whose ways we can walk by connecting to each other and caring for each other, specifically at the moments of illness and grief.

This approach to a Jewish pastoral theology shows the Jewish God as a God Who deeply cares about us and wants us to care about each other. This care becomes most crucial at crisis points when people are most vulnerable, such as times of illness and death. At these times, people truly need to be assured of God's love and presence. And at these times, our own imitation of God's love can be most effective in helping the troubled individual.

While Christianity would probably subscribe to these ideas as well, one of the major differences between Christian and Jewish tradition is that the Torah offers a framework with specific ways of carrying out these ideas. The details of this framework for dealing with illness and grief will be fleshed out in the coming chapters, which will stress that all Jews, not just rabbis, are called upon to follow God's ways in these areas.

The means for imitating God in human relationships are established through empathy. Webster defines empathy as

> The action of understanding, being aware of, being sensitive to, and vicariously experiencing the feelings, thoughts, and experiences of another . . . without having the feelings, thoughts, experiences fully communicated in an objectively explicit manner; also, the capacity for this.[7]

This implies that one need not have had the same experience to be a helping person. One does not have to have suffered cancer to effectively visit a cancer patient. One may offer comfort to a grieving survivor though one's own parents may still be alive. While having had the identical experience may enhance the visit, the Torah does not require this as a prerequisite for the *mitzvah* of visiting the sick or comforting the bereaved. After all, the average Jew cannot "walk in the paths of the Almighty" if this requires us to suffer exactly the way the recipient of our kindness is suffering.[8]

David Switzer, in defining empathy within a pastoral situation, points out that those who offer pastoral care are not necessarily sharing identical feelings.[9] In fact it is possible that clergy, and in particular hospital chaplains, suffer "burnout" when becoming too emotionally involved with their work.[10] Rather, as Switzer suggests, we are referring to a cognitive empathy, one in which the helping person is aware of the feelings of the other person in an imaginative way and communicates this awareness to that person. This type of "accurate empathy and its accurate communication"[11] involves more than simply being empathic. As Switzer writes, "It must be communicated in both verbal and nonverbal ways, but with an emphasis on the verbal."[12]

In other words, a sensitive cognitive empathy actively shared with the person in need helps break down the isolation of the person, helping him or her to feel better understood. This in turn will help the persons to further discover themselves and guide themselves through their crisis period.[13]

This type of pastoral relationship obviously makes demands of the giver. The Talmud tells a lovely story:

> R. Joshua B. Levi met Elijah [the prophet] sitting at the opening of the cave of R. Shimon Bar Yohai. . . .[14] He said to him [Elijah], "When will the Messiah come?" He answered, "Go and ask him himself." "Where is he sitting?" "At the gates of the city."[15] "What is his sign [that I may recognize him]?" "He sits among the poor who suffer from wounds."[16] All of them unbind and rebind [their wounds] in one act.[17] But he unbinds and rebinds [each wound] separately, saying, "Should I be wanted, these [all being dressed at once] should not delay me."[18]

Rashi clearly understands the text to mean "and he is wounded as well," that the Messiah shares in the suffering of those around him. As proof of this, Rashi quotes the passage from Isaiah 53:4, "But our illness he carried and our pain, he suffered."[19] From this we see how the Messiah, descendant of King David and the very symbol of redemption in Judaism, shares the pain of those who suffer, especially of those who are sick. He is able to do this because he himself feels the wounds. In other words, he shares empathy with those who are afflicted. He is able to offer redemption and hope because he understands what suffering is.[20] He may, however, address his own pain in a different manner from the others, since he has special responsibilities.

From this we see a model for care-giving in the sense we have described. The giver should be able to share the pain of the sufferer in the cognitive and imaginative sense, without necessarily feeling the same thing. The giver's understanding and conveying that understanding to the sufferer help alleviate the sense of aloneness and thus alleviate the pain itself.

INTRODUCTION TO PASTORAL CARE AND THEOLOGY FROM NON-JEWISH SOURCES—HISTORY

Much of what we have defined in the framework of *hesed* and empathy would be placed by the Western world (or at least the Protestant world) in the category of pastoral care. Pastoral care in recent years has truly become a major component of the helping field. Yet much of the literature comes from the Protestant tradition.[21] Before we develop a Jewish pastoral theology and practice, some background on the non-Jewish roots of the pastoral field might be helpful.

Historically, pastoral care as developed in Protestantism has been defined as "Cure of Souls," with the pastor acting as a "Physician of Souls," connected to the classic Christian function of shepherding.[22] The pastor as shepherd cares for the flock by translating religious theology into the language of relationships, which can become a curing and lifesaving function. Thus, through the pastor's caring for and curing people spiritually, the Church relates to human need. The ultimate goal of this labor is a renewal of the person, as well as his/her relationship to others and to God, all within the context of the Church. In this century the emphasis moved from theory to practical application of pastoring.[23] Today, the theology upon which pastoral care is based is a central element of Protestant Divinity or clergy training.

OVERVIEW AND BACKGROUND ISSUES IN PASTORAL CARE

The public has realized that the clergy offer much to people who hurt or are in need. But why do people come to pastors, priests, and rabbis for help? My work with individuals has led me to believe that in this country, people of all faiths have certain expectations of their clergy. As told to me by a non-Jewish synagogue employee, "When I experience death, illness, financial problems, issues with children, really any crisis situation, I want my priest to be there, to offer comfort, to help, or just to be present."[24]

The literature on pastoral theology and care offers several reasons why people constantly turn to clergy in times of crisis.[25] The same sources also offer insight on why clergy can be effective as counselors.

1. Clergy have a rich tradition of serving their people's needs and generally continue to maintain that tradition.

2. The various religious groups embody powerful symbols and literature offering comfort, hope, and healing to people in pain. Theological themes that assist those in need include faith, a prophetic context, ethics, the power of blessing, as well as the religious community's own resources.

3. One of religion's basic purposes is to foster love of God and neighbor and thus love of oneself. Counseling helps a person in this direction and thus implements religion's intent.

4. People's expectations of clergy, clergy's context and setting within a religious institution, and clergy's goals of fostering spiritual growth all add to the uniqueness of their pastoral role as counselors.

5. People with any type of religious instinct (even if not religious by any formal affiliation or practice) will generally trust clergy to be caring.

6. Finally, clergy are constantly available, and they are generally cost free.

As a result, people will inevitably come to clergy for help whether clergy desire it or not. Therefore, it is important for clergy to possess training in this area.

Religious professionals are often somewhat limited in their work as therapists by time, training, role, transference (of client onto clergy) and questions of payment.[26] Yet, for ethical and theological dilemmas, religious and quasi-religious questions, familial issues, questions regarding the absolutes and ultimates of life, and the like, pastoral counseling may actually be superior to regular therapy. A pastoral counselor engenders trust, has established relationships, is available, has specific family contexts, and specializes in crisis ministry, tying all the above to their theological training and religious role.

Based on the shepherding paradigm, pastoral work has historically been developed in several specific areas:[27]

1. Healing—in the sense of restoring functional wholeness to the impaired spirit.[28] Restoration may only refer to the process; something new may ultimately emerge. Protestant pastoral theology ties this to Original Sin doctrine, defining sin as a disease that plagues all. Since all people need healing from the sinful condition that is the symbol of the entire human condition, pastoral care becomes the Church's means of cure.[29]

2. Sustaining—keeping the person alive, especially through crises (shock or loss) or degenerative situations. The minister offers this help to all, not merely to those who come within religious contexts. The sufferer is assisted in drawing on his/her own resources to face the issues of faith, doubt, and hope in a critical period. The minister, in other words, helps the person endure the crisis.

3. Guiding—rather than merely reflecting the individual parishioner's feelings or acting in a prescriptive and directive manner, the minister guides that person. Using his/her knowledge, the minister does not force the person's behavior or feelings but instead acts in the classical role of shepherd. The pastor leads but does not persuade, defining options but also acting in a client-centered, non-directive manner.[30]

4. Reconciling Broken Relations[31]—within this context, the pastor helps parishioners reconcile with their fellow humans and Maker,

thus obtaining forgiveness. If the basic purpose of pastoral care and counseling is fulfilling the Church's goal of love for God and neighbor, then ministers who counsel become God's instruments of healing and growth. This in turn overcomes the alienation from God, from others, and ultimately, from ourselves, described by the Christian theological term "sin."

It is possible to see this type of pastoral care within a social sense, with God becoming more alive through reestablishing a person's social wholeness, as well as a catalyst for religious growth. Counseling helps the person nurture a sense of faith and trust. Focusing on God and ultimate meanings in life, pastoral care and counseling mixes religion and psychology, as well as philosophy, ethics, theology, and the helping disciplines. Thus, the pastoral counselor commands respect using these resources and the symbols of the religious community.[32]

Christian thought, which is far from monolithic, uses various theological models as well as rituals to assist people in trouble. These models use elements of their respective theological traditions in defining the role of the clergy in helping those in need. From the clergy's perspective, pastoral care provides healing, spiritual sustenance, guidance, and nurturance of relationships; in addition, religious language can be used to diagnose people's spiritual and emotional condition.[33] The various Christian approaches to pastoral issues differ among themselves in the goal for this care. They also differ in the models for care, using theology, ritual, Scripture, and, to varying degrees, the behavioral sciences as sources.[34]

Judaism also seeks to sustain its people in times of crisis, and many of its goals are shared with other faiths. However, its theological basis is quite different because Judaism is based in the Torah and rabbinic tradition, as will be amplified in the next chapters. A pastoral approach based in Jewish tradition would attempt to integrate psychological insights with Jewish sources and practices. Also, Judaism posits the idea that "pastoral care" is not only the purview of the "pastor"—or in our case the rabbi—but a responsibility belonging to every Jew. We hope to develop these themes more fully in future chapters.

In America, clergy of all faiths are called upon to assume the pastoral role, as defined earlier in this book. Rabbis as well as all religious leaders are expected to offer comfort in times of trouble and strength in the face of adversity. They may be asked to explain God's actions, as if such a thing were possible. They act as shepherds, guiding their flock through the tortuous paths of life.

The pastoral role is fairly well developed in the Protestant tradition, with an abundance of literature on pastoral care, theology, and counseling. While rabbis today are also expected by their congregants to act as counselors and pastors, there is a distinct paucity of material in this area to guide them. Is there a Jewish pastoral theology? Does our tradition have the source material and resources to lead our religious leaders and laypeople into the area Christians call "pastoral"?

It is my contention that the answer to this question is a strong "yes." I would define Jewish pastoral care as using the tools of Jewish tradition, liturgy, and philosophy to guide people through crisis periods. In the coming pages I will attempt to sift through *halakhah*, (Jewish law and tradition), explore the theology that both emerges from and underlies *halakhah*, study the liturgy of illness and bereavement, and use clinical examples to illustrate Jewish pastoral thinking in these areas. This process will show that Jewish tradition offers great therapeutic benefit to those in these painful situations. I will attempt to combine our classic Jewish sources with modern non-Jewish sources dealing with these issues and some of my own original ideas built on all these sources. In this way the material already found in our tradition can be better organized and presented to serve the needs of modern Jews who, like all people, find themselves in crisis and pain.[35]

II

BIKUR HOLIM

2

Roots for Visiting
the Sick

BASIC SOURCES

In our first chapter we offered several talmudic examples of how one can walk in God's ways. The example of visiting the sick was predicated on God's appearance to Abraham following the latter's circumcision in Genesis 18:1-2. The *Midrash* offers a lovely story regarding this.

> When He revealed Himself, the Holy One, Blessed Be He, stood and Abraham sat, as it says, " . . . And he was sitting in the doorway. . . ." It is the custom of the world that when a student is sick and the teacher goes to visit, [other] students go first and say, "[There is] a delegation of the teacher to the house of the patient," meaning that the teacher wishes to visit the student. Not so the Holy One, Blessed Be He. When Abraham was circumcised and was in pain from the circumcision, He told the messengers to go and visit. But before they arrived, God came in first, as the Torah says (Genesis 18:1), "And God appeared to him," and after that (Genesis 18:2), "And he lifted his eyes and saw three. . . ." Is there no greater Humble One than this?[1]

From God's very visit to Abraham, we deduce the commandment of *bikur holim*—visiting the sick. Nahmanides and others assume that this *mitzvah* is biblical in its halakhic origin, putting it on a par with the other divinely ordained commandments. [2] However, Maimonides writes that regardless of its importance, the halakhic basis is less than explicitly biblical:

> It is a positive commandment from the words of the Rabbis [e.g., not directly from the Torah] to visit the sick . . . and this comes under *gemilut hasadim*, the acts of kindness that have no requisite amount. And even though all these are from their words [rabbinic in origin] they come under the [general biblical] category of, "You shall love your neighbor as yourself" (Leviticus 19:18).[3]

It is interesting to note that elsewhere Maimonides points out that the Torah did not need to specify certain commandments in its text.[4] Specifically, this refers to certain *mitzvot* that people regularly do on their own, such as visiting the sick, burying the dead, comforting the mourners, and other acts of kindness. Rather, these commandments are deduced via the hermeneutical rules through which the Torah is halakhically analyzed.[5]

Yet other sources see the *mitzvah* as more generalized and not traceable to a specific source. They deduce *bikur holim* from references in the Talmud that cite the broad obligation to save lives and the quote from Leviticus 19:16, "Do not stand idly by the blood of your brother."[6] The Talmud itself gives a hint at a biblical source from a most interesting analysis of the rebellion of Korah (Numbers 16:29). Here, in response to Korah's actions, Moses appeals to God by asking for a miraculous destruction of Korah and his followers. The Talmud text reads:[7]

> Resh Lakish said: Where is the visiting of the sick indicated in the Torah? In the verse "If these men die the common death of all men, or if they be visited after the visitation of all men, etc." How is it implied? Raba answered [The verse means this] If these men die the common death of all men who lie sick abed and men come in and visit them, what will people say? "The Lord has not sent me," for this task.

This means that the normal way of life is that people get sick and die; [8] others come and visit during the sick period. Moses says that if this is the end of Korah, a normal weakening toward death with the accompanying visitors, then his own (Moses') mission is not valid.

Thus, we see that all of the sources emphasize the significant importance of *bikur holim*, with either a biblical, quasi-biblical, or rabbinic basis.

It should be noted that the dying ill are considered as other invalids in terms of the *mitzvah* of *bikur holim*. Jewish law and theology deems them to have the same rights as all living individuals. There are other issues, such as questions of medical ethics and the like, that relate more specifically to the elderly and dying, but they are beyond the scope of our work. We will, however, touch on these topics when they apply within our context.

A PSALM FOR *BIKUR HOLIM*

The rabbinic approach to Psalm 41 offers an excellent introduction to a theology of *bikur holim*. The first few verses of this psalm read:

> Happy is he that considers the poor
> The Lord will deliver him in the day of evil
> The Lord preserve him and keep him alive, let him
> be called happy in the land;
> And You will not deliver him unto the greed of his
> enemies.
> The Lord will support him upon his bed of illness
> May You turn all his lying down in his sickness.[9]

The Talmud understands this passage as referring to visiting the sick.

> Rab says: He who visits the sick will be delivered from the punishments of *Gehenna*, for it is written, "Happy is he that considers the poor, the Lord will deliver him in the day of evil." "The poor" [Heb. *dal*] means none other than the sick as it is written, "He will cut me off from pining sickness" [Heb. *mi-dalah*—Isaiah 38:12], or from this verse: "Why are you so poorly [Heb. *dal*] you son of the King?" (2 Samuel 13:4). Evil refers to *Gehenna* for it is writ-

ten, "The Lord has made all things for Himself, yea even the
wicked, for the day of evil" (Proverbs 16:4). Now if one does
visit, what is his reward? [You ask] What is his reward? Even as
has been said "He will be delivered from the punishment of
Gehenna!" But what is his reward in this world? "The Lord will
preserve him and keep him alive, let him be called happy in the
land; and You will not deliver him unto the greed of his enemies."
"The Lord will preserve him" from the Evil Urge; "And keep him
alive," saving him from his sufferings. "Let him be called happy
in the land," that all will take pride in him; "And You will not
deliver him into the greed of his enemies," that he may procure
friends like Naaman's who healed his leprosy, and not chance
upon friends like Rehaboam's who divided his kingdom.[10]

The basic rabbinic understanding and translating of this psalm
would then be, "Happy is he who visits the sick;[11] The Lord will
deliver him [the visitor] in the day of evil."[12] The rabbinic interpretation is an authentic textual reading of the Hebrew *dal*, as found
elsewhere in biblical literature. *Dal* means detached, hanging, open,
weak, drawn out, lessened, loosened, or lowered.[13] A Hebrew noun
related to this root word is *delet* or door. Obviously, the word *dal*
refers to the existential state of the patient, not knowing his or her
fate, one whose condition is weakened and whose life is now opened
to harm. It may also describe the emotional state of an invalid, filled
with loneliness, confusion, depression, and detachment.

The classic commentaries on the psalm reinforce this reading
of the verse and its application to *bikur holim*.[14] For example, Ibn
Ezra in his comments emphasizes the intelligence, empathy, and
compassion of the visitor:

> Some say "considers" [Heb. *maskil*] means sees; the more cor-
> rect [interpretation for *maskil*] is to understand with one's heart
> regarding the patient; and some say *maskil* is an active verb re-
> ferring to [actual] visiting, speaking to the heart [of the patient],
> and understanding him/her.

A modern commentary adds that these verses could refer to
the idea of God's reward for one who considers the implications of
sickness and healing.[15]

The Talmud's understanding of this psalm also emphasizes God's presence and sustenance for the invalid.

> Rabin said in the name of Rav: From where do we know that the Holy One, Blessed Be He, sustains the sick? As it says, "The Lord will support him upon his bed of illness" (Psalm 41). Rabin also said in the name of Rav: From where do we know that the Divine Presence rests above the invalid's bed? From the verse "The Lord will support him upon his bed of illness."[16]

From this source, we see that the patient is assured of God's presence and love in time of illness. A visitor would truly be imitating God by sharing his or her presence as well. The idea of the Divine Presence accompanying the patient also plays a role in the demeanor of the visitor, as we will see later in the next chapter.

As a reward for the kind act of visiting the sick the psalmist declares:

> The Lord will deliver him in the day of evil.
> The Lord preserve him and keep him alive, let him
> be called happy in the land;
> And You will not deliver him unto the greed of his enemies.

The commentaries elucidate as follows:

> Rashi: The Lord will sustain him [the visitor]
> when he is on his own sickbed.
> Ibn Ezra: He [the visitor] will live long years.
> Metzudot: He will be praised by his peers and not
> given to the desires of his enemies.[17]

The psalm continues:

> "The Lord will support him upon his bed of illness
> May You turn all his lying down in his sickness."

There is a dispute among the commentaries about whether this divine support refers to the visitor (as a reward—Rashi) or the patient (God's succor of the ill person—Talmud, some moderns). It is most interesting to note that the Targum, the Aramaic translation of the psalm, renders "support" (Heb. *yisad*) as visit! Thus, this verse would be read, "The Lord will visit him while he is on the bed of illness," referring to either a divine visit to the patient (as suggested regarding Abraham), or that the visitor will in turn be visited by the Almighty when taken ill (as a reward for the visitor's kindness in attending the sick).

It seems that this psalm lends strong credence to the notion that true visitation of the sick involves empathy, sensitivity, and understanding. Apparently, the psalmist felt this in his experience, and he assures us that the visit is a major value in Judaism, richly rewarded by God.

We may ask one remaining question regarding a contemporary pastoral understanding of the "divine reward" promised by the psalmist. How are we to understand the reward today given to either the professional pastoral-care giver or to any Jew fulfilling the commandment of *bikur holim*? Even the Talmud itself says, "Antigonus of Sokho . . . used to say, 'Do not be like servants who serve the master for the sake of receiving a reward, but rather be like servants who serve the master without the expectation of receiving a reward.'"[18]

I would suggest that a key concept here is that of God's support, sustenance, and preservation. We are promised God's blessings in a general sense for a sensitive, compassionate visit to the ill. In a deeper way, we may suggest that the visitor is assured of God's presence in his or her time of need. In a secular sense, it could be said that serving others may have a positive impact on one's life, as recent studies indicate that people who engage in frequent volunteer activity may enhance their health.[19] Spiritually, the commentaries suggest that the Almighty will be with the visitor in his or her time of difficulty. Thus, God's presence can be said to be the greatest reward one can have.[20]

3

Bikur Holim
from Rabbinic Sources

THEOLOGICAL ASPECTS

As mentioned in the last chapter, the term *bikur holim* means "visiting the sick." We have already defined "visit" as a caring, understanding presence. This empathic, sensitive visit is in direct imitation of God, Who accompanies the patient. "Sick" refers to anyone with a disease of body or mind.[1] While there are some early views to the contrary, it does not seem that one must view sickness as specific divine punishment for sin.[2] In fact, Judaism has always seen in suffering and illness the chance for growth, return to the Almighty, renewal, and regeneration.[3] For example, on the verse from Song of Songs, "For I am lovesick," the Rabbis comment: "Says the Community of Israel to the Holy one, Blessed Be He, 'Master of the Universe! May all the diseases You bring upon me be only in order to cause me to love You.'" [To return me to a better state—Commentary of Matnat Kehuna.][4]

In other words, sickness is an inevitable part of life. But illness, like any experience, can be seen as a means to help us grow spiritually. In this, God is seen as partner, not punisher. For this reason the Talmud openly says that God's very presence (Heb. *Shekhinah*) rests above the patient's bed.[5]

21

The process of healing also involves a spiritual renewal. As the Talmud puts it:

> R. Alexandri said in the name of R. Hiyya B. Abba: A patient does not recover from sickness until all his sins are forgiven, as it is written, "Who forgives all your iniquities; Who heals all your diseases" (Psalm 103:3). R. Hamnuna said: He then returns to the days of his youth, for it is written, "His flesh shall be fresher than a child's, he shall return to the days of his youth" (Job 33:25).[6]

This passage does not mean that people who cannot recover are unforgiven. But the illustrative quote from Psalms clarifies that healing is coupled with forgiveness and God's love. While all aspire to a physiological cure from illness, we also know this is often wishful thinking. But cure can also be spiritually defined, as the Hebrew term *refuat hanefesh* implies.[7] Forgiveness from sin that may accompany a cure can make one's life spiritually fresher.

At the same time, the Talmud recognized the difficulty in obtaining physical healing:

> R. Alexandri also said in the name of R. Hiyya B. Abba: Greater is the miracle wrought for the sick than for Hananiah, Mishael, and Azariah [who were placed in the fiery furnace and delivered]. [The miracle] of Hananiah, Mishael, and Azariah was fire kindled by a human, which all can extinguish; while that of a sick person is a heavenly fire, and who can extinguish that?[8]

We have already spoken of the great importance of visiting the ill, its merit and reward for the visitor.[9] What does it do for the patient? The Talmud in *Nedarim* says:

> R. Abba said in the name of R. Hanina: One who visits a patient takes away a sixtieth of his pain.[10] Said [the rabbis] to him: If so, let sixty people visit him and restore him to health. He replied: The sixtieth is as the tenth spoken of in the school of Rabbi [Judah the Prince. This means that a sixtieth of the remainder of the pain is removed each time a visitor comes, but visits can never fully remove all the pain;] and providing that the visitor was a *ben gilo*.[11]

Before we define the Talmud's term *ben gilo*, it is important to note that many talmudic commentaries hold that any visitor, *ben gilo* or not, can lighten the patient's pain.[12] The codes do not even mention the term, and apparently the *halakhah* does require the visitor to be a *ben gilo*.[13] However, an analysis of *ben gilo* will be helpful in understanding the issue of empathy in *bikur holim*.

The classical commentaries dispute the definition of *ben gilo*. R. Asher, R. Nissim, and others suggest that the term refers to a visitor of the same astrological sign as the patient (Heb. *ben mazlo*).[14] Rashi here and Jastrow define *ben gilo* as one of the same age. All these commentaries imply that the connections of either sign or age somehow affect the efficacy of the visit. Yet other sources explain *ben gilo* as one "who looks like and behaves like" the patient.[15]

I would suggest a different explanation, based on other references to *ben gilo* and its linguistic definition. Elsewhere, the Talmud[16] refers to Nebuchadnezar and Ahasuerus as *ben gilo*, which means they had the same mind or mentality.[17] This implies an emotional connection. Another *midrash* that goes to the heart of the Hebrew *gil* reads as follows: "God brings *gillin*—groups and circles of friends[18] —into the world. When one of the *gil* dies, the entire *gil* grieves. One member of the group worries about the entire group. . . ."[19]

The commentaries also refer to the definition of *gil* as joy and these groups are, therefore, people who share joy (and sorrow). One's spouse is part of the *gil*.[20] The Hebrew root letters of the word *gil* are identical to those for the Hebrew words for trepidation, appearance, and revelation (*galeh*).

Based on the above, *ben gilo* must refer to some kind of a open relationship. People within the same *gil* share an empathic connectedness, based on emotion, sharing, and similar feelings. Being a part of the same circle appears to be the meaning of the Talmud's text regarding a *ben gilo*. In fact there is a parallel to this text in the *Midrash* that supports this definition.

R. Huna says: One who visits the sick lessens one sixtieth of the illness. It was asked of R. Huna: If so, let sixty people go up [to visit] and then they will all go down to the market together! [The patient will be totally relieved of the illness]. Said he to them:

Sixty![21] But only if they [the visitors] love him [the patient] as their own souls [will an actual sixtieth of illness be lessened]. But even without this [the visit] relieves him.[22]

As the commentaries explain, this deep, soulful love is the definition of *ben gilo*, such as the love of David and Jonathan.[23] If this relationship of empathy is present, then a percentage of the illness is lessened. Establishing a relationship, piercing the loneliness, sharing the suffering, making the patient aware that another can somehow perceive his or her feelings, can all contribute to lightening the emotional burden of the invalid. It is also possible that this cognitive sharing can positively affect the physical condition of the patient.[24] But even if one cannot be a *ben gilo*, a visit can be helpful and a *mitzvah* as well.[25]

PRACTICAL ASPECTS OF TALMUDIC *BIKUR HOLIM*

Amount

It was taught: "*Bikur holim* has no set amount." What is meant by "*bikur holim* has no set amount"? R. Joseph thought it means there is no set amount for its reward [the reward is unlimited]. Said Abaye to him: Does anyone have the set amount of the reward for the *mitzvot*? Do we not learn: Be careful with an easy *mitzvah* as with a heavy one, for you do not know the reward of the *mitzvot*.[26] But Abaye said [it must mean]: Even the greater [Heb. *gadol*] [goes on a visit] to the smaller [Heb. *katan*].[27] Raba said: ["No set amount" means one can visit] even a hundred times a day.[28]

From here we see the limitless aspect of *bikur holim*—whether in terms of its reward, in terms of who must visit whom, or in terms of the quantity of visits.[29]

The Talmud offers an interesting halakhic source on the nature of a visit. The *Mishnah* reads as follows:

One who is sworn off from benefit of a friend[30] and goes to visit [while the friend is ill] stands but does not sit, and may heal a healing of the soul[31] but not a financial[32] healing.[33]

The *Gemara* offers several interpretations of the *Mishnah*. According to Shmuel, there was a custom to pay people to sit but not stand with the patient.[34] This is considered a tangible benefit, as opposed to fulfillment of the *mitzvah*, and therefore banned. Alternately, Shmuel holds that even where the company will sit a long time without being paid, there is benefit, and it is banned under the terms of the vow. *Bikur holim*, as a *mitzvah*, is not forbidden. According to Ulla, the explanation for the *Mishnah* is that there is indeed "benefit" from *bikur holim*, but the vower would not have thought of excluding this within the vow. Therefore, *bikur holim* is allowed while the visitor stands, but the benefit accrued to the patient while the visitor sits is not permitted under the terms of the vow.

Some of the commentaries understand the *Gemara* literally, that the *mitzvah* of *bikur holim* is minimally fulfilled through actual standing.[35] Others say that fulfillment of the *mitzvah* is a question of timing or length of stay, rather than posture; in other words, "If one sits and stands and sits for a long period, this is company [rather than *bikur holim*, and therefore banned under the terms of the vow]."[36]

The *Shulhan Arukh* is not clear on this particular question, but in regard to vows it says that where there is a custom to pay visitors, this practice would be banned by the terms of the vow.[37] However, the *Shulhan Arukh* specifies sitting as an actual part of the *mitzvah* of *bikur holim*. The Code reads, "One who visits the sick . . . should enwrap himself and sit before him because the Divine Presence is above [the patient's] head."[38]

Today, it would seem (according to most authorities) that the length and nature of the visit would be determined by the needs of the patient.[39]

Physical Needs of Patient

The Talmud tells a story:

R. Helbo took ill. R. Kahana proclaimed, "R. Helbo is sick!" but no one came to visit. He rebuked the others as follows: "Did it

not happen that one of R. Akiba's students took sick and none
of the sages came to visit? But R. Akiba [himself] entered to visit
and because [R. Akiba] swept and sprinkled the room before him,
he recovered. 'My master [said the student], you have made me
live!' Following this R. Akiba went and lectured, 'Whosoever does
not visit the sick is like a shedder[40] of blood.'"[41]

We see several things from this story. First, we have another
example of the greatness and importance of *bikur holim*. Second,
this is an excellent example of how the "greater visit the lesser."
Third, we see how tending to the patient's actual physical needs is
part of the *mitzvah*.[42] In fact, the Hebrew term the Talmud uses for
"sweeping and sprinkling" is *kibdo v'rivtzo*. The word *kibed* also
means to honor. Even something as mundane as sweeping the room
is considered an honor for the patient. Today, making sure the ill
person has adequate care, whether at home or in a facility, would
be in fulfillment of the *mitzvah*.[43] Helping the patient to arrange his/
her personal affairs would also fall into this category.

Most clergy tend to deal with spiritual and emotional issues
on a pastoral sick call. After all, hospitals generally provide adequate
medical and physical care.[44] Still, one has the obligation to inquire
after physical aspects of care.[45] From the Jewish perspective this is
a pastoral concern, and this is not always understood by others. Early
in my pastoral training, I encountered this issue. The following is a
segment of a verbatim transcript from one of my early supervised
visits. The patient was not Jewish.

> Rabbi: How much longer in the hospital?
> Patient: Several weeks here and, oh, a few months at home.
> Rabbi: How does this make you feel?
> Patient: I feel hopeful—I think it will work out.
> Rabbi: How are they treating you? Is the food okay?
> Patient. St. Joe's is a wonderful hospital—it couldn't be better—I
> wouldn't go anywhere else. I'm lucky to have my family help-
> ing and supporting.

My Protestant colleagues took me to task in the evaluation for
what they believed was "engaging in chitchat." Asking about food
did not seem significant to them. My response at the time was that

this is what I would have asked any of my Jewish patients, for food is a significant element in traditional Judaism. After all, the food we eat is kosher, prepared in specific ways; an observant Jew will say a short blessing before eating and a longer one after eating. In the words of a contemporary scholar,

> In eating a slice of bread, we discover God; in drinking a cup of wine, we sanctify the Sabbath; in preparing a piece of meat, we learn the reverence for life. . . . Other people engage in diets for their bodies. We have created a diet for the soul. If the first is understandable, why not the second?[46]

Obviously, everything I answered then is still true now. But I now also realize that there is a specific pastoral value in looking after the patient's physical needs. By checking on their food, their facilities, and even their medical care, we show invalids that we are concerned and we share their interests. We empathize with them in their time of difficulty, helping to arrange their affairs when they are unable to do so. In this way, we take our lead from the Almighty, Who loves His people and looks after their needs in their times of distress.

When to Visit

The Talmud writes:

> R. Shisha, the son of R. Idi, said: A person should not visit the sick during the first three hours of the day or the last three hours of the day, for he may dismiss praying for him [the patient]. During the first three hours his illness is easing; during the last three hours his sickness more greatly weakens him.[47]

The thrust of this *Gemara* emphasizes the importance of prayer on behalf of the ill.[48] However, Maimonides in his codification of this rule leaves out the last part of the passage and simply states, "The patient is not visited during the first three hours and the last three hours because they are for dealing with the needs of the patient."[49] Maimonides, being a physician, saw the *Gemara's* idea of "visiting hours" as a medical need.[50] One should simply not visit during the first or last hours because this is when medical treatment is given.

Modern sources say that the Talmud's words here are not part of the *mitzvah* but just good advice.[51] One should attempt to avoid times when medical treatment is given and come when one is able, even if this is during the Talmud's proscribed times. One should also observe a hospital's required visiting times and not overtax the patient.[52]

In addition the Talmud shares the following story:

> Raba, on the first day of his illness, said, "Do not reveal this to anyone, so that my fortune [Heb. *mazal*] should not be affected."[53] Afterward[54] he said [to his servants], "Go and proclaim it in the market, so that those who hate me will rejoice, while those who care for me will ask mercy for me."[55]

No part of this excerpt is codified into Jewish Law in terms of how early in the illness one can visit a patient.[56] However, we can learn from this that social concerns about what others might say can be significant. Raba was apprehensive that if word got out too early about his illness, people would begin gossiping about him. This could indeed affect his condition for the worse. After the first day, once the illness was confirmed, the truth could not be kept back any longer. Those who wished him well would pray on his behalf, while those who did not care for him would take pleasure at his misfortune.

Where/How to Sit during a Visit

> It was also taught: One who enters to visit the sick should not sit on a bed, or a bench, or a chair but should enrobe himself and sit on the ground, for the Divine Presence rests above the bed of the patient, as it says (Psalm 41), "The Lord will support him upon his bed of illness."[57]

This selection underlines the reverence one should have when visiting the invalid. In codifying this, the *Shulhan Arukh* specifies that the Talmud refers to an example when the patient is lying on the ground, as was the case most often in those days.[58] In such instances, the visitor should not be higher than the patient.[59] But if a patient is in a bed, then sitting on a chair or bench is preferable, and this is the practice. Being on the same level[60] is an indication of empathy and sharing. This, hopefully, will alleviate the suffering of the invalid, in imitation of God, Who is present at the very head of the patient and alleviates the suffering.[61]

Today most authorities say the level, position, and posture of the visitor depends on the needs of the patient. If the invalid requests the visitor to be in a certain spot, those wishes are respected.[62]

One modern source interprets "enrobe" as dressing with modesty.[63] According to this authority, one should dress as if going to synagogue, since the Divine Presence will be greeted with the patient. Also, according to this source, visiting the sick fosters thinking about the ultimate life-and-death issues associated with illness. One's demeanor and dress ought to reflect the seriousness of the moment and circumstance. However, one should not dress in a way that will scare or upset the invalid.

Limits on Whom to Visit

> Shmuel said: One would not visit the sick unless they are feverish. Whom does this exclude? It excludes . . . those with intestinal trouble or eye disease or headaches. Now, intestinal diseases [we understood] because of embarrassment.[64] But why eye disease and headaches? Says R. Yehudah: speech is difficult for eyes and headaches [e.g., speaking to the visitor will cause more problems[65] than actually help the patient].[66]

From this we see that there is an etiquette about whom to visit. Nahmanides in *Torat Haadam* applies these restrictions to anyone who has difficulty speaking. In this case, the visitor should check about the patient with another in an outer room, tend to the patient's physical and room needs, and "listen to his pain . . . and ask mercy on his behalf." Today, the etiquette depends on the conditions, but there is still a principle to provide joy and relief for the patient without troubling him/her.[67] Other contemporary authorities advise asking family members first and using discretion.[68] One current source writes that it is a special *mitzvah* to visit when others are not around and the patient in this case is especially lonely, "embittered of the soul," and troubled. A visit may help the ill one to forget his or her worry and pain.[69]

One last talmudic selection is in order:

> "May You turn all his lying down in his sickness" (Psalm 41:4). R. Joseph said: This means he forgets his learning. R. Joseph took ill and his learning was removed [forgotten]. Abaye restored it to him. Thus it is often stated, "R. Joseph said, 'I have not heard this particular lesson,' and Abaye would say, 'You yourself taught it to us and said it from this teaching.'"[70]

This story reminds us that sickness, debilitation, and hospital stays have mental and nonphysiological effects on the patient. The dislocation, both physical and emotional, can cause forgetfulness, among many other symptoms. Any visitor, especially those who tend to or deal with the individual after illness, must be acutely aware of the effects of the stress associated with illness.

In summary, the Talmud offers specific wisdom about the reverence associated with the visit, its length, actions, and timing, and the posture and dress of the visitor, as well as the physical and clinical needs of the patient. While both Jewish law and modern needs have tended to obscure and weaken the Talmud's instructions to a "depending on the case" basis, the Talmud can teach us much regarding our topic.

4

Specific Issues
in *Bikur Holim*

BLESSING ON THE *MITZVAH*

There is no blessing (Heb. *brakhah*) made on the fulfillment of the *mitzvah* of *bikur holim*.[1] Most religious commandments in Judaism are preceded by a blessing with the formula "Blessed are You, Lord our God, Sovereign of the Universe, Who has made us unique with His commandments and commanded us to . . . [the particular *mitzvah* is filled in]." However, almost all *mitzvot* in the broad category of *hesed*, "acts of kindness,"[2] including *tzedakah* (giving of charity), honoring parents, bringing peace to others, escorting and burial of the deceased, comforting the bereaved, etc., lack this blessing. There are several reasons for the absence of a blessing in these cases:[3]

1. *Bikur holim* is not only a personal *mitzvah* of the individual, showing a religious link between that person and his/her Creator, but it involves another person as well. Since the other individual may not always desire the visit, a blessing would be inappropriate.

2. *Bikur holim*, along with the other above-mentioned acts of kindness in this category, is commonly done by compassionate and intelligent people of differing faiths and religions.[4] Blessings are not

31

required on the fulfillment of these types of commandments, because the language of the blessing before fulfilling commandments singles out the Jewish people as being unique through their being commanded to fulfill these acts.[5]

MALE/FEMALE VISITS

Classical Judaism frowned upon too much intergender contact because of the possibility that it might lead to lewdness.[6] Some modern authorities say that there is no problem if men and women visit each other, and this is considered part of the *mitzvah*.[7] Others are stricter in this matter.[8]

VISITING ONE'S ENEMIES

There is a dispute on the question of whether it is appropriate to visit an antagonist. Some say that it is forbidden, since it looks like the visitor is rejoicing at the illness, and the visitor's appearance will bring emotional pain to the patient.[9] Others say that the visit is permitted if it does not appear that the visitor takes pleasure in the pain of his/her enemy.[10] Still others say that the propriety of the visit depends on the nature of the dispute, the hatred, and the relationship.[11] A premodern source recommends that the visitor send a third party to let the patient know that he or she wishes to visit. Assuming that the patient consents, the visit is then permitted.[12] In fact, this source and others recommend that disputants specifically attempt to visit each other, for the sincere visit may help relieve the tension and hatred. As a contemporary rabbinic scholar has written:

> If the visitor is insulted or hurt, the visit will bring peace between them. It is possible that the patient will ask forgiveness from him since he sees that the insulted humbles himself to come and ask mercy [on the patient's behalf]. And even if the patient has been insulted, the visit is still a request for mercy. And in most cases this will bring peace, for one *mitzvah* leads to another.[13]

VISITING NON-JEWS

Halakhically, there is no question that the *mitzvah* of *bikur holim* extends to ill non-Jews. This is based on the Talmud, which states:

> [We] support non-Jewish poor along with the poor of Israel; we visit non-Jewish patients along with the sick of Israel; we bury the dead of non-Jews as we do the Jewish dead, all because of "the ways of peace" [Heb. *darkei shalom*].[14]

Obviously, the acts mentioned in this passage fall into the broad category of *gemilut hasadim*, "acts of kindness" referred to earlier. In all of these we do not make distinctions based on a person's faith or ethnic background.[15] This is codified as normative *halakhah*.[16]

VISITING ON THE SABBATH

There is a talmudic dispute on the subject of Sabbath visits to the ill, with the school of Shammai forbidding it (along with other similar activities such as comforting the bereaved) and the school of Hillel permitting it.[17] The law follows Hillel, as it does in most cases, but not without some dissent. As the Talmud puts it, "Said R. Hanina: With difficulty did they permit comforting the bereaved and visiting the sick on the Sabbath."

The ambiguity of the Talmud finds its way into later sources. Rashi suggests that the reluctance to allow these visits (and the original reasoning for Shammai's negative position) is because these activities cause pain and sorrow, contrary to the spirit of Sabbath joy.[18] As a result, one premodern authority counsels that one should not specifically save the visit for the Sabbath.[19] However, most sources agree that if it is difficult to come during the week, it is certainly permitted to visit on the Sabbath, especially if one knows that the visit will bring joy to the patient.[20] Aaron Levine offers both sides of this issue, pointing out that at most times a proper visit will add to the Sabbath spirit but cautioning that a visit may cause sorrow and pain for someone extrasensitive.[21] Other contemporary sources simply say that the greatness of the *mitzvah* of *bikur holim*[22] transcends this sorrow.[23]

The wishes offered to a patient on the Sabbath reflect the serenity of the day. As the Talmud puts it:

> Our Rabbis taught: One who visits the sick [on the Sabbath] says, "It is the Sabbath [and we] refrain from crying out, and healing is near."[24] R. Meir said: Perhaps it [the Sabbath] will have compassion.[25] R. Yehudah said: [one should say], May the Almighty have mercy upon you and on all the sick of Israel.[26] R. Yose said: [It should read], May the Almighty have mercy upon you amidst all the sick of Israel. Shavna, the man of Jerusalem, used to say [when visiting on Shabbat], "*Shalom*" [Peace unto you] when he would enter; when he would leave he would say, "It is the Sabbath [and we] refrain from crying out, and healing is near, and His mercies are great, so rest in peace."[27]

Shavna's view is the one accepted in Jewish Law.[28] Some variations of these wishes are used in the traditional prayers offered for the ill in synagogue on the Sabbath.[29]

If the patient is in a dangerous or potentially dangerous condition, it is permitted for family members to break the Sabbath to come and visit. Many authorities[30] assign this dispensation only to rabbinically ordained rules, while others apply this to breaking even biblical Sabbath restrictions as well.[31] All this definitely pertains if the patient requests the visit, and according to some even if there is no specific request. There is no question that if the situation is immediately life threatening, all rules on the books can be broken as in any case where there is a threat to human life.[32] This certainly has implications for people regularly engaged in pastoral-care and crisis-intervention situations where there is a threat to human life. Examples might include hospital chaplains on call over a weekend, suicides, or even a case where a congregant falls seriously ill on the Sabbath or holidays and requests another—rabbi or layperson—to accompany them to the hospital.[33]

OTHER ISSUES FOR THE VISITOR

A patient should not be left alone, as stated in the Talmud: "Three individuals require someone to watch—a sick one, a bride, and a groom."[34] Some sources recommend that two go together to visit; others do not consider this a priority.[35] Some suggest bringing children to visit, both as a means of training the children in the *mitzvah* and also to bring joy to the patient. If the patient is poor, one should not visit empty-handed.[36] One should also not go into the room suddenly.[37]

HUMOR

One of the many ways to lighten a patient's burden is through humor.[38] The following is a verbatim account of one of my typical visits.

> [Al was taken by surprise when elective knee surgery turned into a heart problem. I listened to him discuss the difficulty and fear he had in accepting this unexpected turn of events. After he regained his composure, I sensed he felt a bit better.]
> Rabbi: Are you in the mood for a joke?
> Al: Sure, anything to make me feel better.
> Rabbi: There was once a *shohet* [Jewish ritual slaughterer] who cut himself rather severely while *shechting* [slaughtering] a cow. He was rushed to the ICU of the local hospital. He awoke to find tubes coming out of every part of his body. "Oy! Oy!" he cried. "What's the matter?" asked the nurse. "Where am I?" "In ICU." "Oy! Oy!" "What is it now?" "I want a cup of tea!" "You can't have tea—you're in ICU." "How much am I paying in ICU?" "Eight hundred dollars a day." "For eight hundred dollars a day, I want a cup of tea!" "If you say so . . ." She took an IV and chugalugged it into the rabbi's arm. A few minutes later, she again hears, "Oy! Oy!" "What's the matter now, Rabbi?" "For eight hundred dollars a day I want my tea with lemon!!
> Al: [chuckling] That was a good one, Rabbi, it was good.
> Rabbi: Well, I see my time in ICU is up and I'm sure you want to rest. [I turn to his wife.] You make sure he behaves himself, you hear?
> Wife: [laughs] I will. Thanks for coming.
> Al: Yes, Rabbi, thanks for coming.

This type of approach has been referred to as "verbal chicken soup."[39] It brings a smile and a bit of relaxation to what is often a lonely, fear-inducing environment (depending on how the joke is told!). Obviously, it is not appropriate to tell jokes at each and every *bikur holim* visit or to every patient. The visitor must use discretion and judgment in telling a joke or using humor. Sometimes, the visitor runs the risk of appearing too lighthearted. Especially in cases of serious illness, or when the mood of the patient is obviously low, humor might hurt rather than help. Still, in many cases, my experience has shown that a good laugh can be a wonderful diversion and aid to a sick or recovering patient.

LANGUAGE AND NUANCE

It is not always easy to find the right words to share with a patient in pain and suffering. Both Jewish tradition and human experience (at least my own experience and that of colleagues) indicate that the ill person needs companionship rather than scintillating conversation. Similarly, when the patient asks, "Why is God doing this to me?" he or she is not asking a theological question but an existential one. Therefore, the visitor's actual presence is far more important and meaningful than an array of philosophical answers. A smile, a touch of the hand, or some quiet time together is more healing than platitudes. An illustration of this position is our original source for *bikur holim*, God's visit to Abraham following the latter's circumcision in Genesis 18:1-2.[40] There is no dialogue between God and Abraham recorded in the Torah's text. Apparently, the Divine Presence was enough to heal Abraham and act as our model for *bikur holim*.[41]

Sometimes, patients have difficulty articulating their own feelings.[42] A visitor's model for handling this can be drawn from the halakhic etiquette used for visiting a mourner's home during the *shivah* week following the funeral.[43] When one comes to the *shivah* house, one simply goes in and does not expect the mourner to answer the door. Further, one does not initiate the conversation but waits for the mourner to talk. The emphasis is on what the mourner has on his or her mind, allowing them to share their concerns. Rather than engage in meaningless chatter of potentially little concern to a grieving person, caring friends give mourners the chance to work through their grief in their own way.[44]

One might draw a parallel between the ill and the bereaved, for a person in a sickbed or hospital setting may go through a certain level of grief or loss.[45] Using the *shivah*-house model, the visitor attempts to let the patient guide the conversation, speaking of what the patient wishes to share. This does not necessarily mean that one must wait for the patient to begin the dialogue of the visit. A visitor, whether professional chaplain or layperson, can take the initiative by introducing him or herself and starting the conversation. Then the caller picks up on the patient's response and what he or she says.[46] In these ways, we show that our primary concern is the patient and that our visit is centered around him or her.

Generally, one should not visit an invalid and expect the patient to "host" us, since he or she may not be physically able to do so. But it is plausible that emotionally, patients may actually wish to host the visitor. I have seen this often in geriatric situations, where the loss of independence affects patients' well-being. In these cases, some act of hosting may actually be quite therapeutic for the patient.[47]

The words exchanged and how they are exchanged can be colored by the backgrounds of both patient and visitor. There is no question that spiritual concerns are affected by cultural, ethnic, and religious factors.[48] An interesting example occurred several years ago during my visit to "Al."

> Rabbi: How are you feeling, Al? [I take his hand.]
> Al: Physically, I don't know. We're waiting for the results of some tests.
> Rabbi: How are your spirits?
> Al: Oh, Rabbi, you shouldn't have to know.

I correctly understood this to mean, "You should never have to experience what I have gone through." My non-Jewish supervising advisor critiqued me, interpreting the remark as, "You should know how I feel, you should not have to ask." This example shows that nuance in language can affect a visit to the ill and that differences in background affect the nuance. The phraseology and intonation that a Jewish visitor understood from a Jewish patient would be seen differently if either the visitor or the invalid was a non-Jew.

A visitor should take these aspects into consideration during the conversation.

BAD NEWS

One should not bring bad news to a patient, as this may seriously affect his/her emotional condition and therefore the physical condition as well.[49] Halakhic authorities agree that this may be done only in consultation with the family and physicians, while ascertaining the state and needs of the patient.[50]

OTHER FORMS OF *BIKUR HOLIM*

As we have seen, the fullest expression of *bikur holim* is in the personal empathic visit, relieving the emotional pain and isolation of the patient. According to most contemporary halakhic scholars, calling a sick person on the telephone also has the status of the *mitzvah*, and in some cases (where there are too many visitors) may actually be quite desirable.[51] If a personal visit or call is impossible, a letter to the patient may also be in fulfillment of the *mitzvah*, since it accomplishes many of the same purposes.[52] As R. Waldenberg of Israel writes: "A person can visit the sick even if he does not speak a word, such as when the patient is sleeping. For it will probably be that when he is told that so-and-so came to see him, this will bring to him ease of the spirit."[53]

This would indicate that visits through the phone, a warm letter, or even sending another party to convey good wishes are all part of the *mitzvah*.

VISITING CONTAGIOUS PATIENTS

The current spread of AIDS in many communities has focused debate on dealing with patients who suffer from this disease. There is no question that they deserve *bikur holim* and the *hesed* that the Torah commands us to share with all who are ill. The fact that much of the behavior associated with the spread of AIDS (gay lifestyle, hetero-sexual contact outside of marriage, and drug use) is antithetical to traditional Torah teaching should not affect the compassion we are bidden to show all our suffering people.[54] Nevertheless, the questions of potential danger from physical contact with patients who have certain diseases depends on the larger halakhic question of whether one must place him/herself in danger to save another.[55] A full analysis of this question is beyond the confines of this book. It seems to me that the Torah does not oblige one to place his/her own life in danger for visiting someone if that danger is imminent (and this is a highly subjective issue). If there is some danger or slight danger, then it may be permitted, and according to some still obligatory, to visit. Levine suggests utilizing a special team of visitors in these cases, perhaps paying them.[56] Others say that the response depends on whether there is a real chance of saving this person's life, in which case it is permitted.[57] There is no question that the physician is permitted to place him/herself in danger for the sake of the patient,[58] and this is considered a highly meritorious deed.[59]

5

Liturgical Issues

BIBLICAL SOURCES

We have seen from several of our sources the importance of prayer for the ill. This tradition of prayer is an ancient one, and the earliest example is in the Torah itself.[1] Moses appeals to the Almighty on behalf of his sister Miriam, who has been stricken with leprosy. This disease presumably is punishment for Miriam's sin of speaking ill of her brother Moses and his wife.[2] Yet Moses still offers a beautiful, poignant, and short prayer on her behalf: "And Moses cried out to God, saying, 'Please, O God, please heal her!'"

The classical commentaries see in Moses' words the sense of pleading,[3] the request for mercy,[4] and the need for immediacy.[5] In addition, Rashi points out two interesting reasons regarding the brevity of the prayer. He says:

> Why did not Moses lengthen his prayer? So that [the people of] Israel should not say, "His sister is in trouble and he stands and expands his prayers?" . . . Another explanation: So that [the people of] Israel should not say, "For his sister he expands his prayers, but for us he does not expand his prayers."[6]

Though many of the general themes of prayer can be found in this passage and its commentaries, apparently we do not learn any

41

practical lessons of brevity from this biblical selection, as it is not codified in the *halakhah*.[7]

One more comment on this biblical verse touches on the basic thesis of this work. Ibn Ezra writes: "And Moses cried . . . this teaches us that he shared the pain of his sister. [As if to say] O God . . . You Who have the power in Your hand, now heal, [do it] now for her."[8]

Thus, the depths of prayer for the ill can and should come from a sense of empathy with the patient. The biblical example is an especially poignant one, since Miriam was experiencing divine punishment for speaking badly of Moses. Yet, Moses himself is willing to put aside whatever negative feelings he may have had and empathically pray for her in spite of those feelings.[9]

RABBINIC SOURCES AND APPLICATIONS

Rabbinic sources underline prayer as a major goal of the *bikur holim* visit.

> When R. Dimi came he said, "Whoever visits the sick causes him to live, and whoever does not visit the sick causes him to die." How does one 'cause' this? Does this mean that whoever visits the sick will ask mercy [pray] that he may live, and whoever does not visit the sick will ask mercy that he should die?[10] Would you think this? But [it must mean] that whoever does not visit the sick will not ask mercy, neither that he should live nor die.
>
> Raba, on the first day of his illness said, "Do not reveal this to anyone, lest it affect my fortune."[11] Afterward, he said, "Go tell of my illness in the market so that whoever hates me will rejoice . . . while those who care for me will ask mercy for me."[12]

The above sources do not tell us of the content of these prayers. While the Talmud elsewhere offers some of the themes of prayer on behalf of the ill (as we will shortly see) and these are formalized in many of our own prayers for the ill, there are no "official prayers for the ill" from the talmudic period. This leads me to believe that there was once a tradition of spontaneous prayer for the sick in Judaism. Many Christian hospital chaplains, ministers, and priests will offer a prayer at the bedside of a patient. Christian liturgy is not as fixed as traditional Jewish liturgy, and many Christian patients will expect or at least appreciate prayer with a clergyperson. I have worked with ministers who developed this into an art—using the prayer as a summary of the visit and the person's feelings. For example, after a session dealing with the patient's apprehensions about entering a nursing home after surgery, the following dialogue ensued:

> Pastor: I'd like to share a prayer with you. Will that be all right?
> Patient and wife [simultaneously]: Yes, please do.
> Pastor: Dear God, we thank you for this opportunity to get acquainted and to share in our common faith. May you go with P. through the hard places and undergird him in the power of your spirit. Be with his wife and family, and undergird them in faith. May Your love and grace be sufficient for all these things. Amen.[13]

I remember at the time how impressed I was with this technique, assuming it was simply not part of Jewish tradition. But I thought I would try it out with a congregant.

> Congregant: Well, I am looking forward to getting out of here.
> Rabbi: I know you are, and we look forward to having you back at *shul*. Well, it has been good seeing you. Do you mind if I pray with you here for your recovery?
> Congregant: Why would you want to do that?
> Rabbi: Well, er, um, I just hope that the *Ribbono Shel Olam* [Master of the Universe] smiles upon you and guides you as you face the future back at home.

It appears that Jews do not expect or seem to need spontaneous bedside prayer.[14] This may be true because Jews are used to prayer from a fixed liturgy and assume pastoral care deals only with the personal dimensions of the visit, as described earlier.

After discovering the numerous talmudic references to praying or "asking mercy" for the patient,[15] as the rabbinic sources literally put it, I now believe that at one time there was a tradition of spontaneous, unfixed prayer for the ill. While my experience still leads me to assume that many Jewish patients do not care about it,[16] perhaps we ought to attempt to retrieve this tradition,[17] whether in the presence of the patient, or privately.[18] I have started using, when appropriate, the closing moments of a pastoral visit to summarize the feelings I have heard expressed in the form of a quasi-prayer or blessing, such as:

> Rabbi [after, say, a session where the patient expressed apprehension for the future]: It has been good seeing you. Let us hope and pray that the *Ribbono Shel Olam* [Master of the Universe] will strengthen you and guide you through the times to come; and know that all of us are with you.
> Patient: Thank you so much, Rabbi.

Another related clinical issue surrounding liturgy is the need for specifically rabbinic prayer on behalf of or with the patient. I was always led to believe that Judaism frowned on the need for clergy assisting someone in prayer. The following is typical of my early encounters with this issue:

> Patient: Rabbi, would you say a prayer for me?
> Rabbi: There really is no prayer that I can say that you could not say yourself.

Judaism is indeed a people's religion in the sense that one does not need a rabbi for a service.[19] Having grown up in the sixties and seventies, and personally sharing this attitude, I have always felt my role to be that of a teacher rather than an intermediary to God. I saw myself helping to facilitate others' observance and growth. "Praying for them" did not fit into my *weltanschauung*. I was therefore rather surprised to come across the following passage in the Talmud during my research for this work:

> R. Pinhas Ben Hama expounded: One who has an ill person in his home should go to a wise man [Heb. *hakham*] [so that] he may ask mercy for him, as it says (Proverbs 16:14), "The anger of a King is like messengers of death, but a wise man will pacify it."[20]

The commentaries explain that the King is the Divine King whose messengers (or angels, another translation) inflict illness, especially severe life-threatening illness.[21] For these maladies, the prayer of the wise is especially helpful in saving the patient. Thus, classical Jewish thinking teaches that prayers of a wise or righteous person have special efficacy in the eyes of the Almighty. This is not merely folklore, theology, or philosophic theory. It is codified in Jewish Law[22] and also cited as practical guidance in the following medieval commentary: ". . . this is the custom in France. All those who have a sick person would seek the presence of the rabbi who holds forth, that he [the rabbi] may bless him."[23]

Today, most people, Jews as well as non-Jews, believe that the prayers of or at least the presence of clergy add an extra dimension of aid to the invalid.[24] Jewish patients find it reassuring to have a rabbi who represents Jewish wisdom, practice, and history, at their bedside. Encountering this passage has changed my own personal approach to pastoral care. I know and recognize that my congregants need to see me at their side, both for their therapeutic needs and because Jewish tradition demands that of me.[25] Since I have studied these passages, I have also become particularly careful to publicly recite the traditional prayer for the sick[26] in synagogue on the Sabbath.

THE TRADITIONAL PRAYER FOR THE SICK (THE *MI-SHEBERAKH*)[27]

The following is the most commonly used prayer for the ill.

> May He Who blessed our ancestors Abraham, Isaac, Jacob, Moses, Aaron, David, and Solomon, [Sarah, Rebecca, Rachel, and Leah,][28] bless and heal this ill one, [insert the name] son/daughter of [insert the mother's name] and on whose behalf we pray and offer *tzedakah*.[29] With this reward, may the Holy One, Blessed Be He, be filled with mercy upon him/her, to cure and heal, strengthen and sustain him/her; and may He send quickly a complete healing from Heaven to all his/her limbs and nerves. Among all the other sick of Israel [may it be] a cure of both soul and body. [On the Sabbath add: It is the Sabbath and we do not cry out, but healing is near.] May it happen immediately without delay and let us say, Amen![30]

Actually, there is a sizable group of prayers that carry the name *Mi-Sheberakh*. They ask God to reward various individuals, including those who are called up for the Torah reading, those who make donations to the synagogue or other worthy causes, *bar* and *bat mitzvah* celebrants, wedding celebrants, the recipients of circumcisions and baby-namings, and other similar individuals.[31] Most of these prayers date from the Middle Ages.[32] The language of the *Mi-Sheberakh* for the sick also comes from this period, although, as we have seen, it has much earlier thematic origins. The *Shulhan Arukh* makes mention of the *Mi-Sheberakh* as one of the means of helping the ill.[33] A century ago, one work described its use as follows: "It is the custom to bless the sick in the synagogue at the time of the Torah reading,[34] for at that time, the divine mercies are awakened."[35]

The following are the important themes found in the *Mi-Sheberakh*, in order of where they are located within the prayer:

1. *Association with the early ancestors and great figures of Jewish history.* This idea is frequently found in the regular liturgy and especially emphasized on the High Holidays. "The merit of the Ancestors" (Heb. *zekhut avot*), based on their intimate relationship with the Almighty, is often used when praying for one's needs or for forgiveness. From the pastoral perspective, this usage places the patient firmly within the nexus of Jewish history and destiny.

2. *Use of the Hebrew name and the mother's name.* This identifies the patient as a member of his/her people. If the Hebrew name is not known, a name in any language may be used. The reason for using the mother's name is not clear, although its usage is the common custom. Some of the suggested sources include the *Zohar's* (major source of the kabbalistic tradition) reference to Psalm 86, "And save the son of your maidservant," as well as the Talmud's statement, "Abaye said that 'my mother told me all repeated prayers [or incantations on behalf of patients—Soncino] are made with the name of the mother.'"[36]

In addition, the Hebrew for "mercy"—*rahamim*—is directly related to the Hebrew for "womb"—*rehem*—and thus when asking for divine mercies for a patient, it is appropriate to invoke the name of the one who bore the patient.[37]

If one does not know the mother's name in Hebrew or any other language, one may pray for the patient using the father's name or even the name of the town from which they came. Alternatively, the person can be referred to as "son/daughter of Sarah," since the matriarch Sarah is considered the ancestress of all Jews in the spiritual sense, if not in the genealogical sense.

There are some views that suggest we never actually label the person as *holeh*, "sick" or "the patient," in the prayers for the sick. These opinions are based on the talmudic dictum, "A person should always pray that he should not become ill."[38] Rather, we would omit the Hebrew *holeh* and simply ask for "a cure for so-and-so . . . "[39] so as not to imply that the individual is sick beyond help.[40]

3. *Tangible acts on behalf of the patient including prayer and charity.* This is another frequent theme in Jewish liturgy. In fact, it is quite similar to the idea and line in the prayer for the deceased,[41] for whom we also "pray and offer *tzedakah*." Prayer involves the pray-er through specific acts.

4. *Calling directly on God through "asking mercy."* This is in direct fulfillment of the rabbinic dicta that we studied earlier.

5. *Including the patient among the members of the community.* Inclusion of the ill amongst our people's other sick[42] links them to the larger group. Just as we have connected them vertically to their Jewish past, so do we connect them horizontally to the present. In my own experience I have found that this is a powerful tool in lifting the spirits of the sick. When they know that they will be remembered within the living community, their sense of isolation is lessened. A home sickbed can be a very lonely place; a hospital can be downright terrifying. Knowing that one is still part of the Jewish community and that one will be thought of can lift the mood of the ill and spiritually strenghten them.[43] This is an important Jewish notion of pastoral care. Clergy or professional presence is not enough. What non-Jewish faiths define as "pastoral care" actually devolves on both clergy and congregation, according to Jewish tradition.[44]

6. *Healing is both physical and spiritual ("a cure of both soul and body").* Judaism recognizes the emotional and spiritual dimensions of sickness. Therefore, when we pray for the patient's speedy physi-

cal recovery, we are in the same breath and sentence asking for a restoration of the person's spirit. This, in turn, explains why we would even make a *Mi-Sheberakh* for a terminally ill patient. We may not be able to change the physical fate of the sick person, but we still can ask for spiritual wholeness as a form of healing.

7. *Finally, the prayer may be offered on the Sabbath.* While we generally do not ask for our specific needs on the Sabbath,[45] the Day of Rest itself brings comfort and healing in its wake. We may thus make reference to God's healing power on the holy Sabbath.

OTHER LITURGIES AND ILLNESS

The Talmud states:

> R. Hiyya says: Even though it was said that a person should ask for needs in the blessing of "He Who hears all prayer,"[46] still if he has an ill one within his household he should ask this need in the blessing for the sick.[47]

The prayer in question reads as follows:

> Heal us O Lord and we shall be healed, save us and we shall be saved; for You are our praise.[48] Grant a complete healing for all our wounds; for You are God, the King, the faithful and compassionate Healer. Blessed are You O Lord, Who heals the sick of His people Israel.

It is suggested that one who wishes to privately add a prayer for an ill person in their silent *Amidah* add the following in the above-mentioned blessing:[49]

> May it be your will, O Lord my God and God of my ancestors, that You send quickly a complete healing from the heavens, [may it be] a cure of both soul and body for this ill one, [insert the name] son/daughter of [insert the mother's name] among all the other sick of Israel. . . .

Certain scriptural verses may be read when visiting the sick. All of these deal with the themes of disease and healing. They include: Deuteronomy 7:15, Exodus 16:26, Isaiah 57:9, and Psalm 90:10-11.[50]

CHANGING THE NAME

The Talmud says:

> And R. Yitzhak stated that four things tear up the [evil] decree for a person. And they are: *Tzedakah*, "crying out" [prayer], changing the name, and changing one's actions. . . . Changing the name, as it is written (Genesis 17:15), "As for Sarai your wife, you shall no longer call her name Sarai, for Sarah shall be her name."[51]

Changing the Hebrew name for a patient in a dangerous condition is codified in *halakhah* and is used solely for desperate situations.[52] The procedure is done only with a *minyan*.[53] After selections from the Psalms, the following is recited, after which the regular *Mi-Sheberakh* is said:

> And even if it is decreed upon him/her in Your righteous court that he/she die from this disease, behold our Holy Rabbis have said that three things tear up the [evil] decree for a person; and one of them is changing the name. We have fulfilled their words and changed his/her name, for he/she is another one. And if on [insert name] is decreed this, then on [insert new name] it is not decreed; therefore he/she is another and not called by their former name. And just as his/her name has been changed, so may the decree be changed from above to a decree of mercy, from death to life, from sickness to complete healing, for [insert new name]. In the name of all the names in the Torah and in the names of all the angels appointed over cures and salvation, send quickly a speedy and complete recovery to [insert new name]. Lengthen his/her days and years in pleasantness, let him/her spend their days in goodness, with strength and peace, now and forevermore, Amen, Selah!

In earlier days, the new Hebrew name would be chosen at random by opening a Bible and picking the first name that appeared on the opened page. Today, a name denoting healing or life is usually chosen, such as Hayyim or Hayah (life), Rafael (God will heal), or the Yiddish Alter (long life). The old name is not totally dropped, but the new name is used as the first Hebrew name.

While we are not in a position to question the effectiveness of this procedure in the heavenly spheres, we might ask about its usefulness as an expression of pastoral care. I would suggest that as long as those who invoke this—patients, their families, and rabbis— find it helpful, then it certainly has pastoral impact. Changing the name is a desperate act for desperate times. If we define Jewish pastoral care as using the tools of *halakhah*, liturgy, and theology to guide people through crisis periods, then people who take this act seriously will certainly benefit from it.

KAVANOT FOR THE *MITZVAH*[54]

This particular liturgical selection, found in an eighteenth-century prayer book, may be said by the visitor prior to engaging in a *bikur holim* visit. I cite it here because it beautifully illustrates a basic theme of this book—that *bikur holim* is a demonstration of empathy that itself is in imitation of God's ways.

> For the sake of the unification of the Holy One, Blessed Be He and His Presence, in awe and mercy, to unify the Holy letters of the ineffable Name, in perfect unity, in the Name of all Israel. [55]
>
> Behold I am prepared and ready to fulfill the positive commandment "to walk in His Ways."[56] And just as I offer kindness in this world, so with Your kindness may You deal with me in the next world. You will save my soul and spirit from extraneous interferences; with fullness answer me and surround me with kindness. Shield and cover me with Your Divine Shadow, save me from the domain of Gehinom, watch me, sustain me, give me happiness on Earth and do not give me up to the greed of my enemies, as You promised through Your anointed one, David, "Happy is he that considers the poor. The Lord will deliver him in the day of evil. The Lord preserve him and keep him alive, let him be called happy in the land; and You will not deliver him unto the greed of his enemies."

May this *mitzvah* be as significant to you as if I have fulfilled it in all its details and the other commandments linked to
it. Amen, Selah![57]

At this point several of the earlier mentioned biblical verses are
recited followed by this:

May the Almighty have mercy toward you among the other ill of
Israel. . . . May the Holy One, Blessed Be He, show you kindness
and acceptance; may He fill you with mercy. May all Your people
Israel be included in the blessing and the grace, Amen!

This prayer includes all the basic themes of this chapter, including beseeching divine mercy, association with the people of
Israel and community, God's kindness, and a sharing of the moment with the patient. All these are part of the empathic visit, in
imitation of the Almighty and following in God's ways.

6

Preliminary Thoughts
toward a Jewish
Pastoral Theology

PERSPECTIVES ON PASTORAL
THEOLOGY AND THE RABBINATE

Our excursion into Jewish pastoral theology continues with an introduction to the historic bases of rabbinic roles. These comments will shed some light on the contemporary rabbinic models we hope to develop.

Today's rabbi is the heir to several classic biblical and post-biblical models of Jewish leadership. The king (Heb. *melekh*) served as both national symbol and leader. His job, as noted in Deuteronomy 18, included administration of government as well as defense. Maimonides includes kings from the House of David as well as non-Davidic kings.[1] This institution has not existed since the destruction of the First Temple by the Babylonians in 586 B.C.E.[2]

The priest (Heb. *kohen*) officiated in the Temple and assisted those who came to the sanctuary for worship and sacrifice.[3] As progeny of Aaron, they were honored for their position. Today's priestly descendants[4] do not function in any actual capacity but still receive symbolic honors in traditional communities. According to tradition, priests outside the Temple were actually teachers in outlying Jewish communities.

53

The Bible mentions the prophet (Heb. *navi*) as another leadership figure. Maimonides explains that the prophet's role was not to start a new religion or add material to the Torah but rather to offer guidance regarding the Torah's traditions and to warn people ". . . not to transgress."[5] In addition to being moral judges and guides, prophets were also "comforters" (Heb. *menahemim*), offering words of solace to a suffering nation and its members.[6] A good example of this role is found in the second half of Isaiah. Prophecy, according to Jewish tradition, ceased in the early Second Temple period toward the end of the sixth century B.C.E.

The judge (Heb. *shofet* or *dayan*) is yet another biblical model of rabbinic function.[7] These were individuals to whom people came for legal decisions as well as the individuals who enforced those decisions. Maimonides requires those qualified for the position to be "wise, understanding sages, outstanding. . . ." This role still exists today in the traditional rabbinate, as many rabbis continue to act as *dayanim*, judges who settle or decide specific ritual and civil questions. To some extent, congregational rabbis will also act in this capacity to the extent of their knowledge in a given area; this is in large part the basis for traditional rabbinic authority today.

A major rabbinic role that developed during the Second Temple period is that of teacher.[8] In fact, the word rabbi means master or teacher of Torah. While this idea is included in some of our earlier leadership models, the teaching role gained importance after the Second Temple period as the rabbinic role par excellence. It remains as such to this very day. Most rabbis in modern Jewish life see themselves in this tradition as expositors of Torah.[9]

Connected to the teaching and judging roles, and to some extent emerging from them, is the role of rabbi as *posek*, arbiter of religious law. Because classical Judaism involves a community bound by its code of tradition, the sages throughout the generations are called upon to render decisions for religious practice. In Judaism this role does not merely include ritual or ceremonial areas, nor is it exclusively related to interpretation of dogma (though this may be present, at times, as part of the teaching role). Rather, this is a very practical role where the rabbi interprets Jewish Law in questions of religious observance, daily life, life-cycle events, and possibly interpersonal relations and civil law as well.

While there certainly are observant Jews affiliated with Conservative or other non-Orthodox institutions, the observance of Jewish Law today is most often, but not exclusively, followed by those identifying themselves as Orthodox Jews. In the Orthodox community, both in its modern or centrist wing as well as its right wing, the rabbi still operates as a *posek* and final authority on religious law. This is considered one of his primary roles.[10] Laity who have sought the rabbi's guidance as *posek* generally follow that guidance.[11]

All of the above models can be considered precedents for rabbinic leadership. Some, such as those of king and priest, only marginally relate to today's rabbi. Others, such as that of prophet, do not exist as such, but in some symbolic sense (such as that of comforter) can still guide rabbis.[12] Still others, such as judge, teacher, and *posek*, are very much a part of the traditional rabbinate today. Rabbis often see themselves by virtue of training and belief as part of a direct line going back to the early figures in these roles.

Throughout much of this book, we have seen the importance of *bikur holim* and how it is a demonstration of "walking in God's ways," via sharing and lightening the patient's burden. *Bikur holim* in Judaism is everyone's *mitzvah*, not merely restricted to the rabbinate. The duties enumerated in this book, for the most part, are incumbent upon every Jew.[13] Yet the very term "pastoral theology," by definition and implication, is the theology of the pastor, or clergy. Is there any difference between the rabbinic role and the lay role in *bikur holim*? Indeed, is there any particular rabbinic role in *bikur holim*? I would suggest the following pastoral roles as appropriate for today's rabbinate.

THE RABBI AS PASTORAL MANAGER

We have already discussed handling the patient's physical needs as part of the *mitzvah* of *bikur holim*.[14] Sometimes it takes the rabbi's involvement in these areas to alleviate the patient's concern, especially when there is neglect on the part of the hospital staff or the invalid's family. More important, though, a rabbi can help deal with specifically religious issues. Obtaining kosher food in a hospital setting can sometimes present difficulties, as evidenced by this verbatim transcript excerpt from one of my visits:

Rabbi [after just learning that Sadie had been admitted and rushing over]: I just heard you were taken into the hospital, and I came as soon as I could.

Sadie: Thanks so much, Rabbi. Just seeing you here helps me.

Rabbi: I'm glad. Is there anything I can do for you?

Sadie: I don't know. I haven't been eating because the food isn't kosher.

Rabbi: You know they do have kosher TV dinners here.

Sadie: I know that, but the dietary staff gave me a hard time and said I could not get them until tomorrow.

Rabbi: Let me see what I can do. I have lectured to the kitchen staff before on the needs of kosher patients. I'll try to rustle something up for you.

I made a quick phone call to dietary and then visited the kitchen. Sadie had a kosher meal for dinner that night.

There are many other examples of religious observance for which a rabbi's assistance can be invaluable. Obtaining Sabbath, holiday, or Hanukkah candles,[15] Prayer books and other religious objects, as well as ritual or other special foods for Sabbath and holidays, can enable the patient to feel a sense of familiarity at a time when the daily routine has been overturned. While there are times when laity can also assist the patient's religious practice (especially in a home setting) a rabbi, by virtue of learning, training, and community position, is better equipped to negotiate with hospital or nursing-home staff to facilitate these religious observances. If pastoral care means using the tools of religion to help the healing process, then the rabbi acting as pastoral manager can offer the warmth and structure of Jewish living at a time when a patient is most lonely.[16] Assisting these observances offers the invalid a sense of hope when it is needed most.[17]

THE RABBI'S ROLE AS TEACHER

As mentioned earlier in this chapter, the rabbi's teaching role is considered one of the major rabbinic roles in classical Judaism and, indeed, the word "rabbi" means master or teacher. Yet, most people in the midst of crisis situations are not interested in being taught.

Patients, when asking theological questions, are not really seeking theological answers. Questions of a seeming religious nature usually mask other deep-seated emotions such as fear, anger, guilt, loneliness, and so forth. When those struck by major illness ask, "Why is God doing this to me?" they are not looking for a learned dissertation about why evil things happen to good people. They need and seek human care, presence, and concern. At times, though, there are occasions when the theological questions are indeed philosophical rather than existential and can be the basis for a good discussion. Of course, the rabbi must have the training and ear to discern between real discussion and study issues and the existential and emotional issues that require a different response.

There may be appropriate moments when a specific teaching role is helpful in a hospital or illness setting. For an observant Jew, Sabbath and holiday observance, kosher food, and daily prayer are issues affected by hospital conditions. When the patient truly desires it, the rabbi is indispensable for guiding the invalid's personal religious practice. Here is another part of the verbatim transcript from my visit with "Sadie":

> Rabbi: In the meantime, you can certainly get by with fruits, vegetables, cold cereals, and cottage cheese, which I know are all kosher in this hospital.
> Sadie: How come those things don't need special kosher supervision?
> Rabbi: That is a good question. Fruits and vegetables are always considered kosher if they are fresh. Most cold unsweetened cereals are as well, as is milk. And in my checks of the hospital kitchen, I discovered that they only use cottage cheese with the "O-U" [a nationally recognized kosher symbol].

Thus, even teaching about observance can have a pastoral effect in further rooting patients to their tradition and people. In addition, the rabbi can play a valuable teaching role in alerting professional staff to issues of Jewish religious life. Medical, nursing, and social welfare care-givers can better serve their clients if they are aware of the patients' religious needs. What better person to instruct these staff than the local rabbi?

In addition, there are times when the simple study of the Torah itself can be therapeutic if the patient is so attuned. I will never forget when my late teacher Rabbi Herzl Kaplan, a talmudic scholar of note, was ill. The local hospital chaplain, also an Orthodox rabbi, made a point of visiting Rabbi Kaplan each day and studying Talmud together with him. For Rabbi Kaplan, in the opinion of the chaplain, Talmud study truly was pastoral care.[18]

THE RABBI AS MEMBER OF THE EXTENDED FAMILY

Earlier[19] we referred to the Talmud's suggestion that premature visiting and publicizing illness could be detrimental to the patient. Elsewhere in rabbinic literature, we have specific references to added responsibilities of family and close friends. For example:

> What is the difference between one who is sick and one who is considered dangerously ill? One who is merely sick is so in the normal way.[20] "Dangerously ill" refers to one whose sickness came suddenly.[21] For a normal sickness, relatives[22] visit immediately and those more distant visit[23] after three days. But if the sickness came suddenly, both [relatives and those more distant] can visit immediately.
> R. Huna, R. Pinhas, and R. Hilkiah desisted from visiting R. Yosi for three days. Said [R. Yosi] to them, "Through me must you fulfill this teaching?"[24]

From this passage we can see the importance of family visits to most patients at all times. The concerns that a patient might have with outsiders visiting too early do not apply to relatives. Also, a family visitor could have a better chance of alleviating the patient's suffering. Most of the commentaries explain the incident of the three rabbis and R. Yosi as illustrating the wisdom that close friends occupy the same place in this scheme as do relatives.[25] Close friends may and should visit immediately, before the three-day wait. Through their empathic visits, they can alleviate the anguish of one who is sick.[26]

It should be noted that the elements of the talmudic excerpt are codified as law.[27] In addition, all the codes agree that the three-day minimum wait for more distant acquaintances does not apply to actual care-givers or anyone the patient wishes to see.[28]

We have repeatedly pointed out that the responsibility for *bikur holim* falls on every Jew and is not strictly a "pastoral" concern. I would contend that from this talmudic passage, we can develop a distinctly pastoral role for the rabbi as a member of the patient's extended family. In this role the rabbi could visit the patient immediately, rather than wait three days.[29] More broadly, a rabbi who develops this type of relationship with his congregants can offer comfort and alleviate the loneliness of illness, in the same way a relative or close friend would. Obviously, not every rabbi is privileged to have this closeness. We are speaking here of a rabbinic ideal for which to work. But consider how much good could be accomplished if both rabbis and congregants would take the time and effort to foster caring pastoral relationships. Certainly, rabbis who can develop these bonds will be more successful in touching the lives of their members. Conversely, the congregant who makes the effort to connect with his/her rabbi in this way will reap the benefits in times of crisis.

THE RABBI AS DOCTOR OF THE SOUL

Some time ago, I published an article in which I suggested a parallel between the halakhic/historic development of the physician and that of the rabbi.[30] In four or five references from rabbinic literature, I showed that an erring physician who injures the patient in the course of healing duties is considered exempt from penalty, provided the physician was licensed by the *Bet Din* (Rabbinic Court).[31] In fact, Maimonides indicates that members of the higher Jewish courts had to be skilled in the medical arts and sciences in order to license physicians.[32] Similarly, the rabbinic sources make reference to rabbis and teachers who damage a student in the course of duties. In these cases as well, the rabbi is exempt from paying damages. I suggested that the reason for the exemptions is that these professionals are engaged in fulfilling a divine commandment or *mitzvah*—the physician healing and the rabbi teaching the Torah. We do not hold these people liable for damages that occur in this process.

I also discovered that all the premodern and modern commentators and codifiers of Jewish Law agree that today, medical school graduation, peer accreditation, and professional training and licensing would halakhically serve to exempt a physician from punishment or liability in cases of malfeasance.[33] To quote one premodern source, "And today if the . . . healers act with the permission of their sages [e.g., secular non-Jewish scholars], we can assume that all physicians are [halakhically] considered 'expert.'"[34]

And from a more recent source: "An expert is one who has a written document from the great physicians in the places the wisdom [of medicine] is taught, [one] who has learned and knows well. This document is called a 'diploma.'"[35]

In other words, the divine license would not operate unless there was a human license in operation.

Thus, there is a distinct parallel in malpractice issues between the physician and the rabbi. One acts as the doctor of the body and, we might propose, the other acts as the doctor of the soul. According to Jewish Law, both are exempt from liability, provided they were trained properly and did their utmost to fulfill their jobs in pursuit of the divine commandment.

As the medical profession developed into its modern format and standards, so too did *halakhah* take these developments into consideration in its dealing with malpractice. According to Jewish Law, a doctor of the body must be properly trained in the finest and most up-to-date techniques to be granted the divine license. If we extend the parallel between doctor and rabbi along these lines, we might say that the role of the rabbi has also grown in modern times. Today, a rabbi is called upon to give pastoral care, especially in crisis situations such as illness. To continue to engage in this *mitzvah* with a "divine license," the modern incarnation of the traditional rabbi must also have the necessary training and credentials. With these, the "divine license" would continue to operate. This formal training could include courses in counseling (especially pastoral counseling), knowledge of crisis issues and crisis intervention, and knowledge of the Jewish sources in these issues.[36]

Besides the formal training necessary for this modern yet not-so-modern role as "doctor of the soul," I would suggest that the role of rabbi is to become an exemplar in empathy. Rabbis, as spiritual leaders and teachers, are expected to be role models in much of Jewish behavior and Jewish living. Therefore, it is not illogical or difficult to expect rabbis to strive to be exemplars in *bikur holim* as well. A "doctor of the soul" must be an expert in empathy in order to fulfill the specific rabbinic role that others cannot or will not do. A "doctor of the soul" must also be able to train others in these areas.

All this raises an important question: If empathy implies an emotional concern and sharing,[37] how can such a thing be trained or learned? Either one has it, or one does not. It may be possible to hone one's skills in this area, but what if one simply does not have the personality for this kind of work? Does that cut down the effectiveness of a rabbi or disqualify the person from the rabbinate? Can one learn empathy?

Obviously, some personalities are better at pastoral skills than others. But if we use Switzer's definition of empathy as a cognitive process that involves the visitor imagining him or herself being in the other's position, we then have a goal for which many can train.[38] At the same time, we can find a Torah basis for a cognitive empathy. Many times, the Torah offers a commandment of an emotional nature, such as, "Love your neighbor as yourself," and, "You shall not covet." Does the Torah have the right to make commands of an emotional nature? How can one fulfill commandments that involve emotion? While some commentators suggest that the Torah is indeed attempting to legislate emotions, we may for our purposes follow those opinions that say that the Torah is legislating behavior out of which emotions will freely grow.[39] Just as the Torah wants us to behave in a loving manner, even if we do not feel the sense of love every moment, so too does the Torah desire for us to behave in an empathic manner, at least with those in pain who need our pastoral care. This is an ideal for which rabbis may strive, even if they do not see themselves as particularly empathic. This is also a goal for which one can find training and a goal for which gifted people may train others with their own exemplary pastoral skills.

THE RABBI AS REPRESENTING THE COMMUNITY

One final role a rabbi may play is that of *shaliah* or representative. We have seen earlier that while a personal visit is considered the ideal,[40] it is not only permissible, but also a fulfillment of the *mitzvah* to send someone else to convey good wishes.[41] Without detracting from the need and importance of laypeople visiting their peers while ill,[42] we can say that a synagogue rabbi does indeed represent the congregation when paying a hospital call. Further, it may be suggested that a rabbinic chaplain visiting hospitals or institutions represents the entire Jewish community. Certainly, the patient sees the rabbi in this role during the visit.[43] Indeed, one of the therapeutic aspects of the pastoral visits is the knowledge that the patient will be remembered in the living community.[44] Besides, many and perhaps most congregations hire their rabbis with the understanding that they will make hospital or home calls to members who are ill. As the Talmud puts it, "*Shluho shel adam kamoto*," a representative in Jewish Law has the status of the sender.[45] In all these aspects, the rabbi can truly be said to act as the community's *shaliah*.

RABBINIC ROLES IN DEALING
WITH THE RELIGIOUS LEVEL OF THE PATIENT

Any of the above-mentioned rabbinic roles could apply in dealing with patients of varying observance levels. However, the religious feeling and practice of the particular patient may make certain roles more appropriate. Tsvi Schur, a professional hospital chaplain, writes of four types of patients, each type reacting to crisis in a different religious way and each having specific needs.[46] The first is the devout individual[47] with a firm belief in God.[48] This individual, who at times feels fear or doubts and asks questions, still sees his or her mission in life as a positive one of serving the Almighty. While death might be accepted more easily, since it is considered divine will, it is also an end to the person's service on earth. Schur suggests that a rabbi's presence can truly help the person who actively seeks purpose in life, because a rabbi, by virtue of learning, calling, and training, represents such purpose. A devout individual may value the rabbinic teaching role, especially if Torah study was a part of that person's life prior to illness. Rabbinic guidance on issues of observance would be appreciated by one who would attempt to maintain those observances within a hospital or institutional setting. In addition, someone with a well-developed sense of faith might be more interested in the philosophical questions that may arise during this period. A skillful pastoral rabbi would attempt to combine teaching with an empathic presence for this individual. In addition, some effort as pastoral manager might be helpful in facilitating the patient's religious life while ill.

Schur's second category is that of the nonobservant individual who still has religious feelings and loyalties. It is often possible to reach this person with religious language and tools. He/she often asks for prayer and at times displays fear, regret, or guilt.[49] This person's Judaism, while not practiced as often as the observant person's, is still present, and the patient can respond positively to a specifically Jewish form of pastoral care. Some teaching might be appropriate, depending on the needs expressed by the patient. However, the roles of community representative and member of the extended family might be most helpful here. People in Schur's second category, while not always religiously observant, often have a deep and abiding loyalty to Jewish peoplehood and to the Jewish community. A rabbi, in the community-defined role, can benefit such individuals by connecting them to the living community. In addition, many within this category are attached to synagogue life; thus a rabbi who has cultivated the pastoral role as member of the congregant's family can play a major role in guiding the invalid's healing process.

Schur's third category is that of the agnostic who is not really sure of life or belief. This person shares the emotions of the previous type of individual. It is possible to reach this person at the right moment with the comfort of religion and a caring presence.

The last category is that of the atheist. Schur says that the actual self-proclaimed atheist is rather rare. More often he has found those he calls "hysterical atheists." These are people who have gone through suffering and tend to deny God out of bitterness rather than belief. Often, these persons exhibit anger and then aim it at God. Trying to intellectually convince such patients of the need for God and religion is futile. But the presence of a caring rabbi (or a caring religious layperson, for that matter) can often show the benefits of a religious life and make a deep impression. Even people who think they have rejected religion exhibit religious needs in times of crisis.[50] A rabbi must be a caring, loving, and professional visitor even to those who think they have rejected religion. This is in imitation of the Almighty, who loves His children, both believers and atheists.[51]

BIKUR HOLIM COMMITTEES

One area where rabbinic pastoral roles and general lay pastoral roles converge is in the facilitation of *bikur holim* visitation committees. Since talmudic times, there have been groups of individuals organized within the Jewish community for the express purpose of communal needs. For example:

> Rabbi Yehudah said in the name of Rav: If there is a death in the city, all citizens are forbidden to do work [in order to tend to the needs of the deceased]. R. Hamnuna went to Daromta and heard there the sound of the funeral-*shofar*. He then saw some people who were still doing work. He said to them, "These people should be placed under the *shamta*.[52] Is there not a dead person in town?" [But] they told him "There is a *hevrah* [a committee or association] in town"[53] [which does these tasks and fills these needs]. He said, "If so, it is permitted [to do work]."[54]

Or:

> Such was the practice of the *havurot* [associations or committees] in Jerusalem: some went to the house of the mourners; some to the house of [marriage] feasting, some went to a circumcision, others to gather up the bones. . . .[55]

While it is possible that *bikur holim* societies existed in the time of the Talmud, we have no record of groups devoted specifically to the needs of the ill until the fourteenth century. A number of Spanish Jewish communities supported these groups, and the Spanish exiles took the idea with them until it spread throughout Europe in the sixteenth and seventeenth centuries.[56] Rich and poor as well as visiting Jews received care from these *bikur holim* societies, and the members made sure that no one was left alone. Society members paid entrance fees and regular dues. The groups often administered bequests, giving the income to charity. This sometimes led to powerful influence in the community. Besides visiting the ill, *bikur holim* groups aided transients, sponsored circumcisions, aided in childbirth, and safeguarded local physicians. They took care of the physical needs of the sick as well as the needy. Many of the groups had bylaws that regulated the number of visits to a patient and the amount of assistance offered and enjoined their members to submit regular reports on patients.

In the eighteenth century, groups of women called *Nashim Tzidkaniot* (Righteous Women) were formed to act as nurses, offer medical attention, and visit sick women. By the end of the eighteenth century, these efforts led to the formation of Jewish hospitals in Western European cities. This process continued on American shores, where there are still Jewish hospitals operating in many major cities today.

Nowhere in any of the records does the question of rabbinic involvement in the *bikur holim* groups arise, other than in regard to rabbis ruling on questions of Jewish Law pertaining to these groups. There is no doubt that rabbis visited patients, but they did so on their own. The focus of the patients' needs was a communal rather than rabbinic concern. Yet in the Western world, sick care has become institutionalized through the hospital and medical profession. At the same time, rabbis, possibly under the overwhelming influence of surrounding Christian communities, have tended to make sick calls one of their rabbinic priorities. As indicated earlier, this is often expected by congregants.

A rabbi can play an important pastoral role by helping to train and organize *bikur holim* groups. These groups are experiencing a renaissance in the United States.[57] They are based in Jewish federations, synagogues, hasidic communities, and independent community groups. However, many members are often lacking in knowledge of the Jewish sources of *bikur holim*.[58] Similarly, many well-meaning and religious Jews who want to fulfill the *mitzvah* of "walking in God's ways" are unfamiliar with the clinical skills necessary in dealing with the ill. A knowledgeable, caring, and active rabbi can offer a tremendous service in helping to set up a *bikur holim* committee. The rabbi's role would be that of teacher, instructing the members in the Jewish sources for the *mitzvah*, and pastoral manager, helping to set up this committee in conjunction with local hospitals and congregations. In large congregations, this group would aid the rabbi in pastoral calls, since it is usually difficult for clergy of large synagogues to visit all their sick. In smaller congregations, while the rabbi may not require aid in reaching all the ill, the group can still be viewed as a way of deepening the ties that bind the members.

A CASE HISTORY

Through my guidance, a bikur holim committee was formed as an adjunct to a hospital pastoral-care committee and department. Originally, there was only one part-time professional employed by this hospital, a Protestant minister who was unable to cover all of her territory. The New York Board of Rabbis had earlier offered a small salary to a local rabbi to act as a Jewish chaplain. However, even under the best of circumstances, he could not be in the hospital more than a few hours a week. The dozens of Jewish patients there on a daily basis were not visited.

I managed to get a good number of volunteers from my synagogue, along with a few from another congregation. We connected with the Metropolitan Coordinating Committee on Bikur Holim, and with their help as well as with the ongoing support of the Protestant chaplain and the hospital itself, we began to train this group. Gradually, we began to receive support from other area laypeople and congregations. The group has continued to grow and to be active as a "lay visitation" committee, assisting the hospital chaplain and fulfilling an important community need.

In summary, the mitzvah of bikur holim in Jewish eyes is one that devolves on all Jews, rabbis as well as laypeople. Yet we can discern some specific roles that rabbis may play. These include the role of pastoral manager, helping the ill to practice Judaism while they are sick, and training laypeople to fulfill the mitzvah of bikur holim; the role of teacher, sharing the wisdom of the Torah at appropriate moments and teaching others about bikur holim; the role of close friend and member of the extended family, allowing physical and emotional access to patients; the role of "doctor of the soul," trained exemplar of caring empathy; and the role of community representative.

III

DEATH, GRIEF, AND BEREAVEMENT

7

Aninut—The Initial
Stage of Grief

HALAKHIC ISSUES

The study of *bikur holim* in Part II explored some of the therapeutic and clinical benefits found in Jewish tradition regarding illness and has shown how helping the ill is a divine commandment incumbent on everyone. Within this context, several unique pastoral roles were developed for rabbis based on sources in classic Jewish literature.

Part III will analyze the area of death and mourning in Jewish tradition. A great deal has been written already on this subject, and this book will not attempt to explore areas already covered by other works.[1] While selected major issues in the Jewish traditions of mourning will be studied, this book will not attempt to offer a complete English summary of all the laws of mourning. In addition to analyzing therapeutic aspects of the *halakhah* of mourning, the rabbinic models of Jewish pastoral theology will be further developed, focusing on responsibilities of both rabbis and laypeople.

Aninut is both the name and description of the stage the Jewish mourner enters upon hearing the news of death of a close relative. Close relatives are biological parents, biological children,[2] siblings, and spouse. This stage lasts until the time of the burial.[3] During this time, many of the *shivah* regulations[4] apply, including the bans on laundering, grooming, greeting people, haircuts, the study of

Torah, regular work routines,[5] sexual relations, and anything of a joyous nature. In addition, the *onen* (mourner who is in this state) does not eat meat or drink wine, foods associated with joy. The *onen* is exempt[6] from positive time-bound commandments, including the daily prayers and blessings, wearing of a *tallit* (the prayer shawl), *tefillin* (phylacteries),[7] and the like. The mourner is still bound to observe all the negative commandments ("the don'ts of Judaism") such as the Sabbath restrictions,[8] the kosher laws, and so on.[9] *Aninut* restrictions generally do not apply on the Sabbath in public, since the Sabbath joy still transcends the mourning, albeit to a limited extent. The mourner attends synagogue but would not receive any public honors (such as being called to the Torah) or leadership roles (such as acting as cantor).

There is another restriction on the *onen* that emanates from the relationship of the mourner to the community. The *onen* is not counted for a *minyan*, the requisite ten that are required for communal prayer,[10] or to a *mezuman*, the requisite three that can say Grace After Meals as a group. Halakhically, this is derived from the fact that since *onenim* are not bound to pray, they would not be considered part of the community. Psychologically, this reflects the fact that at this grief-stricken moment, the *onen* cannot share in prayer with the group.[11]

Aninut is biblical in origin. Its primary source is Leviticus 10, the story of the death of the high priest Aaron's two sons, Nadav and Avihu. The Talmud sees Aaron's reluctance to participate in the Temple service following the loss of his sons as the precedent for future priests to refrain from various priestly duties during *aninut*.[12] The codes deduce that the day of death (termed the "first day"), is considered biblical *aninut*, while any other subsequent time between death and burial is rabbinical *aninut*.[13]

ROOTS OF THE TERM REPRESENTING GRIEF SYMPTOMS

A linguistic study of the Hebrew term *aninut* will tell us much about the symptoms of grief. The Hebrew roots of this word include *an*, which means "where?" and *ana*, a lament, elegy, plea,[14] or cry of pain. Another significant use of the term is in the Torah, where the Israelites were murmuring[15] (Heb. *"mitonenim"*—note the root of this is identical to *aninut*) about their conditions in the desert.[16] The various commentaries explain this word as doubting,[17] pain- or sorrow-filled,[18] accusing,[19] mentioning calamity and tyranny,[20] grieving,[21] crying out, pleading, and complaining.[22] Elsewhere, the Torah refers to the fact that Rachel originally named her youngest son Benjamin, "Ben-Oni," child of my sorrow or trouble, due to her difficulties in childbirth.[23] In rabbinic literature, the definition and application of the root *an* is expanded to include *ona-a*, oppression, wrong, or fraud,[24] *aven*, curved, hollow, or pressed,[25] as well as sensitive.[26]

Together, these interpretations and applications of the original Hebrew offer a powerful statement about the emotional and existential state of the person learning of a loved one's death. The Hebrew implies rage, emptiness, denial, pleading, anger, depression, bewilderment, grief, sorrow, illness, panic, fear, and a host of other emotions common to this stage. In fact, the Hebrew *aninut* actually anticipates many modern studies of grief symptomatology that diagnose these areas of grief in various forms.[27]

RABBINIC SOURCES AND THEMES

As indicated above, the psychological state of the *onen* is one of shock, coupled with the various emotional reactions mentioned earlier. The Talmud puts it, *"Aninut is only in the heart."*[28]

Rabbinic literature offers guidance for people at this stage with the words "Do not comfort a person while his dead lies before him."[29] This can be understood in an instructional or halakhic sense—one simply should not offer words of comfort before the funeral and burial. The bereaved are not yet ready to accept kind wishes from the members of the community while still in the state of bewilderment that characterizes *aninut*. While this may seem like good advice, I have found that it is often ignored by people with the best intentions. I have seen in my own rabbinate and that of colleagues how the period just before the funeral becomes a sort of reception time. The mourners' home becomes a meeting area at a time when the family is least able to handle it. The interval just before the funeral becomes a "reception line" time at the chapel for well-meaning

acquaintances, when it should be an intimate though sad few minutes for the closest family and friends. The community's time to
comfort is more appropriately the week of *shivah* that immediately
follows the funeral and burial.

One can also translate this rabbinic dictum to be understood
in the psychoemotional and theological sense: "You cannot comfort
the person while his dead lies before him." This can be seen in several
different ways. One commentary explains it as the mourner's personal issue: "When his sorrow stands before him, the mourner will
not accept condolences."[30] Another source sees this as a societal
issue: "An ethical idea in the setting up of human communities."[31]
A third interpretation involves the ill effects the well-intended condolences will have because of the mourners' emotional condition:
"For in his hour of sorrow, the condolence will increase [the mourner's]
anger and he will say things not good [i.e., his/her condition will
worsen]."[32] A basis for this last idea comes from a story of how the
angels wanted to comfort the Almighty as He mourned the destruction of the Temple, and God refused to accept the angelic condolences! "The Divine Spirit responded, 'Do not strain to comfort me,
for the destruction of the daughter of my people'" (Isaiah 22:4).[33]

In summary, the period between the death of a loved one and
the burial is one in which empathy cannot really be accepted or appreciated by most people.[34] Unlike our previous cases of the sick
patient, and unlike the period after the funeral, there is very little
one can do or say to alleviate the mourner's suffering. The most we
can do, both to honor the deceased as well as help the bereaved, is
simply to be there.

The second part of the rabbinic statement regarding the ban
on comforting "while his dead lies before him" requires some analysis. The simplest explanation of the statement refers to earlier times
when the immediate family actually did the preburial preparations,
and the corpse was physically in their presence. However, the Talmud itself deals with this question and answers,

> Since [the obligation] to bury lies before him, it is as if the corpse
> itself lies before him, [even if the physical presence of the corpse
> is not there] as it says (Genesis 23:4-5), "And Abraham rose up

from before his dead and he spoke . . . 'and I will bury my dead from before me.'"[35]

In other words, during the time when the family is busy making the funeral arrangements, the corpse is psychologically or emotionally "before them." Even if individuals in the immediate family are not actually making the arrangements, they are still considered in *aninut*. This is either because they have the potential to make the arrangements and could be part of the process,[36] or because these family members are obliged to honor the dead, and the arrangements are part of the honor (even if they themselves are not making those arrangements).[37]

Another major rabbinic theme of the *aninut* period, as well as the periods that extend beyond it, is *lo'eg larash*. This is based on the first two Hebrew words of a biblical verse, "Whoever mocks the poor [*lo'eg larash*] blasphemes his Maker; whoever rejoices at calamity shall not be [regarded as] innocent."[38] One of the classical commentaries explains that one who insults the product (any human being, even the poorest) also insults the creator (in this case, the Creator).[39] In terms of *aninut* this means that one cannot stand by as though life is normal when this type of tragedy occurs. If one does, this insults the deceased ("mocks the poor") who is not able to respond; this also insults the Creator—the Almighty. This concept can be connected to *aninut* in the sense that the *onen* does not recite the *Shema* or the daily service.[40] The Talmud[41] extends this thought beyond the *onen* to anyone in close contact with the deceased.

> A person should not go to the cemetery with *tefillin* [phylacteries] on his arm and head and recite the *Shema*.[42] And if he does, he transgresses *lo'eg larash*.

> Whoever sees the dead and does not escort him transgresses *lo'eg larash* . . . and if he escorts what is his reward? R. Asi applies the scriptural verses to him, "God escorts the one that lends to the poor";[43] "He that is gracious to the needy honors Him."[44]

As one modern scholar suggests, these are all ". . . reminders that the dead can no longer perform *mitzvot*."[45]

THEOLOGICAL ISSUES

Rabbi Joseph B. Soloveitchik, in a major essay, writes:

> *Aninut* represents the spontaneous human reaction to death. It
> is an outcry, a shout or a howl of grisly horror and disgust. Man
> responds to his defeat at the hands of death with total resigna-
> tion and with an all-consuming masochistic self-devastating
> black despair. Beaten by the fiend, his prayers rejected, envel-
> oped by a hideous darkness, forsaken and lonely, man begins
> to question his own human singular reality. Doubt develops
> quickly into a cruel conviction and doubting man turns to mock-
> ing man.[46]

In Soloveitchik's view, life appears to have lost to death (at least
in the existential sense) after a person has experienced the loss of a
loved one. Even in the eyes of a life-affirming worldview such as
that of Judaism, we cannot expect the mourner to pray or answer
"Amen" when struck with tragedy. Hence, the *halakhah* exempts the
onen from the positive commandments of the Torah, including regular prayer, blessings, and the like. As Soloveitchik writes, "The commitment accepted in Egypt is applicable to the man who is preoc-
cupied with life, and not to one who has encountered death."[47] The
covenant of the Exodus is for the living. When the covenant has
apparently been broken—and this is an accurate emotional description of one who has just suffered a loss—the Torah does not call on
the mourner to affirm that covenant.[48]

> Therefore, the *halakhah* has tolerated those "crazy" torturing
> thoughts and doubts. It did not command the mourner to dis-
> own them because they contradict the basic halakhic doctrine
> of man's election as king of the universe. It permitted the
> mourner to have his way for a while and has ruled that the latter
> be relieved of all *mitzvot*.[49]

Another psychotheological theory ties the *aninut* exemption
from positive time-bound *mitzvot* to the need to make preparations
for the burial.[50] The exemption from these *mitzvot* based on the
obligation to make preparations—even if the individual mourner is

not specifically engaged in the arrangements—forces the *onen* to confront death, while at the same time he or she is expected to

> overcome his wish for identification and incorporation with the lost loved one. The *onen* through his actions experiences the fact that he is "not dead," not still and lifeless, as he may consciously or unconsciously feel or wish himself to be.[51]

Many mourners facing the immediate death of a loved one express a kind of "death wish," as if they are saying, "Why them and not me?" Instead of giving in to these feelings or denying them, the mourner confronts them and works through them.[52] The period of *aninut* mandates the mourner to do whatever he or she can for the deceased. Thus the mourner is released from other religious obligations to facilitate this.

Since the *onen* is released from prayers until after the funeral and burial, there is no real liturgy for *aninut*. However, the Talmud offers an intriguing prayer for the *onen*, to be recited while others are saying the daily service.

> . . . And he accepts upon himself the divine decree. And what does he say? "Master of the Universe! I have sinned before you. Few of my obligations have I wiped clean, and am I not fit for more [of my punishment]? May it be Your will to repair our breaches and to comfort us."[53]

Jack Spiro understands this prayer as a confession of guilt and also as a defense mechanism. In his view, the mourner's hope for more punishment could alleviate his/her severe guilt feelings.[54] Spiro attempts to connect this to David's words after the death of his son Absalom.[55]

A careful reading of the text and parallel talmudic selections would suggest that Spiro's reading of emotions during *aninut* is a contrived attempt to match this passage with Freudian theory. Elsewhere, the Talmud itself rejects the use of this prayer!

> If the deceased is not lying before them, they [the congregation] sit and read [the *Shema*] and he [the *onen*] sits in silence. They stand and pray [the *Amidah*] and he [the *onen*] stands and ac-

cepts upon himself the divine decree. And he says, "Master of the Universe! Much I have sinned before You, and I have not even been paid back one of a thousand [for it]. May it be Your will, O Lord our God, to repair our breaches and the breaches of your nation Israel, and to comfort us."

Abaye says that a person should never ask in this way, for as R. Shimon B. Levi said, and also it was said in the name of R. Yosi, "A person should never open his mouth to the Satan" [one should never invite action or ask for something he or she would not want].[56]

Abaye suggests that the *onen* is already suffering enough, attempting to come to grips with death and loss. We do not know that this death is a punishment for anything,[57] because we do not know the divine agenda.[58] To suggest that the *onen* should ask for more is simply unacceptable. Abaye's view is accepted by Alfasi[59] and codified in Jewish Law.[60] Thus, in contrast to Spiro, normative Jewish tradition does not accept the idea that asking for punishment will alleviate the mourner's guilt. Rather, as the Talmud says, silence and the attempts to grasp the tragedy are the order of the day for the *onen*.[61]

RABBINIC ROLES DURING *ANINUT*

Part II on *bikur holim* described the parallel of community roles to rabbinic roles in Jewish pastoral theology. In Jewish mourning tradition, both roles still exist, but not in parallel form. During *aninut* the community role is minimal, due to the psychotheological and halakhic factors enumerated above. Most laypeople are not able to truly guide or comfort the mourner in the pastoral sense. As the bereaved enters the later stages of mourning, the community's role increases and becomes more crucial with the passage of time. However, the rabbinic role during *aninut* is exceedingly important.

In chapter 6, I outlined several pastoral models and roles for the rabbi. They were: pastoral manager, teacher, representative of the community, doctor of the soul, and member of the extended family. Each one of these models is essential during *aninut*, and they frequently converge during the rabbinic prefuneral visit.[62]

Pastoral management, in the sense of helping the family through the various arrangements, is probably the most immediate role for the rabbi during *aninut*. In ancient times, the family would make all the arrangements themselves and do the actual preparations through the burial.[63] Today, things are quite a bit more complicated. One must deal with government authorities, burial permits, funeral chapels, cemeteries, and much more. In addition, most families are not knowledgeable enough or desirous of making the religious arrangements for washing and dressing the body and conducting the service and postburial observances. In the last sixty years, funeral home businesses have taken over quite a bit of the general arrangements as well as issues of religious observance. This can often cause great difficulty for the family. Part of the role of the rabbi involves navigating these matters, helping the family to plan the service to be authentically Jewish and also meeting their personal needs. The rabbi needs to have a relationship with the funeral director in order to do this.[64] Personally, I also review other questions pertaining to the service and burial, such as pallbearers, the question of gravesite versus chapel services, the participation of the family during the burial, and postburial issues such as services in the home during the week of *shivah*.

I have noticed that in large metropolitan areas, some rabbis tend to ignore this important function. Especially for nonaffiliated Jews or in very large congregations, they let the funeral home make the arrangements and only meet briefly with the family just before the service. I believe these rabbis, besides being cold and unfeeling, are losing precious opportunities to educate fellow Jews and engage in pastoral care at its highest level. More lives would be touched and more Torah tradition would be reclaimed if rabbis would take additional time to meet with mourners before the service.

Closely tied to the manager role is the role of teacher. People who are nonobservant or not knowledgeable in Jewish mourning tradition certainly need the rabbi to guide them through the different practices at each point along the way. Most people are grateful when their rabbis take the opportunity to explain why each law or custom exists, along with its history, meaning, and value. Rabbis should feel a personal responsibility to educate, while recognizing and respecting that some may not choose to observe everything. *Aninut* is the appropriate moment for this type of outreach.[65] Also, even highly educated and observant Jews need rabbinical guidance at this stage. The shock and emotional numbness of this period tends to blur people's familiarity with Jewish tradition, and rabbinic help is both needed and valued at this time. Even people who consider themselves religiously knowledgeable welcome the rabbi during *aninut*, both as teacher and as pastoral manager.

The role of rabbi as representing the community may not be as major as some of the others at the *aninut* stage, but I believe that the rabbi's presence at the home of the family does give them the sense that the community is present with them. Though, as stated earlier, true condolences are not/cannot be offered yet, I have always sensed that my company and availability reassure the family that the Jewish community, as represented by me, does indeed share their grief.

Earlier, it was indicated that *aninut* is a time when most people are not able to accept condolences. As a result, most visitors are not yet able to share empathic feelings with the bereaved. For this reason, condolence visiting is discouraged until after the burial. However, a well-trained rabbi in the role of exemplar in empathy may be able to break through the emotional barriers of *aninut*. A rabbi with a trained ear and sensitive heart can be a comforting presence to the *onen*.[66] Also, the rabbi acting as "doctor of the soul" allows the mourners the chance to express their feelings about the deceased as well as their sense of sorrow and loss. Not all families wish to talk, and obviously, one cannot force people to talk. When this occurs, I respect it. But I have found it extremely therapeutic for the family to share memories, anecdotes, stories, and emotions. In addition, it is most helpful in preparing my eulogy to hear about the deceased, for I like to include a "slice of life" about him or her.[67] This becomes even more crucial when the rabbi does not know the deceased and must speak about him/her. What I was taught in rabbinical school, "Let the family write the eulogy for you,"[68] has truly been good advice.

The rabbi's role as a member of the extended family is not so much a task but a goal and descriptive of the relationship that allows the spiritual leader best access to the family and maximum possibility to fulfill the other roles. When a rabbi is blessed with such a relationship with a congregant, the other roles and tasks will go more smoothly. Just as a family wants all of its members to be there when deep loss is experienced, so too will a caring rabbinic presence add a comforting dimension at times of grief.[69]

8

Keriah—The Tearing of the Garment

HALAKHAH AND THEOLOGY

The tearing of a garment as a tangible show of grief has biblical roots. There are numerous instances in the Torah where individuals tear their clothes to show sorrow.[1] Most of these, however, are occurrences of sorrow after nonnatural disasters, not necessarily involving death. The main halakhic source for our practice of tearing after death is Leviticus 10:6, the chapter describing the demise of Aaron's two sons. There, Moses tells Aaron, "Do not loosen your hair or tear your clothes, so that you will not die."

The Sages understood from the above verse that this specific command to priests officiating in the Temple was a special instruction not to tear, and therefore a divinely ordained deviation from the norm. Otherwise, they would still have been obligated to tear during their grief. As the Talmud puts it, "A mourner who does not tear his clothes (at the time of death) is liable for the death penalty."[2]

In spite of the apparent importance of the practice indicated in this quote, as well as the extensive scriptural background for *keriah*, the commentaries differ on whether the obligation is biblical[3] or rabbinical.[4] Either way, this tradition is extremely important and deeply ingrained in Jewish practice.

81

Classically, the *keriah* is done by individuals in the following situations:

1. Being present near the place where the patient died.
2. Upon hearing of the death of an *adam kasher* (lit. a kosher person), a fine, upstanding human being.
3. Upon hearing the news of the death of a great Torah scholar.
4. Upon hearing the news of the death of one's own personal rabbi or teacher.
5. Upon the death of the relatives over which one is obligated in *aninut* (and subsequent mourning). These include one's biological parents, biological children, siblings, and spouse. One may also tear for other relatives if desired.[5]

It is possible that if *keriah* were performed for everyone in this lengthy list, there would never be an end to the clothing one would have to tear, since these encounters with death in the community happen frequently. Therefore, *keriah* today is generally done for members of the family for whom formal mourning is observed. Obviously, though, the list demonstrates that *keriah* is a graphic act showing the anguish one feels at the saddest occasions associated with the loss of life.[6]

There are several reasons offered for the practice of *keriah*, including:

1. Deepening the sense of pain and sorrow.[7]
2. Confronting the individual with the recognition of the sanctity and importance of life at the time when life is lost.[8]
3. The loss of an article of clothing graphically symbolizes the personal sense of loss to the mourner.[9]
4. Ridding the heart of cruelty and anger[10] by sensitizing the heart to loss, thereby fostering reconciliation, repentance, and return.[11]
5. Tearing the clothing is symbolic of the rending of the relationship between the deceased and those still alive.[12]
6. As a substitute for or sublimation of the ancient pagan rituals of self-mutilation, which are not permitted in Jewish Law.[13]

Originally, *keriah* was accompanied by *halitzat katef*, the baring of the shoulders. Apparently in the rabbinic period up through the medieval period,[14] the clothing would be ripped in such a way as to show the upper part of the body.[15] This may have been an extreme emotional reaction to grief, a way of lowering one's own personal honor for the honor of the deceased.[16] To put it in different terms, it may have been a means of sharing empathy with the deceased. In this sense, it was probably tied to a number of the reasons mentioned above, including deepening of one's sorrow, loss of clothing symbolizing loss of a loved one or the relationship with the loved one, and a substitute for self-mutilation. It was generally done near the deathbed and not elsewhere, nor was it done after the funeral.[17] It could have been performed for anyone but was considered an obligation for loss of parents and also for the loss of major community leaders and teachers.

By the time Jewish Law was codified, this tradition had either been discarded or lost, as stated in the Codes, "There are those who say that now in this time, we are not accustomed to bare the shoulder at all; and this is our practice today."[18] Several reasons are suggested, including the idea that one's own diminished personal honor or dignity must be weighed against the honor due to one's teacher and the honor due to the Torah,[19] or it may be too difficult to tear in this fashion today, given our clothing patterns and style of garments.[20] None of the twentieth-century halakhic sources even mention this tradition. Apparently, if *halitzat katef* is an issue of "honoring the deceased," Jewish tradition and Jewish communities for the last several hundred years have not felt the need to honor in this way. Certainly this tradition would be very difficult to use or reintroduce in light of modern Western sensibilities.[21] Yet, one must ask why this tradition has passed by the wayside when so many others, equally difficult to understand and perform, have remained. Could it be that we have lost the emotional need or capacity to deeply grieve in the graphic way *halitzat katef* suggests?

Keriah is done on an article of clothing near the heart. Rabbinic sources describe this as *megaleh et libo*, or revealing the heart.[22] In many ways[23] the tearing of a garment near the heart symbolizes the emotions felt in the heart at this time.[24] The tear is done on the left side for parents and the right side for other relatives. This may be due to the stronger bond that usually exists between parents and children, or to the fact that a person has only one mother or father but could have other siblings, spouses, or children.[25]

There are other differences between tearing for a parent and for other relatives. One is that the obligation to tear for other relatives is only before and during the thirty-day period following the funeral. For parents, however, the obligation to tear always remains,[26] even long after the initial mourning period has concluded.[27] The Talmud explains this as a function of "honoring one's parents," which continues after the death of the parents.[28] This in turn raises questions in cases, found more and more frequently, when the child feels no emotional bond with the parents. We might well ask whether an abused child or one with a large emotional distance between him/herself and the parent still must tear. Halakhically, the answer is yes, because, at the very least, the biological bond has been severed. One minimally acknowledges the fact that the deceased parent brought the survivor into the world, even if he or she did not fulfill the obligations of parenting.[29]

There are other differences between *keriah* for parents and *keriah* for other relatives. The tear for other relatives can be done with someone's aid and through an instrument such as a knife or blade, while at least part of the cut for a parent should be done by the mourner by his or her own hand. The tearing for other relatives may be done privately, but the tradition for those who are mourning parents is to tear in the presence of others.[30]

The torn garment may be basted (after the *shivah* week) or sewn back together (after the thirty-day *shloshim* period) if it was torn for a nonparental relative. For a parent the garment may be basted together after the thirty-day *shloshim* period but should not be fully sewn together again. In either case this symbolizes the theme that while life goes on, it can never be completely the same after the loss has occurred. For one mourning parents, it also connotes the fact that the mourner is no longer fully able to fulfill the *mitzvah* of honoring them.

The Talmud states that the tear has to be done *beshaat himum*, literally at a time of great emotional heat or pain.[31] While there is some dispute as to when this point specifically occurs,[32] our custom today is to do the tearing at the time of greatest emotional feeling. Usually, this is just before the funeral service, though it is occasionally just afterward, or sometimes at the gravesite.[33]

The tear should be the length of a *tefah*, a handbreadth, three to four inches long. More than this would be considered a transgression of *baal tash'hit*, the prohibition of wasting (in this case, clothing). It must be a clean tear, fully separating the sides of the cut. The color and age of the clothing that are cut are unimportant in terms of religious practice. The tearing is done standing, indicating the importance of this act.[34] After the initial *shivah* week of mourning is over, the garment need not be worn.

Unlike most of the other *mitzvot* that come from the Torah or rabbinic tradition, *keriah* has no specific blessing over its performance. The rabbis were reluctant to attach a blessing to a seeming act of destruction, even one warranted by the Torah. Also, since the *onen* does not perform positive time-bound *mitzvot* or utter their blessings, he or she would also not say a blessing over this *mitzvah*.[35]

However, there is a very important blessing associated with the grief period and, since medieval times, said before performing *keriah*.[36] The blessing is *Dayan Ha'emet* and reads, "Blessed are You, Lord our God, Sovereign of the Universe, the true Judge."[37] While this blessing is traditionally said any time one receives very bad news, it takes on special meaning here. It has been classically explained as the attempt to justify God's actions, be they good or bad. This flows from the traditional belief, expressed in the Talmud, that "whatever God does is for the good."[38] Jewish life certainly affirms this as a general tenet, and some mourners are able to accept the idea. Yet, this explanation is not always satisfying to many in the *aninut* situation. When deep grief and loss strike, one is not always ready to accept conventional theological wisdom or dogma.[39] However, the basic idea behind this blessing acknowledges God's ultimate power over life and death. During *aninut* the mourner attempts to come to grips with the tragedy that has occurred. By referring to God as "the true Judge," the survivor recognizes that death as well as life is part of God's ultimate plan.[40] Much of the funeral service moves the mourner to face the stark reality that has occurred, and *keriah* is the first step. This blessing also may be explained not as an affirmation of faith in the face of tragedy but rather as a goal toward which to work. The ultimate hope of consolation and healing involves the reaffirmation of faith, but this does not happen immediately. Rather, the mourner can view this blessing as a goal, something for which to strive within the mourning and healing process.[41]

RABBINIC ROLES DURING *KERIAH*

In viewing the community/rabbinic roles developed in Part II of this study, we noted that many of the activities that contemporary Christianity considers "pastoral" relate in Judaism to all participants and not only to clergy. This is true in areas of mourning tradition as well, but with some differences. Before the burial, the role of the rabbi is primary and the role of the community is secondary, as shown in the chapter on *aninut*. After the burial, the community's role becomes crucial, as will be seen in coming chapters.

In *keriah* the community role is still minimal; other than tearing for parents being done in public, there really is none.[42] *Keriah* need not be done with a rabbi. Most often, though, it is done so for reasons that emanate from the rabbinic roles discussed in chapter 6. At a time of great emotional need, the rabbi acts as a facilitator and pastoral manager, guiding the individual mourners through a very tangible and possibly cathartic expression of sorrow. Even observant and learned Jews usually require assistance at this point to fulfill the halakhic requirements, and the rabbi often serves as teacher and educator in preparation for and practice of *keriah*. This is especially true with nonobservant or unlearned Jews, who are often unfamiliar with this ancient and graphic tradition. While a rabbi cannot and should not see every pastoral moment as a teaching opportunity, often some education is required at these moments simply to lead the mourner through the basic requirements of Jewish tradition.

The other roles of rabbis are present at *keriah* but in much lessened form. If a rabbi has developed a close pastoral relationship as a member of the extended family,[43] this relationship will ease the role of facilitator and enhance the role of teacher in dealing with *keriah*. Similarly, a skillful rabbi can use elements of pastoral counseling in guiding the mourner through *keriah*. The rabbi as representative of the community really plays no role for the *keriah* observance itself, although the mourner may perceive the rabbi in this role.

There are times when the historical and halakhic importance of *keriah*, along with its therapeutic benefits, are obscured by outright hostility or misunderstanding of its nature. Personally, I have found that my role as educator and teacher has usually ameliorated this. I can recall one case where the family's children, who grew up in my congregation before it became Orthodox, were insistent on tearing a ribbon. Even though a ribbon is not halakhically considered a garment for *keriah* purposes and I would not have torn one with them, this was authentic Jewish ritual to them. They were emotional people, and coupled with the heat of the moment, the potential for explosion was apparent. In the end, we came up with a deft compromise. We agreed to tear neckties and scarves, on which the family members would pin their ribbons. Even if the family were to wear only the ribbons during *shivah* (which was their stated intent), I believed that this would still fulfill the minimum halakhic requirement, since the actual tearing was done properly. The family felt that their needs were met as well. But the story did not end there. To my pleasant surprise, I found that during the week of *shivah*, the family ended up wearing the appropriate garments! A little bit of pastoral sensitivity helped the family fulfill the letter as well as the spirit of the *halakhah*.

Occasionally, one will find an example where the psychological benefits of *keriah* are readily apparent. I had been counseling R. for some time. A Holocaust survivor, she was a woman of great intelligence, charm, and personality. Yet she experienced great difficulty in her family relationships due to what appeared to be a poor self-image. She spoke to me of insults to her parents and herself from her estranged husband. But there was also something underneath all this involving her parents that I could not yet pinpoint.

> R: C. [her estranged husband] said I was like a Nazi and my parents were no good. You can't imagine how hearing these things affected me. After what the Nazis did to my parents . . . how could he say that?
>
> Rabbi: You've mentioned in our conversation several times that your poor relationship with C. is so bad because of how he

connects things with the Nazis. And just now you mentioned
something about what the Nazis did to your parents. What
does it all mean?

R: I miss my parents. I never got to say good-bye. It just destroyed me.

Rabbi: You feel deprived of the chance to mourn?

R: Yes! That's it! I never got to mourn for my parents. Somehow
I never thought of it in those terms, but I never sat *shivah* for
them. They were enlightened Jews, but still pious and learned.
They would have wanted me to sit *shivah*, but the Nazis
wouldn't allow it. They grabbed my father and executed him.
Then I had to go back to work. I was so young. . . . I never got
to say good-bye. . . .

Rabbi: There are Jewish ways of mourning even after many years
if one did not do it at the time. Would you like to explore this
more?

R: Yes, very much so.

I researched the matter and believed that there was a precedent
for this in Jewish Law. Halakhic sources include the case of the *shmu'ah
rehokah* (literally "the distant tidings"), when one does not hear of
the death of the parent until after the thirty-day *shloshim* period.[44] In
such a case, one still tears the *keriah* and sits a symbolic *shivah*[45] of
about an hour. This seemed to be an adequate precedent for our case.[46]
Though R. was aware of the loss of her parents, she never had the
chance to express her grief in a religious fashion through *keriah* and
shivah. I believed this was affecting other areas of her life. All the elements for a proper *keriah* were present. As we indicated earlier in the
chapter, the obligation of *keriah* for parents lasts as long as there are
children who have not yet torn. For Holocaust survivors, it is always
shaat himum, a time of great emotional heat and pain.[47] The blessing
of *Dayan Ha'emet* in its theological sense certainly applied here. I
explained all this to R., and we studied some of the relevant issues
from the sources. She decided to proceed, tearing *keriah* with my
assistance in my office and returning home to sit the symbolic *shivah*.
This proved to be most beneficial to her. She was able to come to
grips with the loss of her own parents in a recognized religious fashion, decades after the loss occurred. She gained strength from these
actions and soon after, she was able to terminate her failing marriage,

experience some reconciliation with her daughters, and finish her counseling sessions with me.

There is no question that historically and halakhically, the tearing of clothing has been a significant part of the Jewish process of grieving. Unfortunately, too many modern Jews have shied away from this graphic psychodrama of sorrow. Even more unfortunately, too many rabbis and funeral directors have abdicated their responsibilities to educate our people in basic Jewish tradition. Some reject *keriah* because they simply reject halakhic practice. Others, more well meaning, desire to spare grieving family members a perceived "barbaric ritual." Thus, the black ribbon was developed as a symbolic substitute for *keriah*. However, the black ribbon seems more in imitation of the non-Jewish custom of wearing a black armband as a sign of mourning. Most people I speak to believe for some reason that the ribbon must be worn for a full month, though there is no source in *halakhah* that indicates that a *keriah* garment be worn that long. Most important, the actual tearing done by the mourner addresses the emotions that all mourners endure. The feelings of pain and loss felt deeply in the heart, the confrontation with the finality of death, and the cathartic ripping of the material symbolizing the ripping of the relationship never to be fully restored are all deep emotional issues that simply cannot be addressed by the paltry ribbon. Indeed, the use of the ribbon may be part of the larger phenomenon in American culture of denying the finality of death and covering up its reality. Along with cosmetic tampering of the body and abandonment of the open grave before burial, these all symbolize the avoidance of facing tragedy. But the healing process cannot begin until one has confronted the loss that has occurred. By acknowledging what has befallen through the ripping of clothing and God's ultimate power over life and death through the *brakhah* of *Dayan Ha'emet*, we begin this process as we address the deepest psychological needs of the mourner. It would be worthwhile for rabbis, funeral directors, and laypeople to study the background and benefits of a proper *keriah* with an eye to encouraging fuller observance of this signifcant *mitzvah*.

In summary, *keriah* is a graphic way of expressing the deep grief one feels at the loss of a close relative. The time-honored tearing of an article of clothing helps the mourner with his or her own feelings and assists in the task of coming to grips with tragedy.

9

The Funeral Service

BACKGROUND

Every culture and religion uses special rites or practices to mark the end of life. For thousands of years Judaism's traditions have reflected the themes of honor to the deceased, honor for the living, the finality of death vis-à-vis this world, and hope for the future. These themes converge and reach an important point, but not a finale, at the Jewish funeral.

The actual service has two major parts—the eulogy and the burial. The eulogy is accompanied by the reading of psalms or other appropriate scriptural selections. The burial at the gravesite is combined with other readings and prayers that will be discussed later. The original Jewish historical practice was to have the entire service, both eulogy and burial, at the cemetery.[1] Early American Jewish practice before the advent of funeral chapels was to offer the eulogy at the home of the deceased. The body had already been placed in the home, where the prefuneral *hevrah kadisha* ritual preparation took place, and it was natural to have the eulogy there as well.[2] Occasionally the synagogue itself was used for the eulogy, although this was (and still is) generally restricted to services for major scholars or leaders in Jewish life.[3] In the last century of American Jewish life, the funeral home or chapel has become the location of choice for the eulogy part of the funeral service. It has been suggested that as the mourners' needs and families grew, homes could not accommodate the funeral gatherings. Inclement weather often precluded regular use of cemeteries for eulogies.[4] As the American Jewish community continued to prosper, especially in the mid-1920s and after World War II, funeral chapels reminiscent of synagogues were built for the eulogy and service.[5] Gravesite services are still done when families prefer a simpler service, or when the numbers of attendees do not justify the expense of a chapel service.[6] When this is requested, both eulogy and burial are done together at the gravesite.

BEFORE THE SERVICE

Traditionally, the family remains together or with their nearest friends at the funeral home prior to the actual service. The comforting from the community does not truly begin until after the burial, as taught by the Talmud, "Do not comfort a person while his dead lies before him."[7] Unfortunately, this is often not the case when well-meaning friends and acquaintances turn the prefuneral time into an inappropriately festive atmosphere.[8] *Keriah* is usually done at this time. The rabbi's role usually centers on that of pastoral manager, making the last-minute arrangements and making sure that the family's requests and concerns are met. There also may be elements of teaching and emotional guidance at this time. The mourners may perceive the rabbi as a member of the extended family, although at this point, this is not primary in the work of the rabbi.

THE FUNERAL SERVICE—THE EULOGY

The service itself consists of several scriptural readings followed by the eulogy. Frequently used selections include Psalm 23, Psalm 15, and Proverbs 31, as well as the amalgam of psalm selections beginning, "O Lord, What Is Man. . . . "[9]

There are two major ideas behind the traditional Jewish eulogy. The first is *hesped*, lamenting or mourning the loss of the deceased, dwelling on his or her qualities. The Hebrew root term for this is s-p-d, implying an introspective lament.[10] The term may be linguistically related to s-ph-t, which means to sweep away,[11] and a-s-ph, which means to gather.[12] Homiletically, we might say that when our lives are swept away, it is proper to gather our memories.[13] The second is *bekhi*, literally to cry or shed tears, to confront the sense of loss and the existential questions of life and death. The source for both of these themes comes from the Torah, where we are told how Abraham "came to eulogize Sarah and to cry for her."[14]

The Talmud questions whether the eulogy is considered *yekara d'shekhiba*, honor to the deceased by describing his or her good qualities, or *yekara d'hayya*, honor to the living (the mourners or survivors).[15] The answer to this question would make a difference in the following two situations: in the case where the deceased willed in his or her lifetime that no eulogy be made after death, and in the case where the survivors did not wish to pay for the eulogizer.[16] If the eulogy is honor to the deceased, then the deceased while alive may give up that honor for him or herself. If not, Jewish Law would compel the survivor to pay for these services, just as we require someone to provide the other burial expenses of a loved one. If the eulogy is honor to the living, then the reverse would be true. The Talmud does not explicitly answer its question, but the codifiers deduce from the various cases cited in the text that the eulogy is *yekara d'shekhiba*, honor to the deceased. The two pivotal cases are codified as such.[17]

How do the Jewish eulogy themes compare to those of Western culture? Irion, in his pastoral analysis of eulogies,[18] looks at their purposes in the Protestant traditions. He rejects the classical Christian mission of evangelism, though apparently this theme was frequently used for eulogies in the Church. This purpose, of course, is totally foreign to Jewish practice and belief.[19] He partly accepts the reason of helping the mourners "bravely stand amidst the storm" but criticizes this as not sufficiently meeting the pain-filled needs of the mourners. Irion introduces two other important purposes for the eulogy. One is to give a realistic view of death.[20] More important, he proposes that the sermon meet the mourners' pastoral needs by dealing with their life situations. Irion downplays emphasis on the life of the deceased in favor of focusing on the emotional concerns of the survivors.[21] In Jewish tradition, however, *yekara d'shek-*

hiba is one of the major reasons for the eulogy. Is there any way to
attend to the needs of the living in the context of Torah teaching
without sacrificing the major theme of honor to the deceased?

Even though the codes accept *yekara d'shekhiba* as the major
reason for eulogizing, the idea of *yekara d'hayya*, honor to the living, still persists in the commentaries.[22] At least one major modern
halakhic source agrees that there is also *yekara d'hayya* in the eulogy, even though practically, *halakhah* allows foregoing the eulogy
when the deceased explicitly requested this.[23] While this source also
agrees that honoring the deceased is primary in the eulogy, it also
backs our thesis that the eulogy can be for the living as well. I would
propose that given these sources, Irion's two purposes for the eulogy in terms of dealing with death itself and addressing the needs
of the mourners are compatible with and appropriate for a traditional Jewish service. A sensitive rabbi, acting as the "doctor of the
soul," would key in on the needs of the mourners and their emotional state. As a sensitive teacher, the rabbi would offer the mourners some guidance on facing the existential questions all confront
when saying good-bye to loved ones.[24] These elements could then
be included in the eulogy, which could then have enormous therapeutic and emotional benefits for the survivors.[25]

My personal and pastoral experience is that the mourners themselves need to remember the good qualities of the deceased. This
can help the mourners begin the process of grieving and healing.
Obviously, one should not invent qualities that are nonexistent, or
turn the deceased into someone he or she was not.[26] Based on my
discussions with the family,[27] I try to give those present a "slice of
life" of the deceased. I include vignettes about the individual and
focus on items such as love for family, devotion to Judaism, care for
work, personal qualities, and so on. I have found there is usually
something good one can say about the deceased.[28]

As stated earlier, our eulogies make reference to the existential
ideas of life and death, the transitory nature of life, and how we must
confront these when faced with tragedy and loss. While some rabbis give "canned" eulogies, a good rabbi will tailor the talk to the
needs of the situation. If those present did not know the deceased
well, the sense of loss is lessened. If the deceased lived a long and
full life, there may be loss but less of a sense of tragedy. When a

person is suddenly struck down, the sense of tragedy and loss are both heightened. A good eulogy should be able to examine all these elements.[29]

No eulogizing, funerals, or burials take place on the Sabbath or biblical feast days.[30] In addition, eulogies are not recited on semi-joyous days such as Hanukkah, the New Moon, Purim, and so forth.[31] While some communities take this literally in the sense that no speeches accompany the funeral on these days, most rabbis will find a way to say kind words or words of praise for the deceased on these days. They will minimize the emotional evocation without compromising the dignity of the deceased.[32] It is a matter of dispute whether a eulogy can be offered at night.[33]

Eulogies are not given for a suicide,[34] an apostate,[35] or one whose death is not verified.[36] A eulogy may be offered by a rabbi or Jewish layperson for a non-Jew because of *darkei shalom*, peaceful and compassionate interactions within society.[37]

ROLES OF THE RABBI AND COMMUNITY IN THE SERVICE

Pastoral manager and facilitator probably best describe the rabbinic role in organizing the funeral service, as well as what is to follow at the cemetery. To guide the family through this difficult period, the rabbi can also strive to show the tenderness of a member of the extended family. A good eulogy might contain elements of teaching, pastoral counseling, and sensitivity for the family's needs with the rabbi as the "doctor or healer of the soul." Certainly the rabbi's officiating at the service puts him in the role of representing the community. But what of the community itself? Is there no role other than that of spectators at the funeral?

The community's mere presence at the funeral can be meaningful to the mourners, for this presence reminds them that they are not alone. The following talmudic excerpt, cited earlier in the book, teaches about those who can represent the community:

> Rabbi Yehudah said in the name of Rav: If there is a death in the city, all citizens are forbidden to do work [in order to tend to the needs of the deceased]. R. Hamnuna went to Daromta and

heard there the sound of the funeral *shofar*. He then saw some
people who were still doing work. He said to them, "These people
should be placed under the *shamta*. Is there not a dead person
in town?" [But] they told him "There is a *hevrah* [a committee or
association] in town," [which does these tasks and fills these
needs]. He said, "If so, it is permitted [to do work]."[38]

According to the Talmud, tending the needs of the dead precludes any other kind of work. Thus, all in the community are obligated to engage in the sacred act of the funeral and burial, unless
the community has a committee that does so. However, these committees or *hevrot* can truly represent the community in terms of
fulfilling the obligations to the deceased for a proper funeral. Therefore, anyone who participates in these actions fulfills this obligation.

Today, most traditional communities have a *hevrah kadisha* that
engages in the washing, dressing, and final preparation of the body.[39]
These people, along with those who accompany the body from the
time of death to the time of the service,[40] as well as the pallbearers,[41] who should come from the funeral party and not the funeral
home, can be said to represent the community. Participation in any
of these acts is considered an honor and a *mitzvah*.[42]

The traditional Jewish service is notable for its simplicity. Flowers[43] and music[44] are generally not appropriate and are not used.

THE BURIAL

The burial is the other major focus of a Jewish service. This tradition again goes back to the Torah, which tells us of how Abraham
bought a plot of land upon which to bury his late wife Sarah.[45] Jewish Law considers it both a positive commandment to bury the
corpse and transgression of a negative commandment to ignore this
requirement.[46] Thus, the burial is considered an integral and required part of the funeral service, requiring all present to confront
the finality of death. The fact that the casket laid in the ground must
be all wood is but another illustration of this idea.[47]

When the body reaches the gravesite, the pallbearers[48] take it
out of the hearse and carry it to the gravesite. Tradition has them

stop several times[49] between the hearse and the grave, forcing all those present to ponder the nature of life and death at this time. Psalm 91 is often recited. The entire party follows behind the procession, participating in the important *mitzvah* of escorting the deceased on his or her final journey on this earth.[50] When the gravesite is reached, the casket is placed and lowered into the grave.[51] The grave is then filled by those present,[52] preferably to the top. When this is not possible, the participants should at least fully cover the casket with a several inches of dirt. The shovel is not handed from person to person but placed in the ground and taken from the ground. Some people use the back of the shovel to show that this is not its usual constructive purpose.[53]

The Talmud suggests two purposes for the burial.[54] Burial is done either because of "dishonor" to the family if the corpse is not to be buried[55] or as "atonement," as a means of finding forgiveness for any sins the deceased may have committed in their lifetime.[56] The Talmud does not clearly decide this issue, but the discussion yields the ruling that even if the deceased requested not to be buried in the ground, we do not honor that request but bury the person anyway. We do so since it is for the benefit of the living as well as the deceased; also even the most righteous of individuals require atonement, for no one is perfect.[57]

While most cultures have some type of burial process,[58] the actual burial itself is not considered that significant a procedure within Western society in general. Irion, besides a page and a half on the Protestant Committal Service recited at the gravesite, says absolutely nothing about pastoral and therapeutic benefits of the burial. My own experience at non-Jewish funerals bears this out, where the casket is left next to or on top of the open grave and the mourners simply depart, leaving the grave diggers to finish the job. All this suggests that the burial has little significance in other Western cultures. In Judaism, the burial is part and parcel of the service and, as mentioned earlier, an important act honoring the deceased and forcing those present to deal with the reality of their loss and death in general.[59]

During this time, the rabbi's role and the role of the community begin to balance out. The rabbi is still acting as the pastoral manager,[60] guiding the family and friends through one of the most difficult moments of life. The rabbi's presence is usually a comforting one at this often traumatic time.[61] In addition, the rabbi should take the opportunity to explain to the participants and family what is going on at each given step of the burial, thus assuming a teaching role. This becomes extremely important with nonobservant Jews and those with little or no Judaic background. Even if the burial procedures are discussed at the prefuneral call, there is a need to reinforce the explanations and alleviate the emotional tension at seeing unfamiliar actions at a sensitive moment. Most people, even those who are well educated and committed, appreciate the explanations.

The actions of those present in filling in the grave represent the emergence of a major community role not yet seen in the funeral preparation and rites. As discussed in the rabbinic sources on *bikur holim* and pastoral themes in chapter 1, everyone is obligated to visit the sick, bury the dead, and comfort the bereaved in imitation of the Almighty, Who does these things. The way in which these *mitzvot* are fulfilled is through empathy, sharing the suffering of those stricken. The community's presence and involvement in the burial is in direct fulfillment of the rabbinic dicta cited in chapter 1 that form the basis of this book. As the rabbis say:

> The Holy One, Blessed Be He, comforts the bereaved, as it says, "And it was after Abraham died and that God blessed his son Isaac . . ." (Genesis 25:11), so too shall you comfort the bereaved. The Holy One, Blessed Be He, buries the dead, as it says, "And He buried him [Moses] in the valley . . ." (Deuteronomy 34:6), so too shall you bury the dead.[62]

Until this point, the *halakhah* has concentrated on properly honoring the deceased, *yekara d'shekhiba*. But as shown earlier, there are also elements of *yekara d'hayya*, honoring the living, in the burial. I would suggest that the community's participation at the funeral and burial does honor to the living. Their presence, in the existential sense, helps to alleviate the grief of the mourners. The participants' labor of filling in the grave helps create an atmosphere and feeling of shared solidarity, which in turn assists the mourners in facing their sorrow and loneliness. Also, the physical act of shoveling dirt into the open grave, difficult as it may be for some, often has a cathartic effect on participants. The physical effort, like that of *keriah*, allows both mourner and members of the community to work through their loss. By being present and sharing the burden of burial, the community truly "walks in the ways of the Lord," imitating the Creator by burying the dead and comforting the bereaved.

SPECIAL ISSUES—A CASE OF CREMATION

There are times when serving the requirements of Jewish tradition and sensitivity to the legitimate psychological needs of the congregant can cause conflict. The following case history illustrates these differences.

A family in my congregation experienced a tragic loss when their thirty-seven-year-old son died on the West Coast. The son had willed in writing that he was to be cremated, his ashes scattered across the ocean. Jewish tradition is quite strongly against this practice,[63] as shown by the following quotes:

> Cremation is never permitted. The deceased must be interred, bodily in the earth. It is forbidden—in every and any circumstance— to reduce the dead to ash in a crematorium. It is an offensive act, for it does violence to the spirit of Jewish law, which never, in the long past, sanctioned the ancient pagan practice of burning on the pyre. . . . Even if the deceased willed cremation, his wishes must be ignored in order to observe the will of our Father in Heaven. Biblical law takes precedence over the instructions of the deceased. . . . Cremated ashes may not be buried in a Jewish cemetery. . . . Jewish Law requires no mourning for the cremated. . . .[64]

> . . . on these, the rabbis have rightfully said that he has denied the [doctrine of the] resurrection of the dead[65] and therefore has no share in the resurrection. It is a holy obligation on all Jews to fight with all their strength against those whose desire is such. It is said that those [who are cremated] are at the gates of *Gehenna*, they cannot return in *teshuvah* [return or repentance] . . . for in cremation there is the sound of idolatry.[66]

When death was close, the father came to me asking if I would officiate at a memorial service several weeks later. I used our discussion to urge the family to fulfill their responsibility to Jewish tradition and fight to gain custody of the body should death occur. My research revealed that there would be no secular legal ramification in going against the son's will in order to provide a religious Jewish burial. The father was willing to consider all this. The mother, however, was on the West Coast with her dying son and was too upset to pursue these avenues. While she sympathized with my view, she believed strongly that she had to respect her son's wishes; I could not change this.

Following death, the cremation took place in California. I was faced with a dilemma. All the sources are quite clear about the severity of cremation in Torah tradition. Yet the family, very much in pain and grief, felt the need to mourn for their son in a Jewish way. Even if the son had "given up his share in the World to Come," in the eyes of our sacred texts, the family still had memories of a living, breathing son now gone. Their sense of loss demanded some kind of closure. How could I provide this and still maintain halakhic standards and my integrity as an Orthodox rabbi?

My personal meeting with the family subsequent to death was quite difficult. I was faced with such questions as, "Where is he now?" How could I, at this emotionally charged moment, tell them that according to Jewish sources their son was being excluded from God's reward? I, of course, did explain the seriousness of cremation in Judaism, but I could not bring myself to exacerbate the family's deep sense of hurt and grief. Though the family revealed their own feelings against cremation, this did not affect their need to mourn in a Jewish fashion.

A clue to resolution was found in one of the halakhic sources, which reads as follows: "But for what applies to honor for the living, R. Hazan in *Hayyei Olam*, p. 108 [another premodern Hebrew work on mourning] allows us to comfort the mourners for a cremated person. . . ."[67]

Based on this, I developed an approach that stressed that any of the practices benefiting the grieving family could be done. If the family chose to sit a facsimile of *shivah* and accept the condolences of the community, this would be proper. We planned a small gathering at the family's home for several weeks after the death. At this intimate service, the emphasis would be on the living family offering to share their feelings of loss and hurt. My remarks centered on this as well as issues of life and death in general, but not on the deceased. We selected aspects of the traditional memorial services, including the study of a *Mishnah*, the *Kaddish DeRabanan*,[68] selections from the psalms, as well as other readings. We also allowed the members of the family a chance to speak. I shared this thinking with several rabbinical colleagues and at least one senior Orthodox rabbinic scholar and *posek* who agreed with my thinking. The gathering proved to be enormously therapeutic for the family. They still feel a sense of anger and loss without the benefit of the focus offered by a traditional burial and service. But the family was allowed the opportunity to grieve in a way consistent with Jewish tradition.

LITURGY OF THE BURIAL

The major prayers of the burial are the *Hazkarah*, or memorial prayer,[69] the *Tziduk Hadin*, or affirmation of the divine decree, and the special Burial *Kaddish* recited at the gravesite. These are not recited on days of moderate joyousness on which funerals might take place, such as New Moon, Hanukkah, and the intermediate days of Passover and Sukkot. At these times, other prayers or readings might be substituted.[70] The joy of these days mitigates the need for the themes of these prayers.[71]

The *Hazkarah* memorial prayer goes back to the time of the Crusades in Western and Central Europe[72] and was probably composed in memory of the Jewish martyrs of those attacks. It reads as follows:

> O God, full of compassion, Who dwells on High, find proper rest[73] under the wings of Your sheltering presence,[74] among the holy and pure who shine as the brightness of the heavens, unto the soul of [the Hebrew name of the deceased and the father's Hebrew name are inserted here] who has gone to his/her world,[75] and in whose memory charity is offered.[76] May his/her repose be in paradise.[77] May the Master of mercy bring him/her under the cover[78] of His presence[79] forever, and may his/her soul be bound up in the bonds of eternal life. May the Lord be his/her possession, and may he/she rest in peace, and let us say, Amen.

The *Hazkarah* prayer in many ways is thematically similar to the *Mi-Sheberakh*. The *Hazkarah* themes include:

1. The affirmation that God is compassionate. This is not always easy to do after experiencing the death of a loved one. Technically, the period of *aninut* has not yet ended, and the mourners are still "angry" at God.[80] At the same time, they are lonely, as the reality of death stares them in the face. The knowledge that God, in the end, is merciful can be comforting.[81] Alternately, this belief can be viewed as a goal for which to strive as the healing process begins.[82]

2. A plea that the soul find its final rest with God and then an affirmation of that tenet. A basic Jewish belief is that the spiritual part of a human being does not die when the body does but returns to its Maker. The prayer asks that the return be a peaceful one.

3. "The holy and pure who shine as the brightness of the heavens" could mean either the righteous who are at peace and at one with God[83] or the angels in heaven.[84] Either way, the prayer affirms that the deceased is no longer in the community of the living but in the "community on high." As with the *Mi-Sheberakh* for the sick, the theme of community finds its way into the liturgy.

4. Again, as with the *Mi-Sheberakh*, a tangible action such as charity or prayer is part of the prayer.

5. As with the *Mi-Sheberakh*, the Hebrew name of the deceased is used, along with the father's Hebrew name. Again, this identifies the person as a member of his or her people. If the Hebrew name is not known, the name in any language may be used.

6. The *Hazkarah* again mentions and affirms the belief of eternal life for the soul, now at peace with God.

The *Tziduk Hadin* is usually recited at the gravesite immediately before or just after the casket is covered with dirt[85] and the grave filled.[86] It reads:

> The Rock whose work is perfect, for all His ways are judgment, a God of faithfulness and without iniquity, just and right is He.[87] The Rock, perfect in all His work; who can say, "What do You work?" to Him Who rules above and below, Who takes away life and gives it, Who brings down to the grave and brings up from there?

The Rock, perfect in all His deeds; who can say, "What do You do?" to the one Who says and acts? Show us free mercy; in the merit of the one bound like a lamb,[88] hearken and act.

You Who are righteous in all Your ways, Rock of perfection, patient and abundant in mercy, have compassion upon us and spare both parents and children, for Yours, O Lord, are forgiveness and mercy.

Righteous are You, O Lord, in taking away or giving life, for in Your hands are pledged all souls; far be it from You to blot us from memory. Look toward us with mercy, for Yours, O Lord, are compassion and pardon.

If a person lives for one year or a thousand, what gain is it? It is as if he had never been. Blessed is the true Judge, Who takes away life and gives it.

Blessed is He for His justice is true, and He scrutinizes all things, rewarding each according to the account; let all give praise to His name.

We know, O Lord, that Your judgments are righteous. You are right when You speak and justified in Your judgment; we are unable to question Your manner of judgment. Just are You, O Lord, and righteous are your judgments.

O true and righteous Judge! Blessed is the true Judge, for all His judgments are righteous and true. The soul of every life is in Your hand, righteousness fills Your right hand. Have mercy on the remnant of Your flock, and say to the angel [of destruction], "Withdraw your hand!"

O You Who are great in counsel and mighty in action, Whose eyes are open to all the ways of people, rewarding each according to their ways and the results of their doings,[89] showing that the Lord is upright; He is my stronghold and there is no wrong in Him.[90]

The Lord has given, the Lord has taken away; praised be the name of the Lord.[91] He is merciful, forgives sin and does not destroy; He greatly turns His anger away and does not awaken His wrath.[92]

The use of these passages goes back to the rabbinic period. When the family of R. Hananiah ben Teradion was taken to be martyred by the Romans, they uttered the biblical verses upon which the *Tziduk Hadin* is based.[93] The actual text comes from the Geonic period[94] and incorporates those biblical quotes in a rhymed scheme.

The themes of *Tziduk Hadin* are as follows:

1. The power over life and death comes from God. This mysterious power cannot be fully fathomed.
2. Ultimately God's divine justice is accepted as the mourners face their loss and pain.
3. Life is transient; all the more reason to affirm the Almighty as source of life and death.
4. In spite of the pain, God's care and compassion are still affirmed; God is asked to share these qualities as those present seek life.[95]

One may ask, how can people who have suffered deep losses affirm these positive qualities about God's justice? Some people, of course, are able to accept these things;[96] some are even able to derive strength from the affirmations. But what of those who have great difficulty with these concepts at the time of burial?[97] It is possible to look at *Tziduk Hadin* as a goal for which to work. A mourner requires emotional healing from the sense of loss, and this process begins with the finality of the burial. There is also a parallel need for religious healing, and this process also begins with the burial. Therefore, the *Tziduk Hadin* can be viewed as an agenda. One may not feel or accept all of its elements, but one can see these themes as points to which we can aspire. People ultimately want to be able to accept a God Who is merciful, compassionate, and cares about them. At the same time, ultimate power over life and death is God's. People want life but eventually must acknowledge that they are not in control, for death is the end of all. The message is almost brutally driven home at the point of burial, and those present are forced to confront it. These words, based on the traditional texts of our faith and people, reassure us that we are not alone as the starkness of this moment is confronted.

The last prayer of importance at the grave is the special burial *Kaddish*. *Kaddish*[98] is a prayer that has many purposes in Judaism.[99] Essentially a doxology or acclamation of God's greatness concluded by a prayer for peace, it serves as an introduction or conclusion to major parts of the service or as a conclusion to a session of Torah study. These purposes go back to the rabbinic period. Sometime later in Jewish liturgical history, the *Kaddish* became a requirement for mourners to say during their period of mourning for close relatives. There is, however, a special version of the *Kaddish* used specifically at the gravesite known as the "Great *Kaddish*" or the "Burial *Kaddish*."[100] The ideas of the first paragraph distinctively connect to the burial.

> Magnified and Sanctified be His great name, in the world *which He will renew, reviving the dead and raising them to eternal life, rebuilding the city of Jerusalem and establishing His sanctuary therein; uprooting alien worship [idolatry] from the earth and restoring the worship of heaven; and the Holy One, Blessed Be He, will reign in His majestic glory,*[101] during your life and your days, and the life of the whole house of Israel, speedily and soon, and let us say, Amen!

The major themes of this paragraph are the messianic and eschatological ideas involving the uprooting of idolatry, the ultimate universal acceptance of the One God, the rebuilding of Jerusalem (which for the believing Jew is not a symbolic idea but a very real one), and the resurrection of the dead.[102] Even at the point where, to paraphrase Rabbi Soloveitchik,[103] death has truly beaten life and the finality of death directly faces us, our hopes for the future are still affirmed.

The issue of the resurrection of the dead troubles many Jews, even observant ones. While it does not play the kind of role in Judaism as it does in Christianity, where it is a core of the faith, it is still a part of traditional Jewish belief. Maimonides includes it in his thirteen essentials of Judaism,[104] as do other major medieval Jewish philosophers. Yet, when one moves away from classical Jewish thought, this is one of the first doctrines to be jettisoned, for it is awkward for many to accept the notion that God will one day bring the dead back to life. Yet the thought of eventual reunion in a better world is often the only source of comfort to the grieving survivors. It may be difficult to understand how or when such a thing can take place, but the affirmation that God has the power to do so can, from the pastoral perspective, be enormously therapeutic. This is done precisely at the moment when the finality of death is confronted, following the burial and before the *shivah* period.[105]

To summarize, the funeral service, through the eulogy, burial, and other traditions, offers honor to the deceased in various ways. Further, the service focuses on the needs of the mourners as well as the deceased. Along with these, the liturgy forces the mourner to confront the earthly finality of death within a religious context. The rabbi plays a most important role in all this, sensitively educating and guiding the mourners through this difficult period. The community[106] also begins to play a role in offering honor to the deceased as well in beginning the healing process for the survivors.

10

Postfuneral Observances

TRANSITION TO *SHIVAH*–THE WEEK OF MOURNING

As shown in the chapters on *bikur holim*, both rabbis and laity play important roles in the emotional healing of the ill. This is done with the quality of empathy, in imitation of God Who heals the sick. The preceding chapters on mourning have explored how halakhic practice compels the mourners to face the finality of death, which is in turn a prerequisite to emotional healing following the loss of a loved one. The rabbi, through the roles developed in this book, can foster and assist this process. The laity or community can help at these early stages by their presence and assistance; however, their role up to this point is secondary.

A real transition in roles occurs during the *shivah*, or week of mourning following the funeral. At this point, the community, through its empathic presence, becomes the primary conveyor of spiritual healing and assistance. This transition is graphically demonstrated by a tradition practiced immediately after the conclusion of the gravesite service. After the prayers and burial are completed, all present form two parallel lines. The mourners[1] walk between those two lines on their way out of the grave area. The others present recite the traditional words of comfort, "May the Omnipresent[2] comfort you amidst the other mourners for Zion and Jerusalem."[3]

This brief wish, also used when visitors have completed a condolence call at the *shivah* house, invokes the Divine Presence, which those present are imitating when they comfort the bereaved. The words connect the mourner to the tragic periods of Jewish history, specifically the destruction of the Temples and Jerusalem.[4] The two lines symbolize the entire community's empathic comfort, in imitation of the Almighty, who is also present at this tragic moment. Thus, we let the mourners know that they are not alone by connecting them to the Jewish world vertically (our history) and horizontally (our community of those present.) The rabbi, while perhaps explaining and guiding this process, is only a facilitator and teacher.[5] The passing of the mourners between these two lines marks the actual transition between the *aninut* and burial period into the *shivah* mourning period.

Upon leaving the cemetery, those present pull some grass with earth out from the ground and throw it over their shoulders.[6] This very poignant custom goes back to the medieval period. Several reasons have been suggested for this practice, including the following:

1. Just as the grass has been pulled out and will eventually regrow, so too we recall the idea of the resurrection of the dead who will be brought back to life.[7]

2. To remind us that we are but dust and to remind us of our mortality.

3. To recall that in biblical times, dust was one of the elements involved in purification of a person from contact with the deceased.[8]

4. As a sign of pain over one's loss.

5. As a part of the healing process in terms of "letting go" of the deceased.

After one leaves the cemetery, the hands are ritually washed in the same way one would wash before the eating of bread by pouring water from a cup two or three times over each hand.[9] While this can be done simply after leaving the cemetery grounds[10] or before entering one's own home, the common practice is to have water and cups available at the door of the *shivah* house, or home where the mourners will be for the week following the burial. People coming to the *shivah* house after the cemetery wash before entering the home.[11]

The first few hours following the burial are crucial for the mourners. During this time, a special meal is eaten.[12] This is a meal prepared for but not by the mourners.[13] Traditionally, the meal includes round objects symbolizing the cycles of life, such as hardboiled eggs, lentils, bagels, or rolls. The talmudic source for this tradition reads:

> R. Yehudah said in the name of Rav: A mourner is forbidden on the first day [following burial] to eat bread of his own, as Scripture states in Ezekiel,[14] ". . . and do not eat the bread of others;" Raba and R. Yosef [while they were both in mourning] would trade meals[15] with each other.[16]

The Hebrew term for the meal is *Seudat Havraah*, which is often translated as "Meal of Condolence." Actually, the term *havraah* is grammatically related to the words for health and for creation, both of which have the same root letters, *b-r-a*.[17] Rather than a party or social gathering, the meal is an intimate time for family and friends to begin the healing process and recreate their lives.[18] In addition, as Lamm points out, the mourners may be harboring a death wish of their own following the burial, in the sense of, "Why am I alive when my loved one is deep in the earth?" This meal, offered through the caring kindness of others, is a way of gently helping the mourners begin the long road back to emotional and spiritual wholeness. As the *Shulhan Arukh* puts it: "A mourner is forbidden to eat of his own on the first meal [following burial] but may do so for the second meal, even on the first day.[19] And it is a *mitzvah* for the neighbors to feed him of theirs, so he [the mourner] should not eat of his."[20]

In other words, the best pastoral care that can be offered to one feeling an emotional and spiritual vacuum after the burial of a loved one is not necessarily from the pastor but, in a very graphic and physical way (through food), from the community of empathic, caring friends.

The meal is concluded by the traditional Grace After Meals.[21] However, the mid section, calling for the rebuilding of Jerusalem and thanking God for the goodness in the world, is changed to take into consideration the themes of the moment, as follows:

> Comfort, Lord our God, the mourners for Jerusalem and the mourners who mourn this bereavement. Comfort them from their sadness and cheer them in their sorrow, as it is written, "As a man is comforted by his mother, so will I comfort you, and through Jerusalem will you be comforted."[22] Blessed are You, O Lord, Who comforts Zion by rebuilding Jerusalem.
>
> Blessed are You, O Lord our God, Sovereign of the Universe, the God Who is our Father, our Sovereign, our Creator, our Redeemer, our Holy One, the Holy One of Jacob, the Living Sovereign, Who is good and does good. [He is] the true God and true Judge, Who rules with righteousness and takes back souls in rulership,[23] and His dominion is in His world doing His will, for all His ways are just, and we are His people and His servants. For all this we are bound to acknowledge and to bless Him. He Who binds up the wounds in Israel, may He repair this breach from us for life and for peace; may He forever grant to us grace, kindness, mercy, and all good, and may He never deprive us of any good thing.

These passages thematically have a great deal in common with the other liturgical selections quoted in the last chapter.[24] The themes include associating the mourner with the destruction and rebuilding of Zion and thus all of Jewish history, accepting God as the ultimate arbiter of life and death, and looking to the Almighty as the source of comfort and healing.

GUIDELINES FOR *SHIVAH* OBSERVANCE

Shivah, literally meaning seven in Hebrew, refers to the week following the burial. The various positive time-bound commandments from which the mourner was exempt during the *aninut* and burial period, such as daily prayer, blessings, and so on, are once more incumbent on the person. As Rabbi Soloveitchik puts it,

> The halakhah [now] commands the mourner to undertake an heroic task: To start picking up the debris of his own shattered

personality and to reestablish himself as man, restoring lost glory, dignity, and uniqueness. . . .

Death must not confuse man; the latter must not plunge into total darkness because of death. Death teaches man to transcend his physical self and to identify with the timeless covenantal community. Death . . . not only does not free man from his commitment, but on the contrary enhances his role as a historic being and sensitizes his moral consciousness. . . .

No matter how powerful death is . . . however terrifying the grave is . . . no matter how black despair is . . . we declare and profess . . .[25] that we are not giving up . . . that we will carry on that work of our ancestors. . . .[26]

All this does not mean that the mourner in Judaism is forced to plunge back into life. On the contrary, the mourner remains at home, with the community coming to visit and offer comfort. The daily services are held at the house, allowing the mourner to say the *Kaddish* prayer without leaving the house.[27] There are a number of restrictions on the mourner during the week of *shivah*. Haircuts and shaving are prohibited.[28] Laundering is not done.[29] Anointing, washing, and grooming,[30] all of which are pleasurable activities, are not done.[31] Leather shoes are not worn.[32] Marital relations are forbidden.[33] The study of Torah, being a joyous activity, is not done, other than the sadder selections of Torah literature appropriate for the *shivah* week.[34] In general the restrictions reflect the fact that this week is not one of business as usual but rather a time to ignore the aesthetic aspects of life in favor of allowing the mourner to grieve with the support of the community.[35] At least one scholar sees in these practices[36] the symbols of alienation and loneliness.[37] After being touched by the desacralization of death and the absence of life, the mourner is now moving between life and death. "In effect, the law asks the mourner to behave as if he himself were dead. He is now an incomplete person and his daily life begins to reflect [this]."[38]

The task of the mourner during the week following the funeral is often referred to as "sitting *shivah*." This refers to the fact that the mourner sits at a lower level than he or she would normally sit. The funeral homes often offer so-called *shivah* chairs to the family, consisting of uncomfortable cardboard fold-up boxes. However, any type of lower-than-usual seating will do, such as sitting on the floor, cushions, pillows, the sofa without the cushions, or footrests. The mourner may also stand up, walk around, or lie down. The mourner's goal is not being uncomfortable; it is identifying with the sense of loss by sitting below the usual level.[39]

There is a delicate etiquette about visiting a *shivah* home. One does not offer greetings to the mourner[40] upon entering the house; in fact, usually one does not even knock. Generally, the doors are left open and visitors simply walk in. The visitor waits for the mourner to initiate any conversation. This may seem awkward at first. In fact, sometimes it seems as though there is pressure on the mourner to "entertain" the visitor. But this visit is not meant as a social call. The visitor does not even ask "How are you?" since the mourner is obviously not well. The visitor's job is not to make small talk. It is simply to be with the bereaved person, sharing an empathic presence. There is no agenda or script. The mourner sets the tone and pace for conversation, if there is any. Many well-meaning people feel the need to take the mourner's mind off the grief. But the bereaved person needs to work through the grief at his or her own pace. All the visitor can really do is alleviate the suffering and share the moment by reaching out with human-to-human contact.[41] Again, this is imitation of the Almighty Who comforted Isaac and blessed him with the Divine Presence after the death of his father Abraham.[42] At the conclusion of the *shivah* call, the visitor, rather than saying good-bye, offers the traditional words of condolence that were said at the cemetery upon completion of the service: "May the Omnipresent comfort you amidst the other mourners for Zion and Jerusalem."

The Sabbath, while counted as one of the days, generally lifts most of the public restrictions of *shivah*.[43] This is because the Sabbath maintains its own transcendent joy even in the face of death. The *halakhah* mandates that there is no public mourning on the Sabbath. In addition, the mourners rise from *shivah* several hours before sunset on Friday to allow adequate time for Sabbath preparation. *Shivah* resumes after nightfall on Saturday night.

If the burial takes place before a major holiday,[44] the holiday cancels *shivah*. If the burial takes place during the intermediate days of Passover or Sukkot, the *shivah* is delayed until after the entire holiday is concluded.[45]

RABBINIC ROLES DURING *SHIVAH*

The rabbi's role during *shivah* is secondary to the community's. Thus, the rabbi's duty to pay a *shivah* call is no more or less than that of any other member of the community. However, a rabbi, due to personal qualities and professional training, can still play a valuable role in helping bereaved persons through the grieving process during *shivah*.[46] Using the rabbinic roles developed earlier, a rabbinic *shivah* call can be most beneficial.

There is only a small amount for the rabbi to do as a pastoral manager. This may simply consist of organizing, publicizing, and conducting the daily services at the *shivah* house.[47] As a teacher, the rabbi's role can be very useful. If desired, *shivah* can be an appropriate time to deal with some of the theological, philosophical, and halakhic questions that could not be approached before the burial.[48] The mourners may want to pursue some of the reasons for the practices that they have done or simply explore Jewish views of death.[49] In terms of representing the community, it is true that some mourners consider a rabbinic *shivah* call a symbolic community presence. But as has been shown, the community is really obligated to represent itself, and not by proxy. Rabbis can nurture an enriched fellowship if they encourage other members of their communities to pay *shivah* calls.[50]

In the end, the most important roles for the rabbi during *shivah* are those of extended family member, doctor of the soul, and exemplar in empathy. The rabbi who has honed skills in listening, who possesses the ability to care for people in times of need, and who has developed a warm family-type relationship will be the one whose presence is most valued by the mourners. These qualities, formulated in chapter 6 to ensure a successful *bikur holim* visit, are the very traits that will enhance a *shivah* call. Just as the ill patient suffers from loss of independence, loneliness, weakness, and confusion about ultimate fate, so too the bereaved experiences these symptoms in grief.[51] An empathic rabbinic visit can help ease the burden by virtue of the rabbi's caring presence.

POST*SHIVAH* OBSERVANCES

The seventh day of a regular *shivah* is not a complete day; the family sits for only an hour or so in the morning before *shivah* is completed. Upon the completion of *shivah*, many have the custom to walk outside for a bit. This symbolizes their reentry into the community after being at home during the week of *shivah*.

When the mourner begins to reenter the community of the living and return to his or her life, he or she cannot be forced to simply go back to the daily routine as if nothing had happened. The *halakhah* offers a gradual process involving stages of reentry. As the Talmud puts it,

> R. Levi says: A mourner during the first three days [of *shivah*] should see himself as if a sword lies on him between his two thighs;[52] from the third to the seventh day it is as if (the sword) faces him in a corner; afterward, it is as if it moves along with him in the market.[53]

The vacuum of loss causes severe dislocation in most people. Generally healthy individuals will find that the healing process will commence of its own accord but needs to be assisted. The structure of the *halakhah* for Jews provides that assistance. Gradually, step-by-step, the mourner returns to the routine of normal life. The pressure and stress of grief, as illustrated by the talmudic selection, slowly eases away.

Following *shivah*, the various restrictions are lifted. The mourner may return to work and go back to a somewhat normal routine with certain exceptions. These continue until the thirtieth day following the burial. This period is called *shloshim*, which means thirty in Hebrew. As Maimonides puts it, "[We know] from rabbinic rulings [as opposed to biblical law] the mourner should practice some aspects of mourning all thirty days."[54] These aspects include a ban on taking haircuts,[55] wearing new clothes or professionally laundered clothes, and attending festive affairs with live music.[56]

For relatives other than parents, basic mourning ends at thirty days, the end of *shloshim*.[57] For parents,[58] however, aspects of mourning continue for a full year. This includes saying the *Kaddish* at daily services as well as leading those services if one is able to.[59] Also, the mourner still restricts him or herself from particularly joyous public activities, especially those with music. In cases of family gatherings tied to religious observances, such as *bar* or *bat mitzvahs* or weddings, the mourner may attend by doing work on the affair, thus playing a functional role[60] rather than a passive role of simply enjoying the festivities.[61]

During *shloshim* and the first year of mourning for parents, there are no specific pastoral responsibilities for laypeople. Rather, the entire community is called upon to share kindness, empathy, and comfort in imitation of the Almighty. The rabbi, extending friendship and in any of the other roles we have outlined, can also be an invaluable aid to mourners as they return to normal life.[62]

Many mourners need more than just a sense of routine after the initial period. They need an extension, as it were, of the *halakhah*'s structure for grieving. To this end, Rabbi Jacob Goldberg has formulated a program called Pastoral Bereavement Counselling.[63] Using the Rogerian approach,[64] Goldberg trains clergy of all faiths to offer structured counseling for mourners in the months following the funeral. The goals are to encourage the mourner to become aware of the feelings that all mourners share in times of grief, to recognize, legitimate, and explore them, and to gently help the mourner move and work through these emotions as if on a journey, with the hope that this journey will be completed. While there may be no cure for the difficulties, there will be a sense of healing. The counselor uses ten basic skills: listening, reflecting, identifying and labeling, assurance of support, assurance of normalcy, "staying with" the client, "working through" with the client, commending progress, using religious language and other forms or ideas, and therapeutic termination at completion of the process. Much of Goldberg's work offers a practical and organized realization of the theology presented in this book—empathy, the need for religious language, emotional acceptance, and existential presence on the part of the clergy. This program is an encouraging development in meeting the needs of people who grieve.

The Talmud teaches:

"Do not weep for the dead or moan for him" (Jeremiah 22:10).
"Do not weep for the dead" in excess, "or moan for him," more
than the required amount. What does this mean? Three days for
weeping and seven for eulogizing and lamenting, and thirty for
wearing freshly laundered clothing and haircuts. After that, the
Holy One, Blessed Be He, says, "You cannot be more compassionate to him [the deceased] than I."[65]

The rabbis teach that if the Almighty does not demand more
than the requisite amount of mourning, then we also should not
demand this of ourselves. While this is halakhically interpreted as
meaning that after *shivah* one gets up, and after the later periods
one cuts the hair and gradually returns to the normal routine, I
believe the rabbis are referring to an emotional issue as well. Some
people do not experience a sense of healing in the period following
burial. Even with all good intentions, religious observance, rabbinic
and community support, and everything else expressed here, some
are truly mourning long after death has taken place. I have worked
with people who say even years after a death, "I am still sitting *shivah*
for my beloved so-and-so." In these cases, mourning has become
complicated or pathological. There is not much either the rabbi or
community can do in this case other than be supportive to the extent that they are able. The rabbi can help by making a referral to a
professional therapist. Use of programs such as Goldberg's can be
helpful in preventing this type of extended grieving.

AFTER THE COMPLETED MOURNING PERIOD

Glen Davidson points out that under normal circumstances, the physical and emotional symptoms of grieving slowly ease over the first year
after the loss of a loved one.[66] His documentation of the physical
symptoms[67] such as shock, excessive numbness and sensitivity to
stimuli, stunned feelings, outbursts, anger and guilt, restlessness,
disorientation, depression, weight gain or loss has shown that these
tend to abate as the first year wears on. This decrease is coupled by
reorganization, better personal eating and sleeping habits, renewed

energy, and better judgment.[68] He notes that some aspects of disorientation, such as guilt and depression, as well as physical symptoms such as illness and weight gain, tend to peak during the middle months of the first year.[69] He recommends that mourners examine their values and philosophies of living during this time, along with having a physical exam. Within this framework, the observances that Jewish tradition provides for the entire year form a matrix of support for the mourner. This includes the religious and social aspects of being a part of the daily prayer service, as well as the reinforcement involved in the saying of *Kaddish* on a regular basis. In addition, the *halakhah* minimizes extensive joyous social interaction.[70] The combination of support and social restrictions allows the mourner the time and space to continue the emotional reorganization process during the middle phase of the first year.

Davidson notes that these clinical grief symptoms reappear on the first anniversary of the death, as well as at other times, such as anniversaries and holidays.[71] He recommends "telling your story," meaning such activities as sharing experiences with others and doing something tangible on special occasions to ease the pain and promote the emotional healing. He specifically points out the *Yizkor* service on Yom Kippur as an example. While *Yizkor* originated on Yom Kippur, this solemn memorial service coupled with a pledge to donate to charity is recited on the final days of all the major festivals including Passover, Shavuot, and Shemini Atzeret. It goes back at least one thousand years and possibly back to the rabbinic and Maccabean (Second Temple) periods.[72] As the Prayerbook of Rashi (tenth century) described the idea, "One publicly disburses charity for both the living and the deceased."

The *Yizkor* service is part of the larger main service for that festival day. There is a custom that those who have no one for whom to say these prayers leave the sanctuary for the duration of *Yizkor*. The service contains readings from the psalms, prayers for the deceased of the congregation, as well as prayers in memory of Jewish martyrs throughout the ages. The core of the service is a personal prayer that each individual recites silently:

> May God remember the soul of my dear [insert the Hebrew name and father's name of the deceased, as well as which relation the

person was to the mourner], who has gone to his/her eternal
rest; in his/her sake I pledge charity. As a reward for this may
his/her soul be bound up in the bonds of life, with the souls of
Abraham, Isaac, and Jacob, Sarah, Rebecca, Rachel, and Leah, and
with the other righteous in Gan Eden, Amen!

This prayer has a great deal in common with other liturgical
selections for illness and grief quoted in this book in its use of the
themes of connection with the figures of Jewish history, practical
acts of righteousness, affirmation that the soul is at one with God,
and affirmation of the eternity of the soul.[73]

Anniversaries of the death are often considered "marker events,"
occasioning a reopening of the wounds of grief. The anniversary of
the date of death on the Hebrew calendar is known as *Yahrzeit*,
Yiddish for "Year Day." Customs for this day include lighting a special twenty-four-hour candle in memory of the deceased, attending
synagogue services and leading them if possible, the reciting of the
Hazkarah prayer, the saying of *Kaddish*, and for some, the study of
selections from the *Mishnah*[74] and fasting. Again, a religious structure for the mourner assures that the feelings of reopened grief are
recognized and the loved one will not be forgotten. The rabbi's role
is minimal, other than sometimes facilitating these observances when
called upon. Rather, the mourner's participation in the services of
the living community offers fellowship and guidance, along with
continuity.

The custom has arisen in the Western world to have a formal
unveiling or dedication of a monument for the deceased on the
gravesite. The idea of a grave marker is an ancient one, going back
to biblical times.[75] While a formal dedication service is a relatively
recent innovation, the idea has been embraced by all segments of
Jewry. It can be done anytime after the thirtieth day (in fact in Israel
it is done at this point) and generally is done within the first year.[76]
The service is a brief one, consisting of readings, selections from
the psalms, a eulogy, the *Hazkarah* and *Kaddish*.[77] These gatherings
can be enormously beneficial to the family. It gives them a chance
to collect their memories and feelings in a way they could not do at
the funeral. As with the eulogy, rabbis should try to address these
feelings when called upon to officiate. While there is no reason the

entire community could not attend these, most people prefer to keep these services as intimate family- and close-friend-oriented gatherings. And while it is not ritually necessary, a rabbi is invariably called to officiate. Obviously, a rabbi who has the relationship with the family described elsewhere in this book can greatly enrich this type of service. However, if the rabbi did not know the deceased or even the family, it is still possible to add a pastoral dimension of empathy and sensitivity by carefully listening to the needs of the family as well as finding out about the life of the loved one.

In summary, Jewish tradition offers a framework for mourning following the funeral. The constructs of the seven-day *shivah* period, followed by the thirty-day *shloshim* period and the entire first year of mourning, allow time and space for grieving and healing, while gently and gradually bringing the mourner back to society. The postmourning period observances, including the monument unveiling, the end-of-festival *Yizkor* service, and the anniversary *Yahrzeit* observances can assist in the mourner's handling of the senses of loss and grief that often appear after the initial mourning periods. The rabbi's role, while still important, recedes as the community comes to the aid of the mourner.

Conclusion—Some Reflections on a Jewish Pastoral Theology

Many years ago, during my years as a student developing an interest in and beginning my studies in counseling psychology, our rabbinical school received a major donation for a chair in pastoral counseling. The dean at that time, a well-known name in the *yeshivah* world of American Orthodoxy, got up after daily services one morning and began lambasting the notion of pastoral care. I remember his words well. "The Torah," he cried, "is not a means for comforting people. . . ." He understood Judaism as a religion that challenges its adherents rather then making them feel good. It seemed that he saw pastoral care as a threat to Jewish tradition rather than an enhancement or integral part. While I agreed (and still do) that religion at times must challenge us, I felt quite uneasy hearing this, for I was growing into the realization that the Torah can indeed be a means for comforting people and offering meaning to pain-filled and shattered lives. My conviction in this matter has grown over the years, and this book is in essence the result. With all due respect to the noted scholar, I firmly believe he was wrong. The eternal wisdom of the Torah, as shown throughout this work, has much to say to us in times of illness and grief. These ideas transcend the so-called denominations in American Jewish life, for all Jews are commanded to alleviate the suffering of the ill and comfort the bereaved, in imitation of the Almighty. I also hope that

121

the non-Jewish world might benefit from these ideas, for many of them truly apply to all people.

I chose to focus on both illness and mourning in developing this pastoral theology, because many of the clinical, theological, halakhic, and liturgical themes in these two areas are connected. Illness and death are part of every life.[1] Rabbi Soloveitchik interpreted Numbers 19:14, "This is the law of the Torah, when a person dies in a tent . . . ", in this way. The "law of the Torah" in the verse is not only the Temple ritual that the text enjoins to be performed when a person is in contact with a corpse but is death itself,[2] ". . . a fate which awaits us all, a trauma of human helplessness awaits us all."[3]

In my opinion, Americans have great difficulty in coming to grips with the reality of sickness and death. We do our best to cover up this inevitability in the way we attempt to look and feel young, in our daily habits, and yes, in the way we "do death" and mourn.[4] The sooner we face the fact that we will all at some point be sick, and at some point die, the sooner we can begin to live fully.

We have already seen how death causes very real symptoms of dislocation among the mourners.[5] Sickness also causes loneliness and anxiety in the patient.[6] Jewish tradition and *halakhah* provide a needed sense of structure at the very times when all structure seems to collapse. This notion is often taken for granted by those who are observant of *halakhah*, and totally or partially ignored by those who do not subscribe to *halakhah* and the halakhic system.[7] But based on the theses developed throughout this book, I believe *halakhah* offers enormous benefits to those who take the time and trouble to study and observe it. When one's life is shattered by the illness or death of a loved one, when one's basis for day-to-day living is ripped out from underneath, the approach of *halakhah* can offer structure. The reassurance that the community stands with the patient and mourner is coupled with the requirement that the community address the person's physical and spiritual needs.

The liturgy, as shown in chapters 5 and 9, offers the comforting themes of Jewish identity, history, and community, as well as the reassurance of God's presence with the patient and the mourner. These extend emotional and spiritual strength to individuals in crisis, allowing them to find their own resources for healing. They are assured that they are not alone and are assured that hope always remains for the future. With these points embodied within, the traditional liturgy can be a powerful tool for the individual's sustenance.

Specific actions within the structure of *halakhah*, specifically in bereavement, help the mourner through a very difficult period. The symbolic catharsis of the *keriah* can be most therapeutic. The finality of the burial, along with a sensitive eulogy that recalls the goodness of the deceased but also takes the mourner into consideration, offers a sense of closure to the mourner and a focus for beginning the healing process. The stages marked within the *halakhah* of bereavement parallel the emotional stages of recovery. Too often in Western culture, the mourner is left to his or her own devices following the funeral. Mourners are expected to move back into society and fend for themselves, dealing with their loss in whatever fashion they can. Over this period of time, Judaism offers the expectation of the community's assistance to the mourners, as well as the emotional space to foster the healing process.

The structure of Judaism is tempered with sensitivity. A pastoral theology such as the one developed here demonstrates that the letter of the law is implicitly accompanied by a loving and tender spirit of empathy and caring. This does not mean that there will never be conflict between Jewish tradition and the needs of the ill or the bereaved. But I believe that a sensitive rabbi, learned in Jewish tradition, possessing the requisite therapeutic training and skills, and who has honed the pastoral skills outlined, would be able to resolve perceived conflicts between Jewish tradition and pastoral needs. Part of the job of the rabbi, then, is to make the Torah come alive for the laity via fulfilling the rabbinic roles suggested in this book. God's system in theory may look lovely, but it takes real human beings, led by educated and caring human rabbis, to make the system work.

Cognitive empathy, a major means of addressing the patient or mourner's pastoral needs, is inherent in Jewish tradition as well as in the basic Jewish texts on pastoral care. A structured empathy is another way of making God's presence manifest to the mourner or patient via a caring human presence. Besides an immediate human presence in the *bikur holim* visit, the *shivah* call, or the various rabbinic roles, this empathy can be conveyed through use of liturgy and prayer, phone calls, and other activities. Sometimes, the visitor ought to verbally communicate to let the person know of the caring interest. Sometimes words do not help, but conveying care through one's presence is sufficient.

Though America is becoming an increasingly secularized country, it is obvious that people will still turn to clergy in times of crisis.[8] It is therefore imperative that professionals who will inevitably be engaged in pastoral care have the proper training. While the situation in the rabbinate is better than in the past, there still are not enough rabbis who have even basic training in clinical, pastoral, counseling, or referral skills. In addition, while rabbis may be aware of the basics of the Torah tradition on grief and illness, they are not aware of the Torah's rich pastoral guidance. Almost nothing is in print, either in Hebrew or English, on *bikur holim*,[9] and while there is some excellent material on death and mourning in English, very little of it approaches this topic in the pastoral way of this book. If rabbis are to be effective in serving people, healing their wounds, and bringing them closer to a Jewish way of life, then they must have the pastoral skills necessary to reach their laity at times of illness and grief. They must also study their own tradition with an eye to dealing with the emotional needs of their fellow Jews in illness and mourning.

Rabbis today play many roles in their work. This book has shown five approaches to the pastoral roles rabbis can play today. These are: pastoral manager, teacher of the Torah's wisdom at difficult times, member of the extended family, doctor of the soul or exemplar in empathy, and representative of the community. While in many ways these seem like recent inventions, they actually connect to the classic rabbinic roles as mentioned in chapter 6. Serving people's needs through pastoral management is a type of administrative task, related to the administrative work done by the king in ancient times. The king, in Jewish Law, was considered a civil servant responsible to the Torah. The king was also a representative of the nation, not unlike the way the rabbi represents the community. The rabbi as empathic doctor of the soul and member of the extended family is also in some ways a continuation of the role and image of the prophet as comforter, who is together with the people in times of trouble. The rabbi as teacher, of course, is part of the rabbi's classical role as teacher and decisor of Jewish Law. In these ways there is a real continuity between today's pastoral roles for rabbis and the roles of Jewish leaders since the founding of our people.

A main thesis of this book centers on the pastoral role of the community and the laity. The lay and rabbinic roles parallel each other for *bikur holim*. In terms of grief and mourning, however, we can assign a scheme to the relative importance of lay and rabbinic pastoral care, depending on the timing. Using the chart below, it becomes obvious that the conclusion of the burial service marks a turning point in the priority of which type of pastoral care (i.e., lay or rabbinic) *halakhah* and Jewish tradition suggest. This does not totally exclude either lay or rabbinic care at any given point, but it does assign priority to one of these two types of care, depending on the point within the scheme. Before the burial, the mourner is not in a position to receive the care of the community, other than its presence up to and at the service and burial. The rabbi's guidance is most important before and during the service. Afterward, however, the community's concern and care transcends that of the rabbi, although the rabbi's role may be helpful in other ways.

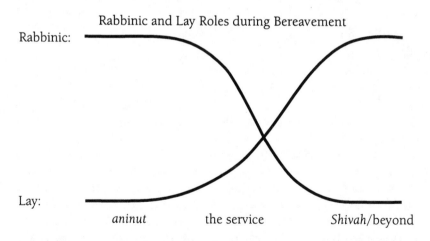

Rabbinic and Lay Roles during Bereavement

Rabbinic:

Lay:

aninut   the service   *Shivah*/beyond

Rabbi Soloveitchik, using Adam and Eve as his models, defines community as two lonely individuals reaching out to each other in the way members of a family would reach out to each other.[10] In this sense, not only could the rabbi be considered a member of the extended family as suggested but a community itself could be considered an extended family. A rabbi could empower laypeople to assume all the roles originally defined for clergy: member of the extended family, teacher of the Torah, pastoral manager, exemplar in empathy and doctor of the soul, and representative of the community.

Rabbi Harold Schulweis has attempted to do this by training "Para-Rabbinics."[11] His acclaimed program was born out of necessity, as Schulweis' Conservative congregation has seventeen hundred families. He selects individuals who are, "empathic, still growing, see this project as a *mitzvah*, and not restricted to the most Jewishly informed people around." He trains them to actually assume some of the rabbinic functions in the congregation including baby namings, some *bar mitzvah* work, and assisting (though not officiating) at funerals. He has a separate *bikur holim* group. Also, Schulweis sees his own role as a facilitator and his relationship to the pararabbinic as one of collegiality.

Not all rabbis want to empower their members to take upon themselves "pastoral" *mitzvot* that rightfully belong to the laity. I hope that more laypeople demand from their rabbis the training and teaching to do these things. At the same time, I hope more rabbis take the professional training and Torah study to act in the pastoral roles described.

While this book has focused on showing how Judaism addresses pastoral needs or opportunities in illness and grief, it is also possible to discover this interaction in other aspects of Jewish living, such as life-cycle events, crisis intervention, and issues of day-to-day life.[12]

It is also my hope that some of the themes described herein will find their way into the non-Jewish world as well. Christian divinity students studying pastoral theology and care might be curious and interested to study a pastoral tradition offering a somewhat different perspective from their own. I hope my work can be useful to them on that basis alone. But at the risk of sounding radical, I would even go a step further. While we do not and cannot expect non-Jews to observe Jewish tradition, I believe that the material described in these areas can actually help those outside my own tradition. Empathy and an empathic presence with those who are ill, teaching and empowering laypeople to assume pastoral functions, use of a structure[13] that is cognizant of the loss of the mourner and that allows mourners to work through their grief in gradual ways, and existence of a supportive community are ideas and processes that can assist all people at critical times. Some of this may be happening already, as one source indicates, "Protestants are increasingly emphasizing the significance of the 'pastorhood of all believers,' in which the care-giving responsibility to the bereaved is shared by the whole congregation and not just undertaken by the professional minister."[14]

The Catholic Church has also recently addressed these concerns. In a recent report, a major diocesan commission has redefined pastoral care as being incumbant on all members of the Church, not just ordained clergy.[15] Its introductory statement in part reads:

> Pastoral care . . . addresses the emotional, social and spiritual needs of the patient. . . . It is personal ministry to individuals and their families by professionally trained persons who are educated to understand the theological issues of the sick, trained to give . . . care . . . and who understand . . . contemporary health care.

The report looks at the physical, emotional, and spiritual struggles of the sick that often precipitate a crisis of faith for the patient. It suggests that ministry to the sick must be seen as a symbol of hope for the patient. Originally, the ordained priest-chaplain was considered the sign of the Church's presence to the sick and their families. The commission statement, however, expands the definition of chaplain to include trained chaplains who may not be ordained. It also recommends extensive use of lay volunteers such as Eucharistic ministers and pastoral visitors as a means of sharing a religious presence with Catholic patients. This is another illustration of the growing non-Jewish recognition for the value of laypeople as worthy pastoral-care-givers, corresponding to *bikur holim* committees.

The overall rewards of this process must be addressed as well. Besides creating a more sensitive empathic world with the use of these skills, people can also bring the *Shekhinah*, the Divine Presence, closer to fellow individuals and the human community by imitating God in pastoral work. This makes the world a better, warmer, holier, more loving, more spiritual, and more livable place. And, as has been shown in the analysis of Psalm 41, the care-giver is also ultimately rewarded with both a sense of fulfillment and the Divine Presence. What better gain could there be for both the individual and society?

In addition to the above, participation in the *mitzvot* of *bikur holim* and comforting the bereaved offers the care-givers a sense of continuity. Rabbi Meir in the Talmud, commenting on the verse "It is better to go to a house of mourning than to a house of feasting,"[16] says: "If one eulogizes others, others will eulogize for him; if one buries, others [will assist] at his burial; if one carries [the casket], others will carry him; if one raises his voice in lament [for others], others will raise their voice for him."[17]

The Talmud assures those who offer kind acts to others in need that they will ultimately be the recipients of similar acts of kindness when their time of need comes. Thus, the sense of community so often mentioned in this book is not only horizontal, connecting Jews with each other, but vertical as well. All who engage in *bikur holim*, burial, eulogizing, and other deeds of *hesed* are part of a great chain reaching back to the beginning of the Jewish people. The links of the chain extend into the future, affirming the eternity of the Jewish people via loving deeds and pledging that those who engage in these actions will be remembered and not be forgotten.

In the end, Judaism affirms that God is with us in everyday life but also, and perhaps especially, in sickness and in times of sorrow. Ultimately, our comfort comes from the Almighty. But at the same time, both rabbis and laity, in their appropriate ways, are expected to help those in need of spiritual sustenance, guidance, and shepherding. We do this in imitation of the One Who is the source of compassion, because, as the Talmud puts it:

> Abba Shaul says [interpreting the biblical verse, "This is my God] and I will glorify Him"—Be like Him, for just as He is merciful and compassionate, so you too be merciful and compassionate.[18]

תם ונשלם שבח לא-ל בורא עולם

Appendix 1

The Laws of *Bikur Holim*

Note: This selection is taken from *Shulhan Arukh*—the Code of Jewish Law, section *Yoreh De'ah* 335, authored by R. Yoseph Caro (sixteenth-century Sefardic scholar) with annotations by R. Mosheh Isserles (sixteenth-century Ashkenazic scholar). These annotations will be preceded by Isserles' Hebrew acronym, "Rema." This translation is my own work and will be helpful for the references in my book to the areas codified in Jewish Law. In addition, I have included selected commentaries on the *Shulhan Arukh* (seventeenth and eighteenth centuries) in my notes to elucidate the text.

1. It is a *mitzvah* to visit the sick. Relatives and close friends may enter immediately, more distant friends after three days. If the illness took hold suddenly,[1] all may enter immediately.[2]

2. Even a *gadol* should go to visit a *katan*,[3] even several times a day, even a *ben gilo*;[4] and he who increases [visiting] is considered praiseworthy. This is as long as he does not trouble the patient.

Rema: Some say that one who hates the patient[5] may go to visit the sick one, but I do not accept this. Rather, one should not visit the sick or comfort the mourner when he hates them, so it should not be thought that he rejoices at the other's evil fate while he has pain. Thus it appears to me.

3. One who visits the sick should not sit on a bed or on a chair or bench but should enrobe himself in reverence and sit before him because God's presence is above the [patient's] bed.

Rema: This refers specifically to a patient lying on the ground, that one who sits would be higher than him. But for a patient lying on a bed, it is permitted to sit on a chair or bench, and this is the practice.

4. One does not visit the sick during the first three hours of the daylight because the illness is easier on the patient in the morning and the visitor will not ask mercy upon the patient. And also not in the last three hours of the daylight because the illness is more severe and the visitor will give up from beseeching mercy.

Rema: And all who visit and do not ask for mercy have not fulfilled the *mitzvah*.

5. When one prays on behalf of a patient in front of him, he can pray in any language he chooses. But if he prays not before the patient, he should pray in the Holy Tongue [Hebrew].

6. [When praying] he should include him [the patient] with the other Jewish ill and say, "May the Almighty be merciful to you among the other ill of Israel"; on the Sabbath he should add, "It is Sabbath and forbidden to cry out but healing is near to come."[6]

7. One tells the patient to consider if he lent or left objects with others, or if others left objects with him, and not to be afraid that this consideration is due to [fear of] death.[7]

8. One does not visit those with intestinal disorders, eye disease, disease of the head, or any disease that causes the world to be heavy for him and makes it hard to speak. One does not visit in his presence but sits in an outer room and asks about his needs, sprinkling or sweeping the room and listening to his pain and praying for him.

9. We visit the ill of idolators for reasons of "the paths of peace."

10. With intestinal disorders, a man should not serve the needs of a woman[8] but a woman can serve the needs of a man.

Rema: Some say that one who has a patient in his home should go to the sage of the city who should ask mercy on the patient's behalf. And it was thus customary to bless the ill in the synagogue, and to offer a new name, for a change of name can tear up the evil decree. Comforting the mourners comes before visiting the sick.[9]

Appendix 2

Resources

The following organizations can be helpful to people in illness or bereavement situations.

The Samuel W. and Rose Hurowitz Coordinating Council of Greater New York for Compassionate Care for the Sick, Frail, and Home-bound—*Bikur Cholim*
130 East 59th Street
New York, NY 10022
212-836-1197
212-836-1372/212-249-7010 (FAX)
Rabbi Isaac Trainin, Executive Vice-President
    Networks and connects, organizes conferences for, and offers resources to *bikur holim* groups.

The Jewish National Healing Center
9 East 69th Street
New York, NY 10021
212-969-0030
    Offers resources for spiritual healing within a Jewish context.

Chevra Kadisha of the Vaad Harabonim of Queens
85-18 117th Street
Richmond Hill, NY 11418
718-849-9700
718-571-4579 (emergencies)
Rabbi Elchanan Zohn, Director
    One of the best organized *Chevra Kadisha* groups in the country and a good source of information on this sacred *mitzvah*.

Tripartite Committee on Jewish Funeral Standards
1350 East 54th Street
Brooklyn, NY 11234
212-444-8080
Rabbi Sidney Applbaum, Director
    A joint project of the Union of Orthodox Jewish Congregations of America, the Rabbinical Council of America, and the Jewish Funeral Directors of America. Provides for the maintenance of halakhic standards in Jewish funerals.

Mourners' After-Care Institute
620 Fort Washington Avenue, Suite 1-C
New York, NY 10040
212-568-5255 212-787-2126 (FAX)
Rabbi Jacob Goldberg, Director
    Offers structured guidance and counseling for mourners after the initial bereavement period.

Notes

CHAPTER 1

1. See also Maimonides, (twelth-century Spain/Egypt) *Yad Haha-zakah* (Code of Jewish Law), Laws of Knowledge, 1:5, who codified "Walking in the way of the Lord" as the "Middle Way" or "Golden Mean."

2. *Talmud Bavli* (Babylonian Talmud, hereafter listed as TB) *Sotah* 14a; also *Midrash Genesis Rabbah* 8.

3. Literally, "acting within the line of judgment."

4. TB *Baba Metzia* 30b; also TB *Baba Kamma* 100a.

5. TB *Shabbat* 127a; cited in the *Daily Prayerbook*, trans. Philip Birnbaum (New York: Hebrew Publishing, 1949), 16-17. This translation, however, is mine.

6. It may be argued that to have God observe His other Divine Laws besides *hesed* would stretch the boundaries of anthropomorphism; thus the ways of kindness and *hesed* are really the only ways we can imitate the Almighty. Yet there are references to God observing His Law in both biblical and rabbinic literature. For example, see Abraham's challenge to God over the destruction of Sodom in Genesis 18:25: "Far be it from You! Shall not the Judge of all the Earth do justice?" as well as the reference to what is written in God's *tefillin* in TB *Brakhot* 6a.

7. *Webster's Ninth Collegiate Dictionary* (1988), s.v. "empathy." It has been my experience in teaching this material to various groups that some people often confuse the definitions of sympathy and empathy, believing

133

that empathy involves actually feeling the other person's feelings and sympathy sharing without feeling. It is not my intention to enter a war of semantics. The quality of which we shall speak throughout most of this book is the one Webster and Switzer (see below) define as empathy.

8. This does not necessarily imply that theologically, God shares human emotions. This issue is an important and controversial one in medieval Jewish thought. Heschel's notion of a God of pathos and feelings, as outlined in his major work *The Prophets*, is considered a major contribution to modern Jewish thought. Yet it has been seriously critiqued. See Eliezer Berkovits in chapter 6 of *Major Themes in Modern Philosophies of Judaism* (New York: Ktav, 1974.) There he states that a God possessing human feelings and emotion is a Christian idea, having no place in Judaism. Not wanting to enter this dispute, I have purposely chosen the word empathy, as opposed to sympathy, which Webster (p. 1196) defines as "common feelings . . . an affinity, association or relationship wherein whatever affects one similarly affects the other . . . the inclination to think or feel alike." Thus, the way in which we follow the loving, caring, but nonhuman Deity is by loving and caring in a very human way. On the strictly human level, however, there will be times when sympathy and empathy can be very close.

9. David K. Switzer, *The Minister as Crisis Counselor* (Nashville: Abingdon, 1986), 58-60. Switzer's work, as the title implies, deals with clergy. Later in this work, we will deal with Jewish models for both clergy and lay pastoral care.

10. Switzer hints at this on page 59 but does not say it outright.

11. Switzer, 58.

12. Ibid. Switzer puts a great deal of emphasis on the spoken word as being the act of the whole person (page 47). I would suggest that in Judaism, there are times where no words are a more appropriate empathic sharing. See, for example, chapter 10 on the post-funeral *shivah* call and, to a lesser extent, our material on a *bikur holim* sick call.

13. Switzer also suggests that the helper will grow through this process as well. See page 54.

14. Shimon Bar Yohai was a great mystic who lived sometime during the second century. He spent a number of years in hiding from the Romans. According to tradition, he was the author of the *Zohar*, the important basis and compendium of *Kabbalah*. Many mystical experiences, including this one, are connected with him.

15. Rashi (R. Shlomo Yitzhaki, eleventh-century France) interprets "the city" as referring to the Garden of Eden, based on midrashic traditions that the Messiah waits in Eden. The Vilna Gaon (R. Elijah–eighteenth-

century Lithuania), basing himself on early manuscripts of this text, says the city is Rome. Maharsha (R. Shlomo Eidels, Poland—sixteenth and seventeenth century) refers to the same texts but says they could still be connected to Eden, because the words for "of Rome" in Aramaic—*Daromi*—also mean "southern," perhaps the southern gate of Eden. Yet he still questions Rashi's position, asking what the rest of the passage has to do with Eden, for example why would the wounded people come to the edge of Eden?

16. While these words are not in the text, this is how Rashi reads it, and this explanation of the passage becomes clearer as it continues. His understanding of this point is most important to our thesis.

17. Rashi: They take off all their bandages, wipe and dress all their wounds, then return and rebandage them.

18. TB *Sanhedrin* 98a.

19. As is well known, some Christian thought uses this passage as a basis for its theology. No Jewish commentator sees Isaiah 53 in reference to Jesus, though some, such as Rashi on the Talmud, see it in a messianic context. See below in footnote 20. Some, including Rashi's commentary on the actual Isaiah text, understand the "Suffering Servant" passage to refer to the entire Jewish people.

20. *The Wounded Healer* (Garden City, NY: Image, 1979) by Catholic theologian Henri Nouwen is predicated in large part on this talmudic passage. His interpretation of the healing Messiah in the Talmud as Jesus is, of course, completely unacceptable from a Jewish point of view. Besides being theologically incompatible, it is historically inaccurate to think that the Rabbis who wrote down and taught this selection (fourth- to sixth-century Palestinian and Babylonian) as well as Rashi, who commented on it, were Jewish Christians. Nevertheless, Nouwen's pastoral understanding of the need for the healer to feel and understand those whom he/she is attempting to spiritually heal is very compatible with the basic thesis of this book.

21. This is not to imply that Christianity has a monopoly on these areas. In fact, the major purpose of this book is to show that there are important Jewish sources for these areas of life, many of which predate the Christian sources. However, the terms themselves and most Westerners' perceptions of the field come from Christian tradition.

22. Seward Hiltner, *Preface to Pastoral Theology* (Nashville: Abingdon, 1958), 1-29.

23. Note must be made of Anton Boisen, who pioneered the Clinical Pastoral Education movement. Boisen believed that studying people and their experiences is the best way to derive theological insights. His work has greatly contributed to the modern field of pastoral care and counseling.

24. Interview with Barbara Conelli, March 3, 1989. Ms. Conelli noted that when her priest was unavailable (as was often the case since he served a two-thousand-member parish), she would often turn to Rabbi Samuel Z. Glaser, her boss and my predecessor at Elmont Jewish Center. Working in the synagogue office, she saw him daily. Differences in theology and religious denomination were of no concern on most issues.

25. Howard Clinebell, *Basic Types of Pastoral Counselling* (Nashville: Abingdon, 1966), 49-52; Paul Pruyser, *The Minister as Diagnostician* (Philadelphia: Westminster, 1976), 44-59; Wayne Oates, *Pastoral Counselling* (Philadelphia: Westminster, 1974).

26. Clinebell, 52-56.

27. Hiltner, 89-173.

28. Ibid., 91-92, characterizes impairments as defects (psychopathology), invasion (outside social factors affecting the person), distortion (of internal perception), and decisions (the inability to make them as affecting personality).

29. There is a great deal in Jewish ethical and philosophical literature regarding the concept of sin as a disease. See, for example, P. Peli, *Soloveitchik On Repentance* (New York: Paulist Press, 1984), and A. I. Kook, *Lights of Penitence*, ed. B. Z. Bokser (New York: Paulist Press, 1978). However, the doctrine of Original Sin is foreign to Jewish thought and would have no place in a Jewish pastoral theology.

30. The terminology here is directly based on the counseling techniques of Carl Rogers. While this summary is an accurate reading of Hiltner and Clinebell, my own notes from people currently in the field indicate that this type of traditional Rogerian technique is being eclipsed by an eclectic variety of pastoral response approaches. Written communication, Dr. Frank Stalfa, associate professor of Pastoral Theology, Lancaster (PA) Theological Seminary, October 1990.

31. Clinebell, 39, based on the work of Clebsch and Jaekle, *Pastoral Care in Historical Perspective* (Englewood Cliffs, NJ: Prentice-Hall, 1964).

32. See chapter 6, where we connect some of these ideas to the rabbinic roles in Jewish life.

33. See Pruyser, 60-79, who makes extensive use of religious language in his work on pastoral diagnosis, including:

1. Awareness of the Holy—in the sense of reverence for sacredness (however defined), feelings of awe, the person's knowledge of his/her own creatureliness.

2. Providence—exploring the sense of purpose in life, related to the capacity for trust.

3. Faith—the sense of embracing life and one's attitude toward life.

4. Grace—gratefulness in the sense of gratitude and kindness, both given and received.

5. Repentance—the capacity for growth and change, tying in with regret and sorrow.

6. Communion—how one relates to the world and others around. This defines how one acts as part of the human community, whether reaching out and comfortable or isolated and estranged.

7. Vocation—a person's willingness to play a decisive part in the divine scheme of things. This also touches upon the person's attitude toward that involvement.

While this terminology obviously comes from a Protestant background, a minimum of retranslation and reinterpretation would easily allow the use of these religious terms for pastoral diagnosis within a Jewish context.

34. In a series of interviews as part of a study I did several years ago, I discovered that quite often, the pastoral approach reflected that denomination's specific approach to theology or religious practice. Some Catholics along with certain sacramentally based Protestants such as Lutherans and Episcopalians used their sacraments as part of pastoral counseling. Some conservative or Fundamentalist-Evangelical Protestants attempted to integrate theology with modern psychological insights; others followed the notion of "biblical counseling," with a highly directive approach attempting to find all answers to problems in Scripture. Some saw their role as following in the ministering footsteps of the founders of Christianity. Still others were far less concerned about theology, ritual, and Scripture and far more concerned about their presence and interaction with the parishioner, representing God in their ministry to those in need. See Joseph S. Ozarowski, *Jewish Pastoral Theology and Care at Life's Crisis Points* (Ann Arbor, MI: UMI, 1992), 9–16.

35. The approach and models I have developed here primarily relate to the Western (and specifically the American) rabbinate. After completing the first draft of my work, I had occasion to talk extensively with Rabbi Fred Naftali Hollander, director of the Israeli Region of the Rabbinical Council of America. Rabbi Hollander was one of the earliest Jewish CPE instructors before moving to Israel and is now developing a pastoral care practicum for Israeli rabbis and rabbinical students. He reports that Israeli rabbis are most interested in the clinical aspects of this program rather than the Judaic bases. This, he says, is because they may not trust the Judaic backgrounds of their American counterparts, and the secular background

of these Israeli rabbis (all Orthodox) is much weaker than that of most American Orthodox rabbis. (Conversations with Rabbi Fred Hollander, June 1991 and June 1994.)

CHAPTER 2

1. *Midrash Tanhuma Vayera* 2.

2. In addition to the 613 biblical *mitzvot* we understand from the Written Torah (the Five Books of Moses), there are also *mitzvot* that are considered "rabbinic." The Rabbis (Second Temple through talmudic periods—sixth-century B.C.E. through sixth-century C.E.) either enacted these themselves or extracted and extended them from the Torah's own commandments. While rabbinic *mitzvot* traditionally are also considered binding on a Jew, they do not have the strength or force of the biblical commandments. Our discussion revolves around the question of whether *bikur holim* is biblical or rabbinic in its origin and strength.

See Nahmanides (Ramban—thirteenth-century Spain), notes to *Sefer Hamitzvot* 1:3; *Behag* (*Baal Halakhot Gedolot* of R. Shimon Kayara—ninth-century Babylonia), positive commandment 36; R. Yonah (thirteenth-century Spain) on TB *Brakhot* chapter 3; and many others.

Besides the *Midrash* of God's visit to Abraham, the sources cite the earlier-mentioned references to imitating God and walking in His ways as biblical roots of the *mitzvah* of *bikur holim*. See *Tur Shulhan Arukh* (fourteenth-century Spanish post-Maimonidean but pre-*Shulhan Arukh* code of Jewish Law), *Yoreh De'ah* 335.

3. Maimonides, Laws of Mourning 14:1.

4. Maimonides, *Sefer Hamitzvot*, section 2. Note also that Maharitz Chayot (Tzvi Hirsh Chayes, nineteenth-century Austria) on TB *Nedarim* 39b explains Maimonides' opinion as "*Halakhah LeMosheh MiSinai*," unwritten divine law traceable to Sinai.

5. These rules are found in the introduction to the *Sifra*, a rabbinic commentary to Leviticus, in the name of Rabbi Yishmael, and are included as part of the daily service. See, for example, the text and commentary in Birnbaum, *Daily Prayerbook*, 41-45.

6. *Responsa, Maharil* 197 and *Ahavat Hesed* 3:3, both quoted in Aaron Levine, *Zikhron Meir* (Toronto: Zikhron Meir, 1985), 66-67 n. 1.

7. TB *Nedarim* 39b. Rashi and Tosafot understand from this story a possible biblical basis for the *mitzvah*. Meiri (Menahem ben Shlomo—thirteenth-century Provence) sees this only as a biblical hint and holds, like Maimonides, that *bikur holim* is definitely a rabbinical commandment.

The translation in this citation is not mine but from Isidore Epstein, ed., Soncino *Hebrew-English Edition of the Talmud* (London: Soncino Press, 1983).

8. See the discussion in chapter 1 regarding sickness and death as an integral part of existence, and the last chapters of this book for my critique of people in Western culture who are unable to face the fact that life is limited and we all are mortal. The talmudic quote is certainly a good illustration of these points.

9. The translation used at this point is that of the Jewish Publication Society (hereafter referred to as JPS) as found in A. Cohen, trans. and ed., *The Psalms* (London: Soncino Press, 1945). I have taken the liberty of editing out some of the older unwieldy English, while keeping the basic thrust of the JPS text. However, the rabbinic understanding of the text will offer a somewhat different rendering.

10. TB *Nedarim* 40a.

11. It may also be possible to see in this a special *mitzvah* to visit the ailing poor.

12. This thought is echoed elsewhere in rabbinic literature. See *Yalkut Shimoni* 2, #640 (midrashic commentary on this psalm), also *Midrash Leviticus Rabbah* 34:1 (on Leviticus 25:35) on the verse "When your brother becomes poor . . ." interpreting poorness here as sickness.

13. See biblical examples in Mandelkorn's *Concordance* (Tel Aviv: Schocken, 1978), 295, and modern Hebrew listings in *Shilo Dictionary* (New York: Shilo, 1963), 32.

14. But see the commentary of Metzudot, who renders this verse, "Happy is he who gives *tzedakah* [charity] to the needy."

15. A. Hachen, *Daat Mikra on Psalms* (Jerusalem: Mosad Harav Kook, 1979), 235. Hachen concludes that according to this, the entire psalm was written by the psalmist after a personal encounter with illness and healing. This follows Ibn Ezra, who also considers this psalm a moving personal account on the nature of illness and visitation.

16. TB *Nedarim* 40a.

17. For the talmudic interpretation, see the above-mentioned quote from TB *Nedarim* 40a.

18. *Ethics of the Fathers* 1:3.

19. A positive attitude toward life, followed up with compassionate acts to others, could indeed affect a person's physical condition. Many who are quite ill are assisted in their recovery by their own attitudes. See Howard F. Andrews, "Helping and Health: The Relationship between Volunteer Activity and Health-Related Outcomes," *Advances* 4:1 (1990): 25-34, and Bill Moyers, *Healing and the Mind* (New York: Doubleday, 1993), 157ff.

20. See the comments in chapter 3 regarding God's presence near the patient's bed.

CHAPTER 3

1. There is a great deal of responsa literature dealing with the status of mental illness in regard to halakhic questions, especially medical *halakhah* and ethics (such as birth control, abortion, etc.) This is a complex subject, ranging far beyond the purview of this book. For our purposes, we shall follow the vast majority of halakhic scholars who hold that mental illness does indeed have the status of illness in Judaism.

2. TB *Baba Kamma* 85a, comments of Rashi and *Tosafot*; TB *Brakhot* 60. See my article "Malpractice" in the *Journal of Halacha and Contemporary Society* 14 (Fall 1987): 111-127, where I suggest that because illness is not punishment, there is a divine *mitzvah* for the physician to heal.

3. See Aaron Levine, 23-26, where an impressive array of rabbinic, medieval, and modern sources are offered supporting this position. However, it is easy to see how one in the midst of devastating illness or loss may find it difficult to subscribe to this idea.

4. *Midrash Shir HaShirim Rabbah* 2:1.

5. TB *Nedarim* 40a.

6. TB *Nedarim* 41a.

7. See chapter 5, where this term is used and defined in the liturgy.

8. TB *Nedarim* 41a.

9. See the end of chapter 2, where we define the visitor's reward in terms of God's sustenance.

10. A variant text has this as "one sixtieth of his illness." See TB *Baba Metzia* 30b.

11. TB *Nedarim* 39b.

12. See Alfasi (tenth-century northern Africa) and Meiri on this text.

13. Maimonides (Laws of Mourning 14:4) words it quite simply: "Anyone who visits the sick, it is as if he has lifted part of his sickness and eased it from him."

14. Also Rashi on TB *Baba Metzia* 37b follows this; however, Rashi here suggests a different explanation.

15. *Maavar Yabok, Siftei Tzedek* 1, cited in Levine, 79 n. 74.

16. TB *Megillah* 11a.

17. This follows Rashi in TB *Megillah* 11a, who uses the Hebrew term *ben mazlo* but defines it as we have here. Soncino renders it "counterpart"; Jastrow has it "same character."

18. For this translation I am following the commentary of R. David Luria.

19. *Midrash Ruth Rabbah* 2:7.

20. See the commentary *Yefe Anaf* for this idea.

21. The *Midrash* does not really answer the query here but the commentary *Matnot Kehuna* (R. Yissachar Hakohen—sixteenth-century Poland) says that the answer must be the same as in TB *Nedarim*—the sixtieth is fractionalized.

22. *Midrash Leviticus Rabbah* 34:1.

23. Commentaries of Matnot Kehuna and R. Zev Einhorn (nineteenth-century Lithuania).

24. My anecdotal experience, as well as that of my colleagues, is that sick people often feel better physically as well as emotionally after a good *bikur holim*/pastoral visit.

25. Interestingly, the remainder of this *midrash* goes on to associate this thought with Psalm 41.

26. *Ethics of the Fathers* 2:1.

27. There are differing interpretations of this particular passage. Rashi understands it to mean greater and smaller in stature. Also thus *Shita Mekuvetzet* (digest of talmudic commentaries by R. Betzalel Ashkenazi—sixteenth-century Egypt and Jerusalem), "Even the greatest personage should visit the humblest . . ." and Soncino. See Perisha (Commentary on *Tur Shulhan Arukh* by R. Yozhe Katz—premodern Europe), who uses God's visit to Abraham as an example of greater visiting humbler. Maimonides, however, understands it to mean age, that an older person should visit a younger one.

28. TB *Nedarim* 39b.

29. Compare this talmudic passage and its interpretations to these two parallel ones: Radbaz (R. David Ibn Zimra—sixteenth-century Egypt) on Jerusalem (Palestinian) Talmud (herein referred to as JT) *Terumot* 1:5: "No set amount means [visiting can be] at day or night, just as certain oils were burnt in the Temple at day or night." Also *Yalkut Tehillim* (*Midrash on Psalms*) 41, "*Bikur holim* has no set amount so that the person should pray for the patient and his/her prayer will be received."

Maimonides in his code (Laws of Mourning 14:4) writes, "One can visit many times in the day. Whoever adds [to this] is praiseworthy, providing one does not trouble [the patient]." Note how Maimonides, himself a physician, made the patient's need a major point in his halakhic formulation of this issue.

30. This could be either A, who has sworn off having benefit from B, or A, who has sworn off giving benefit to B. The idea of a vow (Heb. *neder*)

for limiting one's pleasure was one frequently used in biblical and talmudic times. See Numbers 30:1-17 and the entire tractate TB *Nedarim*.

31. This means a physical healing as well. Note that the *Mishnah* equates body and soul in terms of healing.

32. This could refer to the charging of wages for the healing; "healing of the soul," which is permitted, then means healing that comes from the goodness of the soul. This explanation would have implications for a professional physician who "swore off" a patient. The *Gemara* rejects this explanation in favor of one that defines forbidden financial benefit as "healing of his animal," which would be banned under the terms of this vow. There is no intrinsic *mitzvah* for this—*Tosafot* (commentary on Talmud—various rabbis, twelfth to thirteenth-century France and Germany).

33. TB *Nedarim* 38b-39a.

34. Rashi calls this *tzavta*, simply keeping the patient company, as opposed to *bikur holim*. This would be similar to paid nursing companions that we often use today.

35. See R. Nissim (fourteenth-century Spain).

36. Radbaz on Maimonides, Laws of Vows, 6:8.

37. *Shulhan Arukh, Yoreh De'ah* 281:4.

38. Ibid. 335:3; see the *Shulhan Arukh*'s full English text on *bikur holim* in Appendix 1.

39. But see further for more detail.

40. Rashi—since people who visit take care of the patient's basic needs.

41. TB *Nedarim* 40a.

42. This entire idea is cited in Maimonides' code but not in the *Shulhan Arukh*.

43. This would include medical and other forms of therapy, as well as general care. Tending to the patient's food and dietary needs, in my opinion, would come under this rubric; I will have more to say about food in the next chapter.

44. This is a common truism. My experience, though, is that many hospital chaplains and clergy staff would not accept this statement. In fact the very day I wrote this paragraph, I participated in a pastoral-care committee meeting at a local hospital. This specific issue took up a great deal of that meeting. The inclusion of this section in the book, hopefully, will share some wisdom from Judaism on this important topic.

45. In fact, there is another version of the Talmud's story hinted at in the Meiri commentary and quoted in the commentary of the Netziv, Rabbi Naftali Tzvi Berlin of Volozhin (Lithuania—nineteenth-century), which has Rabbi Akiba visiting his student but not doing the sprinkling and sweeping himself. Rather, the attendant, upon noticing the presence of Rabbi

Akiba, was moved to sweep and sprinkle, causing the student to say, "My master, you have made me live!"

We can learn a most significant lesson for our mode of care from this version of the story. Even though we assume that the physical needs of the patient are attended to by paid staff, and we do not have to "sweep and sprinkle" ourselves, still these things are not always adequately addressed. However, our mere presence in visiting the patient can often prompt the physical care staff to better do their jobs of "sweeping and sprinkling."

I thank Rabbi Yitzhak Knobel of Yeshiva Gedola Ateres Yaakov, who brought the alternate reading of the talmudic story as well as this interpretation to my attention.

46. Samuel Dresner, *The Jewish Dietary Laws* (New York: Burning Bush Press, 1959).

47. TB *Nedarim* 40a. Rashi and R. Nissim comment: When the visitor sees the patient stronger in the morning, the visitor believes the prayers are not as necessary. When the patient weakens in the last three hours, the visitor will not pray because he/she has given up hope for recovery.

48. See chapter 5 for amplification of this important theme.

49. Maimonides, Laws of Mourning 14:5.

50. This is how the commentary of the Radbaz understands Maimonides.

51. *Arukh Hashulhan* 335:8 (premodern reworking of the Code of Jewish Law by R. Yehiel Epstein—nineteenth-century Lithuania); *Ramat Rahel* (R. Eliezer Waldenberg—twentieth-century Israel) mentions that according to Radbaz on JT *Terumot* 11:5, one can even visit at night.

52. Aaron Levine, 77 n. 62, mentions an interesting point. The author heard from the late Rabbi Y. Ruderman of Baltimore in the name of R. Hayyim of Brisk (Lithuania—nineteenth century) that the maximum amount of time for a *bikur holim* visit is six minutes. He arrived at this figure by taking this talmudic passage allowing six hours for visits (if the first three and last three are excluded), making a total of 360 minutes. If the visit of a *ben gilo* takes away 1/60th of the illness, as indicated above, then 1/60th of 360 minutes is six minutes! This could also explain our earlier talmudic reference regarding the difference between *bikur holim* (the minimal visit of six minutes, fulfilling the *mitzvah*) and company (a longer visit).

I also recently heard in the name of R. Hayyim of Volozhin (Lithuania—eighteenth century) an interpretation of one of the biblical verses upon which our pastoral theology is predicated in chapter 1 (Exodus 18:20), "And you shall show them the way that they shall walk on it and the act that they shall do. . . ." R. Hayyim understood the term "The way that they shall walk," explained by the Talmud as referring to *bikur holim*, to mean that there comes a point in the visit that the visitor should walk out (e.g., know when to leave) and not tire the patient! (Conversation with Rabbi Fabian Schonfeld, January 15, 1992.)

53. Rashi: "Because perhaps I will recover right away, or so that people should not talk about me." R. Asher (Germany and Spain, fourteenth century): "Since the people who dislike me and seek my ill fortune will only minimally pray for me, the sickness will increase." Meiri: "Because [the ill condition] might be a coincidence and it is not worthwhile to alarm [the patient] until sickness grows stonger."

54. Rashi: Since he did not recover immediately, he said "Go and tell. . . ."

55. TB *Nedarim* 40a.

56. But see later in chapter 4 for differentiation of timing for visits to close friends or relatives.

57. TB *Nedarim* 40a.

58. *Shulhan Arukh, Yoreh De'ah* 335:3.

59. See Maimonides, Laws of Mourning 14:6: "One who visits . . . should not sit on a bed, chair, bench, or any high place, and not higher than [the patient's] head but should enrobe and sit below his head, ask mercy for him, and leave."

60. I can truthfully say that encountering this particular selection from the Talmud has affected the way I do my hospital calls. I am much more sensitive to how I enter a hospital room and to where I place myself when I enter the room. It is not always possible to be on the same level as the patient, but I always try to do so.

61. The Bet Hillel commentary on the *Shulhan Arukh* states that the main issue in all this is the height of the visitor, not the seating position. But Rashi on TB *Shabbat* 12 quotes the *Zohar* that says a person should not be at the head, because of the Divine Presence, or at the foot, because of the Angel of Death. This may not matter when visiting a particularly righteous person (Heb. *tzadik*), where the Angel of Death is not present, or a confirmed evildoer (Heb. *rasha*), where the Divine Presence may not abide.

62. N. A. Tuckaczinski, *Gesher HaHayyim* (Jerusalem, 1960), 28.

63. *Ramat Rahel* section 10, based on earlier sources.

64. R. Nissim—the constant use of (the toilet) for the patient's bodily needs is embarrassing.

65. But R. Elijah of Vilna comments that speaking is good for one with a fever.

66. TB *Nedarim* 41a.

67. Aaron Levine, 70-71.

68. *Arukh Hashulhan* 335.

69. *Ramat Rahel* 3.
70. TB *Nedarim* 41a.

CHAPTER 4

1. For a summary of guidelines for blessings, see Blu Greenberg, *How to Run a Traditional Jewish Household* (Northvale, NJ: Jason Aronson Inc., 1989), 143-156.

2. See chapter 1 for the rabbinic sources and context of *bikur holim* within this framework.

3. Aaron Levine, 68.

4. On the question of the *mitzvah* to visit non-Jews, see further.

5. See chapter 9, where we offer the identical reason for the rule that no blessing is recited over the *mitzvah* of burial.

6. See, for example, *Ethics of the Fathers* 1:5: "Do not overly gossip with a woman; [if] it is said with one's own wife, how much more so with the wife of another. . . ."

7. *Arukh Hashulhan* 335:11, with the caveat that the ban on *yihud*—being totally alone together with no one else having access to them—is not transgressed. It would be hard to imagine this type of situation in a hospital setting, though it is conceivable in a home.

8. Aaron Levine, 71 n. 24, 25. The stricter guidelines are followed primarily in the so-called right-wing Orthodox community.

9. *Shulhan Arukh, Yoreh De'ah* 335:2, comments of R. Isserles, as well as others.

10. *Yekara D'Hayei*, 39-40 in the notes, quoted in Aaron Levine, 72 n. 35.

11. Commentaries on *Shulhan Arukh, Yoreh De'ah* 335:2—Bah (R. Yoel Sirkes—sixteenth-century Poland), Shakh (R. Shabtai HaKohen—seventeenth-century Lithuania), and also *Hokhmat Adam* (R. Abraham Danzig—early twentieth-century Lithuania) 151:2.

12. *Arukh Hashulhan* 335.

13. *Ramat Rahel* 9.

14. TB *Gittin* 61a. Rabbi Moshe Tendler, (professor of Talmud and head of biology at Yeshiva University) in an oral presentation (January 16, 1990) and in a subsequent written response to me (February 28, 1994), defined *darkei shalom* as

the cement that permits a pluralistic society to function. Diverse religious communities must interact at many social levels. Sensitivity and compassion to those in need is a neccessary component for such interactions. It would be unrealistic to expect cooperation in areas of mutual social concern if each faith community ignored the sick and hungry in their midst because they were not of the same faith.

15. R. Moshe Feinstein (twentieth-century United States in *Igrot Mosheh, Yoreh De'ah* 2, responsa 130, rules that a convert to Judaism, who generally gives up any religious connection to their non-Jewish parents, may still be obligated to visit a sick parent if so requested. He suggests that in addition to the issues we have listed here, there may still be a responsibility of "honoring parents" in this family.

16. Some medieval authorities such as Rashi, Alfasi, and R. Asher attempt to narrow the interpretation of obligating a Jew to visit non-Jews to, "only when they [non-Jews] are actually [living] with Jews," so as not to antagonize them or cause animosity. Others, such as R. Nissim and Ritva (R. Yom Tob Ben Avraham al-Asevilli—thirteenth- to fourteenth-century Spain) follow the broader understanding of the Talmud cited in our text. The various codes of Jewish Law definitely accept the intrinsic value of visiting non-Jews and, as mentioned above, are considered the authoritative guide in this matter. See Maimonides, Laws of Mourning 14:12 and *Shulhan Arukh* 335:9 for the codification on *bikur holim*.

17. TB *Shabbat* 12a. Rashi suggests that Hillel's school allows this because only worldly, weekday "desires [are forbidden on the Sabbath] but not heavenly desires." Since visiting the sick is a *mitzvah*, it is obviously considered a "heavenly desire."

18. R. Hananel (eleventh-century North Africa), R. Asher, and Alfasi add that one may be tempted to pray for the patient with troubled cries, not appropriate to the *Shabbat* spirit. This fits in with the other passages in the Talmud referring to the types of prayer for the ill that may be used on *Shabbat*. See below.

19. *Mishnah Brurah* (R. Yisrael Meir Hakohen—late nineteenth- early twentieth-century Poland), quoting Magen Avraham (R. Avraham Gombiner—seventeenth-century Poland), on *Shulhan Arukh, Orah Hayyim* 287:1.

20. It seems to me that a visit on the Sabbath should be done in a "Sabbathlike" manner in terms of pace, dress, etc.

21. Aaron Levine, 78-79.

22. Comforting the bereaved on *Shabbat*, which could be seen as parallel to *bikur holim*, has a different halakhic guideline. We do not engage in the traditional "*shivah* call" of formal condolence on the Sabbath,

since there is no public mourning on the Sabbath. It is certainly permitted to offer a friendly visit, though. See further in chapter 10 regarding *shivah* calls in general.

23. R. Waldenberg in *Ramat Rahel* 14 and *Tzitz Eliezer* 13:36.

24. Rashi in his commentary says this means that one should broaden the mind with words of comfort so as not to feel sorrow on the Sabbath.

25. Rashi: Since you honor it by refraining from crying out.

26. Rashi: Since one includes this patient with others, the prayer is heard through the merit of the many.

27. TB *Shabbat* 12a-b.

28. See *Shulhan Arukh, Yoreh De'ah* 335:6

29. See the next chapter, where we deal with the liturgy for the sick.

30. *Tzitz Eliezer* 8:15:9; also *Minhat Yitzhak* 3:70 (Rabbi Yitzchak Weiss—twentieth-century England and Israel), and many others.

31. *Helkat Yaakov* 1:64. See earlier in chapter 1, where we cite the distinction between biblical law, more stringent in doubtful cases because of its divine source, and rabbinical law, where more leniency can be adopted because of its human origin.

32. Obviously, a subjective decision must be made as to when a given situation is considered life threatening. The parameters of what constitutes a threat to life are beyond this book. But as we have shown before, the *halakhah* considers the emotional needs of a patient in a dangerous state along with his/her physical needs. If the patient requests a particular visitor or action, and the visit or action will affect his/her physical or emotional condition, the *halakhah* allows compliance, even if this involves breaking other rules of Jewish Law.

33. I have experienced cases of people collapsing in my synagogue during services on Saturday mornings. While using a phone is something I would never do on a normal Sabbath, I myself made the calls for help more than once in my career.

34. TB *Brakhot* 54b. Others include a mourner in this category.

35. Aaron Levine, 80.

36. Ibid.

37. See TB *Niddah* 16b and TB *Derekh Eretz Zuta* 5—that a person should not enter anyone's room suddenly. How much more so should this apply to a sick person?

38. See also Aaron Levine, 80; "Comic Relief," *Prevention* 40:3 (March 1988): 38-42; Joel Goodman, "Laughing Matters," *Journal of the American Medical Association* 267:13 (April 1, 1992): 1858; and Jane E. Brody, "Per-

sonal Health (Laughter as Potential Therapy for Patients)," *New York Times*, 7 April 1988.

39. Paul Irion, in private conversation with me.

40. Cited at the beginning of chapter 1 in the talmudic selections developing a Jewish pastoral theology; also cited at the beginning of chapter 2 in the quote from *Midrash Tanhuma Vayera* 2.

41. Even Rashi's comment, "God came and asked about [Abraham's] welfare," (based in part on TB *Baba Metzia* 86b) need not contradict this understanding. Rashi's interpretation does not specify a dialogue of words but could indeed suggest an empathic relationship as we have outlined so often in this book.

42. This is true for clients in many counseling or crisis situations. The model developed in these paragraphs can be used in other cases as well.

43. Rabbi Dr. Jack D. Frank of Chicago, Illinois, suggested this idea to me orally in June 1984. See Part III of this book (Death, Grief, and Bereavement) where the Jewish tradition of *shivah* will be explored further.

44. See Maurice Lamm, *The Jewish Way in Death and Mourning* (New York: Jonathan David, 1969), 122-125 and 140-141, for an explanation of these traditions.

45. However, Rabbi Jacob Goldberg, author of *Pastoral Bereavement Counselling* (New York: Human Sciences Press, 1989) and developer of the "Mourner's After-Care Institute," has stated publicly and told me privately that he does not consider "true" afterdeath grief to be analogous to the other emotional conditions that some refer to as "grief," such as "anticipatory grief," during the period before the imminent death of a terminal patient, or the other types of loss that do not involve death.

46. Written communication, with Rabbi Charles Spirn, chaplain, Mount Sinai Hospital, New York, August 9, 1990.

47. I will never forget one particular visit to a hospitalized congregant. While in bed with several tubes coming out of her, she offered me a glass of water. I told her, "Thanks, but I'm not really thirsty," not wanting to trouble her and truly not being thirsty. Yet, when she persisted, I realized that she wanted the dignity and pleasure of hosting me in "her home," to the extent that she was able. I graciously accepted the glass of water. Though it was not easy for her to pour it, this simple act gave her great joy and lifted her spirits.

48. In fact, Edward Wimberly has developed an approach to pastoral care from an African-American person's perspective. See, for example, his *Pastoral Counselling and Spiritual Values: A Black Point of View* (Nashville: Abingdon, 1982).

49. *Shulhan Arukh, Yoreh De'ah* 337:1. Some of the commentaries indicate that this applies even to informing the patient of a death in the family, which would then impose halakhic obligations on the patient as a mourner (see later in this book for details of these). Elsewhere (*Shulhan Arukh, Yoreh De'ah* 402:12), it is suggested that withholding or changing the truth is permitted if knowledge of this information might affect the patient's condition. This issue has many serious ethical implications. Ultimately, Judaism considers life to be of the highest value and in some cases higher than truth. My own feeling is that every case is different. The guiding principle would be that whatever benefits the physical condition and then the emotional condition of the patient would be appropriate. Sometimes, a rabbi with a close relationship to the patient, rather than a physician, is the best judge of what will emotionally affect a person. Obviously, the family's guidance is essential here. See chapter 6 for my discussion on the rabbi as a member of the extended family.

50. Aaron Levine, 81.

51. See *Responsa Igrot Mosheh* on *Shulhan Arukh, Yoreh De'ah*, vol. 1, #223; also many others concur with this ruling.

52. Aaron Levine, 99, and see below.

53. *Tzitz Eliezer* 8:5 and *Ramat Rahel* 8, quoting the medieval comment of R. Asher on Genesis 18:1 (God's visit to Abraham following the latter's circumcision—one of our earlier important bases for *bikur holim*).

54. For an excellent summary of the issues connected to AIDS and Judaism, see J. David Bleich, "AIDS: A Jewish Perspective," *Tradition* 26:3 (Spring 1992): 49–80.

55. In essence, the question revolves around the issue of obligation to act versus permissibility to act. An obligation is a *mitzvah* and binding; a permissible act may be laudatory and encouraged, but it is not binding.

56. Aaron Levine, 99.

57. Y. Y. Greenwald, *Kol Bo Al Aveilut* (New York: Feldheim, 1973) 1:2 n. 5.

58. See my development of the rabbinic roles for pastoral care in chapter 6. According to my position there, a trained pastoral-care giver would fall into the same category as a physician.

59. Both Greenwald and Aaron Levine muster an impressive array of sources for their positions. Both of them also cite the comment of the Sema (*Sefer Me'irat Einaim* of R. Joshua Falk—sixteenth-century Poland) on *Shulhan Arukh, Hoshen Mishpat* 426:2, who in turn quotes a passage from the Jerusalem Talmud to the effect that one has the obligation to save a life even if one's own life is in immediate danger.

CHAPTER 5

1. Numbers 12:13. I have translated this myself.

2. Rabbinic tradition considered the biblical skin disease often translated as "leprosy" (but actually not related to the disease modern medicine knows as leprosy) as punishment for *lashon hara*, speaking ill of another. See Leviticus chapters 13-15 and commentaries.

3. Or Hahayyim (R. Hayyim ben Attar—eighteenth-century Italy/Jerusalem) Tosafot, *Targum Yonatan* (Aramaic translation and interpretation of the Torah, rabbinic period—Israel).

4. Or Hahayyim, *Targum Yonatan.*

5. Or Hahayyim, Tosafot, Ibn Ezra (twelfth-century Spain) and Sforno (sixteenth-century Italy). Note that Tosafot understands the themes of pleading (Heb. *bakashah*) and of immediacy from the double use of the word "please" (Heb. *na*) in the biblical verse.

6. Rashi on Numbers 12:13.

7. In fact the Talmud in TB *Brakhot* 34a mentions the following story: Once a student went to lead the prayers in front of R. Eleazar and made the prayers too short. The other students questioned how short [in prayer] this one is! R. Eleazar replied, "Certainly not shorter than Moses, our teacher, as it is written 'Please, O God, please heal her!'"

Interestingly, this story is preceded by a similar one of a student who was rather long winded in prayer and whose cohorts also questioned him. R. Eleazer answered in a similar way, that the student went no longer than Moses, who prayed for forty days and forty nights!

8. Ibn Ezra on Numbers 12:13.

9. This is not the only hint of Moses using prayer in the empathic sense. *Midrash Yalkut Shimoni* 393, commenting on Moses' praying to God for forgivenesss following the Golden Calf incident, suggests a linguistic connection between the Hebrew word for pleaded, *vayehal*, and the word for illness (*holeh*). The *Midrash* states, "From here we learn that Moses stood in prayer until he became ill." If we view sin as a form of spiritual sickness, then Moses here takes upon himself the illness of his people—not only in empathy with them but also in sympathy, as Webster has defined them! Perhaps tongue in cheek, the *Midrash* continues, "Abaye said, '[Moses prayed] until he made God ill with his prayer.'"

10. R. Nissim's commentary on this section deals with an important question: Can one actually pray for the death of an ill person? He suggests that "there are times when one must ask mercy for the ill person that he should die, such as when he suffers so much in his illness and it is impossible for him to live." R. Nissim goes on to compare this with the case in

TB *Ketubot* 104a where the maidservant of R. Yehudah Hanasi prays for her master's death, as she sees him suffering so much. R. Nissim suggests that R. Dimi endorses the maidservant's prayers over those who prayed for R. Yehudah's health.

See Marc Angel, "Halacha and Hospice," *Journal of Halakha and Contemporary Society* 12 (Fall 1986): 25, where he writes, "Giving up in such a [hopeless] case is not a sin but a virtue." However, R. Moshe Feinstein in *Responsa Igrot Mosheh, Hoshen Mishpat* II, #74, rules that the Talmud's case may not be seen as a source for allowing prayer for a terminally ill patient's demise, since we do not really know how our prayers are accepted by the Almighty. R. Eliezer Waldenberg in *Ramat Rahel* (5:5:28, 7:49:3, 9:47) limits praying for the patient's demise unless there are absolutely no ulterior motives, the suffering is so great it cannot be accepted, and all other medical alternatives, as well as prayer and charity for recovery, have been exhausted. R. Waldenberg allows the patient to pray for his own death.

11. *Mazal* could be translated literally as referring to one's astrological sign. Rashi, however, reads it as, "lest people talk of his illness and affect [his fate.]"

12. TB *Nedarim* 40a.

13. The Reverend Glenn Dietrich, unpublished verbatim, Lancaster Theological Seminary, Doctor of Ministry Program, July 1, 1981.

14. This has been my continuous experience in eighteen years in the rabbinate; it is echoed by many other fellow pulpit rabbis. However, see footnote 16 regarding the differing views and experiences of colleagues in the hospital chaplaincy. In addition, there are other types of prayer that have a desired pastoral effect, as we will see later in this chapter when we deal with prayer in the synagogue.

15. But see the commentary of Meiri, who proposes that the ultimate goal of the visitor's prayer is to encourage the *patient* to pray on his/her own behalf. Meiri connects this idea with the earlier-cited talmudic selection, "One who enters to visit the sick should not sit on a bed, or a bench, or a chair but should enrobe himself and sit on the ground . . ." (TB *Nedarim* 40a). He suggests that a visitor sitting at the same level as the patient will encourage the patient to pray.

16. In my teaching this material as part of lectures or courses in the last few years, most of the students I asked about this question responded thusly: Some told me they "tolerate" the bedside prayers. However, many Jewish hospital chaplains believe there is value in bedside prayer with rabbis. One, for example, uses the liturgy from the service, such as the *Mi-Sheberakh* (see further) at the bedside. This differs to some extent from spontaneous prayer (written communication with Rabbi Charles Spirn, Mount

Sinai Hospital, September 1991). Another uses an abridged *Mi-Sheberakh*, encouraging the patient to participate with a resounding, "Amen!" (oral communication with Rabbi Jacob Goldberg, February 14, 1992). Yet another Orthodox hospital chaplain has told me that he does indeed use spontaneous bedside prayer. His experience leads him to believe that the reluctance to accept this form of prayer is a cover-up, and claims that such prayer can be dramatically effective once done (oral communication with Rabbi Israel Kestenbaum, New York University Hospital, January 3, 1992). I suggest that this issue be further studied in the rabbinic community.

17. See, for example, this talmudic selection from TB *Brakhot* 34a:

> It happened that when R. Hanina Ben Dosa went to study Torah with R. Yohanan Ben Zakkai, R. Yohanan's son took ill. He [Yohanan] said [to Hanina], "Ask mercy for him that he may live." He [Hanina] put his head between his knees, asked mercy, and he lived. Said R. Yohanan, "If Ben Zakkai would put his head between his knees all day, no power [for evil] could sway him!" His wife then said, "Is Hanina greater than you are?" He said, "No, but he is like a servant before the King [who can enter and depart at will and who will always receive a response], while I am like a prince before the King [who does not always receive a royal audience]."

I thank Rabbi Spirn for bringing this talmudic illustration of spontaneous prayer to my attention.

18. I believe that spontaneous public prayer would not fit into the traditional synagogue service framework, due to its fixed liturgical nature. However, there are now groups such as San Francisco-based Jewish Healing Center that are attempting to develop creative or alternative liturgies and "healing services," involving spontaneous prayer. These are not meant to substitute for adequate medical care (as in certain Christian traditions) but rather to help the ill and their loved ones face the emotional and existential difficulties of illness.

19. See chapter 6 for my summary of rabbinic roles and precedents.

20. TB *Baba Batra* 116a. My translation follows Rashi's interpretation of the verse from Proverbs, as does the JPS translation of Proverbs. The Metzudot commentary (R. David Altschul—seventeenth- to eighteenth-century Galicia) renders it, "[The wise man will] take off and wipe clean the anger with the sweetness of his words." Rashi, in his commentary on the Talmud, also uses the term, "Wipe clean." But Maharsha on the Talmud translates the Heb. *yekaperna* literally, as, "The wise man will atone for him," meaning that the prayer of the wise man will obtain forgiveness for the sin that caused the patient's illness. However, see earlier in our work

where we rejected the theological idea that illness is considered punishment for sin.

21. Rashi, R. Gershom (tenth- to eleventh-century Germany), Maharasha.

22. *Shulhan Arukh, Yoreh De'ah* 335:10, comment of R. Isserles in the name of *Yesh Omrim*—"There are those who say. . . ."

23. Nimukei Yosef (R. Yosef Habiba—early fifteenth-century Spain) on TB *Baba Batra* 116a.

24. See my earlier summary in chapter 1 of why people go to clergy for pastoral care.

25. Personal note: Whether or not I qualify as the "wise man" of the Talmud is highly questionable. The important thing is that the people I visit consider me so.

26. See below.

27. The Hebrew is taken from the first few words of the prayer "May He Who blessed. . . ."

28. The names of the "foremothers" can be inserted, especially when the prayer is for a female patient.

29. Often translated as "charity," and usually referring to gifts for the needy or worthy institutions, the actual Hebrew meaning is "righteousness."

30. The translation is mine. The complete Hebrew text can be found in the *ArtScroll Prayerbook*, 442, and Hyman Goldin's *Hamadrikh: The Rabbi's Guide* (Orthodox) (New York: Hebrew Publishing Company, 1956), 94. The version in the *Rabbinical Assembly Manual* (Conservative), 89–90 has essentially the same themes, albeit in somewhat altered order and without the reference to *tzedakah* or prayer on the patient's behalf. An abridged version can be found in the Birnbaum *Daily Prayerbook*, 462.

31. For a selection of these, see *Hamadrikh*, 87–95.

32. See Judah D. Eisenstein, *Otzar Dinim Uminhagim* (*A Digest of Jewish Laws and Customs*) (Israel, reprinted 1970), who traces these back to R. Jacob Moellin ("the Maharil"), an important early fifteenth-century Ashkenazic rabbi and redactor of liturgy. Also see *Encyclopaedia Judaica*, s.v. "*Mi-Sheberakh*."

33. *Yoreh De'ah* 335:10.

34. Note that the *Mi-Sheberakh* for the ill, along with the other *Mi-Sheberakhs* for their various purposes, are usually said in between the *aliyot*, when various individuals are called to the Torah.

35. *Arukh Hashulhan, Yoreh De'ah* 335:12.

36. TB *Shabbat* 66a; also see TB *Avodah Zarah* 12a and TB *Gittin* 69b, where there are references to prayers for the ill using the mothers' names.

37. I have not been able to find a written source for this but have

heard it many times. It has also been suggested that a person in a difficult situation desires his or her mother, in the way a child might call out "Mommy!" when scared. In addition, we might speculate that since Jewish identity is traditionally transmitted through the mother, we invoke the mother's name when praying on the patient's behalf.

38. TB *Shabbat* 32b.

39. See Aaron Levine, 90 n. 107.

40. This, of course, might reinforce denial in a terminally ill patient. Still, Jewish tradition encourages both patient as well as family and friends never to give up hope. However, those who hold that the term "sick" not be used in the *Mi-Sheberakh* are a minority opinion, and the prevailing custom is to include the word *holeh*.

41. See section at the end of chapter 9, "Liturgy of the Burial."

42. It is not clear whether one may make the traditional *Mi-Sheberakh* for a non-Jew, since this part of the language does not apply. However, it is certainly permissible and praiseworthy to "ask God's mercy" for the sick of all peoples.

43. See also Harold Kushner, *When Bad Things Happen to Good People* (New York: Schocken, 1981; Avon, 1983), 121-122, where he defines general prayer in a similar fashion. More will be said on this important idea in the sections on grief and mourning.

44. This topic will be further developed at the end of this section.

45. It seems that the Almighty also deserves to rest on the Sabbath!

46. This blessing is part of the *Amidah*, the private silent prayer that is the core of the three daily weekday services. The blessing is an overall conclusion to the petitionary section of the prayer. See the Birnbaum *Daily Prayerbook*, 89-90.

47. TB *Avodah Zarah* 8, TB *Brakhot* 34. Note that the codes do permit prayer for the sick in the Daily *Amidah*'s blessing of *Shomeya Te'fillah* ("He Who hears all prayer") as well as in the private meditation following the *Amidah*. See *Mishnah Brurah* on *Shulhan Arukh, Orah Hayyim* 122:8. However, the preference toward praying for the ill in the blessing for the sick is codified in Maimonides, Laws of Prayer 6:3, and *Shulhan Arukh, Orah Hayyim* 119:1.

48. The source for this language is Isaiah 65:24, where it is written in the singular rather than the plural.

49. *Mishnah Brurah* 116:3, and see *ArtScroll Prayerbook*, 104-105.

50. See *Hamadrikh*, 97-98.

51. TB *Rosh Hashanah* 16b. This is echoed in numerous other rabbinic and medieval sources. The midrashic version in *Genesis Rabbah* 44:12 uses Abraham's change of name, rather than Sarah's, as its scriptural basis.

It was only after Abraham's and Sarah's names were changed by God that they gave birth to their divinely promised son, Isaac.

52. *Shulhan Arukh, Yoreh De'ah* 335:10.

53. The quorum of ten post-*bar mitzvah* age (thirteen) men without which communal prayer cannot take place. Many non-Orthodox circles today count women as well, though this is not sanctioned by traditional *halakhah*.

54. *Kavanot* can be translated as meditations to enhance intent. The Hebrew word *kavanah* is grammatically related to the word for direction (*kivun*). A *kavanah* can thus be considered a means for the doer of a particular *mitzvah* to direct his or her intent. They are frequently found in the kabbalistic and hasidic traditions.

55. These lines are a standard opening formulation for a pre-*mitzvah* *kavanah*.

56. See chapter 1.

57. *Siddur* of R. Yaakov Emden (eighteenth-century German rabbi and scholar) who in turn traces it to R. Isaiah Horowitz ("The Shlah"—seventeenth-century central Europe and Jerusalem).

CHAPTER 6

1. Maimonides, Laws of Kings 2:2.

2. However, descendants of the Davidic house occupied leadership positions among the Jewish people for quite some time, perhaps into the sixth century or later. See *Encyclopaedia Judaica*, s.v. "David, House of."

3. Maimonides, Laws of Temple Vessels, chapter 4.

4. Jews with surnames such as Kohn or Cohen are often descendants of this priestly tribe.

5. Maimonides, Laws of Torah Fundamentals 9:2, based on Deuteronomy 18:9.

6. See Robert Katz, *Pastoral Care and the Jewish Tradition* (Philadelphia: Fortress Press, 1985), 21.

7. Deuteronomy 19:1; Maimonides, Laws of Sanhedrin 1:1.

8. Maimonides, Laws of Torah 2:1.

9. During an exercise prior to my entry into a doctoral program at a Protestant Theological seminary, we completed an extensive series of questionnaires to determine our ministerial roles. My overriding and master role, which emerged from the self-study, was teacher.

10. For some accounts of the traditional rabbinate today as well as descriptions of current rabbinical training see Louis Bernstein, *Challenge and*

Mission (New York: Sheingold, 1985); Herbert Bomzer, *The Kollel in America* (New York: Sheingold, 1985); William Helmreich, *The World of the Yeshiva* (New York: Free Press, 1982). Also see *American Jewish Archives* "Centennial of the Rabbinate" issue (Cincinnati, 1980), including articles on the organized rabbinates of the Orthodox, Conservative, and Reform groups.

11. During my Resources Evaluation prior to entry into a Doctor of Ministry program, this was the one role for which my Protestant colleagues could find no parallel in their work.

12. It can be argued that the adminstrative functions of the rabbinate stem from the "kingly" role of ancient times, that a rabbi's religious role is often seen by congregants as "priestly," and that when a rabbi sets moral standards for the congregation, the role is "prophetic." But unlike the latter roles enumerated, I do not believe most rabbis see these roles as theirs on a regular basis.

13. Note that we have already dealt with the notion of liturgy and the efficacy of rabbinic prayer in chapter 5.

14. See my analysis of the talmudic story of Rabbi Akiba's student in chapter 3.

15. Hospitals and nursing homes generally do not allow actual candle-lighting in rooms because of fire and safety regulations. For many years the Women's Branch of the Union of Orthodox Jewish Congregations of America has provided electric candelabra for hospital use upon request. Alternatively, the rabbi can arrange candle-lighting in a safe place within the hospital or nursing home setting.

16. Much of the invalid's response will depend on religious interest. See the end of this chapter for Tsvi Schur's categories of patients' religious levels.

17. Obviously, a rabbi (or layperson, for that matter) should never force or pressure a patient into observance. The ill are physically and emotionally vulnerable, and pushiness can actually alienate the person from Judaism as well as affect physical and emotional conditions. There are times in my hospital work when I have been asked to stop well-meaning rabbis from forcing themselves on to patients because of the patients' objections.

18. Told to the members of my ordination class at the Hebrew Theological College, Skokie, Illinois, in 1977 by Rabbi Dr. Norman Berlat, then chaplain at Lutheran General Hospital, Des Plaines, Illinois, and now of Toronto, Canada.

19. See chapter 3 and the story of Raba in TB *Nedarim* 40a.

20. Literally, "In the way of the land." The *Pnei Mosheh* commentary (R. Mosheh Margolis—eighteenth-century Germany) in JT *Pe'ah* says this term specifically refers to the method of *bikur holim*.

21. Literally, "One whose sickness jumped upon him." Pnei Mosheh suggests that in practice, the definition of this term refers more to the suddenness of the illness than its danger.

22. Literally, "Those who are close."

23. The *Korban Ha'edah* commentary (R. David Fraenkel–eighteenth-century Lithuania/Holland) suggests that the reason that those more distant wait to visit is because they "should not impair the patient's fortune and cast upon him the name of sick one." It is possible to explain this talmudic passage and its commentaries by defining "fortune" as luck in the astrological sense, which is in fact a connotation of the Hebrew *mazal*. It is also possible to define this as we did earlier in chapter 3 regarding the similar story of Raba (from TB *Nedarim* 40a), who asked that his illness not be revealed. There, we suggested defining "fortune" in the practical, social sense of not wanting to alarm the patient by publicly proclaiming him/her as "sick." According to either explanation, there is no danger of "impairing the patient's fortune and casting upon him the name of sick one," when the visitors are relatives and close people. These interpretations may also explain why there is reluctance by some authorities to label the invalid in the *Mi-Sheberakh* prayer as *holeh* or "sick one" (see chapter 5).

24. In other words you, who are my good friends and are close to me, should have visited me immediately and not waited. JT *Gittin* 6:5, repeated in slightly altered form in JT *Pe'ah*, end of chapter 3.

25. *Pnei Mosheh* and *Korban Ha'edah*.

26. See our reference in chapter 3 to the *ben gilo*.

27. *Shulhan Arukh, Yoreh De'ah* 335:1.

28. Aaron Levine, 76.

29. Unless, of course, the patient does not wish to see the rabbi. In that case, the rabbi, like any visitor, must respect the patient's wishes.

30. Ozarowski, "Malpractice," 111–127.

31. This, of course, assumes that the physician was properly trained and gave the best effort to heal the patient. Jewish Law tends to give the physician the benefit of the doubt for the reason mentioned in the next line. Civil suits and an adversary court system are generally not a part of the Jewish legal process, but there are financial penalties for damage, as well as the penalty of exile to a city of refuge in the case of manslaughter (Numbers 35:9-29). See my article for further details.

32. Laws of Sanhedrin 2:1.

33. Subject to the same conditions in above note.

34. Shiurei Brakhah on *Shulhan Arukh, Orah Hayyim* 328:1.

35. Divrei Shaul (R. Joseph Saul Nathanson–nineteenth-century Lemberg) on *Shulhan Arukh, Orah Hayyim* 328:1.

36. As I indicated in my introduction to this book, I firmly believe that Judaism has much to offer its own adherents as well as those of other faiths in these areas. It is my hope that this work can serve as a basis for this type of training.

37. See above in chapter 1.

38. Switzer, 58-60.

39. For a fuller explanation of this theme, see Nehama Leibowitz, *Studies in Shemot* (Exodus) (Jerusalem: World Zionist Organization, 1976), 178-182 ("Actions Shape Character") and 342-351 ("Thou Shalt Not Covet").

40. See chapter 4 and the question of phone visits, letter visits, and sending a third party to convey good wishes to the patient.

41. In fact, R. Waldenberg in *Tzitz Eliezer* 8:5 and *Ramat Rahel* 8 writes this as accepted Jewish Law.

42. In fact, while there are many *mitzvot* that one can do vicariously via a *shaliah*, the fact that a rabbi or another may represent the community in this does not take away one's personal obligation to fulfill the commandment of visiting the sick.

43. There is some precedent for this notion in the Talmud. In TB *Taanit* 9a, the rabbis note that Moses, the first rabbi, was regarded by God as representing the community. As it states, "Because he prayed for the public, he is considered as the public."

44. See chapter 7 regarding the *Mi-Sheberakh* prayer.

45. TB *Baba Metzia* 96a, TB *Brakhot* 34b, TB *Kiddushin* 41b, and many other places in rabbinic literature.

46. Tsvi G. Schur, *Illness and Crisis: Coping the Jewish Way* (New York: NCSY—Orthodox Union, 1987).

47. In his work, Schur tends to identify the "truly religious person" as an observant or practicing Jew, though he does not specifically use the word Orthodox. Schur is an Orthodox rabbi who ministers to a wide variety of individuals, yet his standard is certainly Orthodox. One might also ask whether there can be a truly religious Jew who is not observant. From our perspective, the question may be moot, for pastoral care can benefit everyone and should be available to all regardless of their religious level or observance. Schur's point in his construct, as I understand it, is that the approach to a given patient may differ depending on the practice and level of commitment of the individual.

48. Also see chapter 1 and my citation of Pruyser's use of religious language in evaluating the patient for pastoral diagnosis. Some use of this language may be helpful in determining the patient's sense of religiosity, and how this religious commitment affects his/her life.

49. Schur does not spell it out, but even deeply devout and observant individuals might feel fear, anger, regret, and guilt while ill.
50. Again, see Pruyser in chapter 1.
51. There is a story (based in part on *Midrash Tanhuma Genesis Lekh
Lekha* 12 and TB *Sotah* 10b and quoted in full by Rabbi Jack Riemer, "Word
for the Week," *St. Louis Jewish Light* [November 10, 1979]) regarding the
Patriarch Abraham's hospitality. After feeding his guests, Abraham would
encourage them to bless and thank the Lord for their food, thus teaching
them about monotheism. One old pagan refused to thank God, preferring
to acknowledge his idols. Abraham drove him out. That night, God appeared to Abraham and told him that if He had been able to put up with
this idolator for so many years, certainly Abraham could do so for one meal.
52. A limited form of excommunication.
53. Rashi says that these groups took care of the burial needs of their
members, similar to the Jewish burial associations that are prevalent today
in New York and large communities. Smaller communities often offer burial
privileges through synagogue affiliation. In addition, it is often possible to
purchase burial rights from both synagogue and association plots without
being a member. In both larger and smaller communities, the religious
preparation of the body—the washing and dressing—is done through groups
organized for this purpose, known as the *Hevrah Kadisha*. To my knowledge, people are not turned away due to lack of funds or nonmembership.
See further for more details on preparation for burial.
54. TB *Moed Katan* 27b.
55. TB *Semahot*, chapter 12. This was an early Jewish burial practice.
Some time after the body was buried, the remains would be collected again
for reburial in a final resting spot.
56. See *Encyclopaedia Judaica*, s.v. "sick care, communal."
57. Note the organization of such groups as the Metropolitan Coordinating Council on *Bikur Holim* of New York.
58. It is my hope that the material contained in these chapters will
serve as a guide to *bikur holim* groups across the country.

CHAPTER 7

1. Some of the basic reference works on death and mourning in
Judaism include Maurice Lamm, *The Jewish Way in Death and Mourning*
(New York: Jonathan David, 1969); Arnold Goodman, *A Plain Pine Box*
(New York: Ktav, 1981); Jack Riemer, *Jewish Reflections on Death* (New York:

Schocken, 1976); Jack Spiro, *A Time To Mourn* (New York: Bloch, 1985); and Abner Weiss, *Death and Bereavement—A Halakhic Guide* (New York: Ktav, 1991). We will be referring to these works when appropriate.

2. Judaism obligates one to mourn for biological parents and children, as will be shown later in the book. One is permitted, rather than obligated, to engage in religious rites of mourning for an adoptive parent if one wishes. See Lamm, 80.

3. Primary halakhic sources for these regulations can be found in *Shulhan Arukh, Yoreh De'ah* 341. Y. Greenwald, *Kol Bo Al Aveilut* (New York: Feldheim, 1973), section 2, and Y. M. Tuckaczynski, *Gesher Hahayyim* (Jerusalem, 1960), chapter 18, also deal with *aninut*. Both of these are considered modern classics in the area of Jewish mourning law. Also see Lamm, 21-26.

4. *Shivah* regulations, which apply during the week following the burial, will be more fully explored in chapter 10.

5. This is somewhat tempered by the needs of reality. For example, if a major monetary loss may be averted by working, the mourner may do so. Also, the mourner may attend to communal needs if needed. For example, a kosher ritual slaughterer can serve the community during this period if there is no one else to do so.

6. It is a matter of dispute whether this exemption is biblical (Greenwald in the *Kol Bo*) or rabbinical (*Sedei Hemed*), as cited in Aaron Levine, 257 n. 52. Most authorities hold that the mourners should not even take upon themselves these observances voluntarily.

7. See TB *Moed Katan* 15a, describing *tefillin* as *pe-er*, in turn based on Ezekiel 17:24, ". . . Make no mourning for the dead, bind your *pe'er* upon yourself . . . ," which the rabbis understood to mean *tefillin*, worn when there is no mourning. The word *pe'er* means ornament, decoration, honor, or glory; *tefillin* is considered thus. See both Rashi and Tosafot on TB *Sukkah* 25a, who say that the *onen* is not a *Bar-Pe'er*, a "son of glory or ornamentation," because of the tragedy that has transpired; if *tefillin* would be worn, the *onen* would feel a lessened sense of mourning.

8. The other positive observances of the Sabbath also still apply except for Torah study, sexual relations, or other joyous activity.

9. The therapeutic effects and philosophy behind this exemption will be discussed later in this chapter.

10. This can be overridden in cases of great need, such as when another mourner requires a *minyan* to recite the *Kaddish*. Also, it apparently does not apply on the Sabbath, nor would it apply if the mourner is removed from the city in which the actual arrangements are being made for the deceased.

11. See further in this chapter, the discussion of Rabbi Soloveitchik's approach to the emotional/theological state of the *onen*.

12. TB *Zevahim* 99a-101a, echoed in *Sifra* (halakhic *Midrash*) on Leviticus 19:10.

13. There is little to no practical difference between the two, other than questions of extenuating circumstances. In such cases, there is always more halakhic leeway with rabbinic law than with biblical law, as discussed in chapter 2. See *Shulhan Arukh, Yoreh De'ah* 369:13, *Kol Bo* 1:258-259, *Gesher Hahayyim*, 180-181.

It is conceivable that given the mandate in Jewish Law for as speedy a burial as possible, the burial in earlier times was often on the same day as the day of death. Today, burial usually takes place within twenty-four to forty-eight hours of death, depending on the needs of the family. Nevertheless, burial must still take place as soon after the death as feasible, so that the *aninut* is not prolonged, and the healing process following burial may begin.

14. See, for example, Psalm 118:25.

15. This is the JPS translation, found in Joseph Hertz's *The Pentateuch* (London: Soncino Press, 1962).

16. Numbers 11:1. Rabbi Soloveitchik suggests that Moses' changed role after this incident, becoming a "nursing father" (Numbers 11:12) is an illustration of the need for rabbinic empathy in times of difficulty. See chapter 14, "Teaching with Clarity and Empathy," in Abraham Besdin, *Reflections of the Rav* (Jerusalem: World Zionist Organization, 1979), 158.

17. *Targum Onkelos* (Aramaic translation and interpretation of the Torah, first-century Palestine).

18. *Targum Yonatan*. Note that Nahmanides and Rashbam (R. Shmuel ben Meir—Rashi's grandson—twelfth-century France) in their comments to the same verse echo the *Targums'* explanations and point out that these put the murmurers in a positive light, "finding merit" for them.

19. Rashi.

20. Ibn Ezra, though he also ties it into issues not connected to our thesis, such as personal strength and vanity.

21. Tosafot: "They were as *onenim* [our term for people in this stage of grief] and mourners over the dead."

22. Kli Yakar (R. Ephraim Lunshitz—sixteenth- to seventeenth-century Poland/Bohemia).

23. Genesis 35:18.

24. See, for example, TB *Baba Metzia* 58-59, TB *Sanhedrin* 47, TB *Moed Katan* 14, TB *Ketubot* 53a, and many other places in the Talmud.

25. See Marcus Jastrow, *Dictionary Of Talmud* (New York: Pardes, 1950), 27.

26. See TB *Hullin* 112a.

27. Elisabeth Kübler-Ross's stages for people facing death in *On Death and Dying* (New York: Macmillan, 1970), 38–112, correspond most closely to our Hebrew definition of *aninut*. These include denial (complaining) or isolation (the very condition of the Israelites in the desert), anger (crying out, rage, fraud, wrong), bargaining (doubt), and depression (sorrow, pain). One might argue that Kübler-Ross's stages deal with people who are facing death and not people who have suffered loss. Yet there is a close correspondence between these two for they both remind us of our own mortality and the effects on us as we face death, whether our own or that of a loved one.

Some of the other major studies of grief stages include Erich Lindemann's classical study of the victims of the Coconut Grove fire ("Symptomatology and Management of Acute Grief," *American Journal of Psychiatry* 101 [September 1944]: 141–148, now found in Arthur Carr, et al., *Grief: Selected Readings* [New York: Health Sciences Publishing, 1975] and reprinted in abbreviated form in Geoffrey Gorer's book, *Death, Grief and Mourning*). Lindemann's basic stages include somatic distress, preoccupation with images of the deceased, guilt, hostile reactions, and loss of patterns of conduct. Distorted or extreme reactions could include uncharacteristic bursts of action or activity, social withdrawal from family and friends, isolation from relationships, deep hostility, schizophrenia, self-punishment, psychosomatic illness, assuming symptoms of the deceased, and extreme depression. Also see Paul Irion, *The Funeral and the Mourners* (Nashville: Abingdon, 1979), 41–49, whose grief reactions are tearfulness, bewilderment, fear, ambivalence, hostility, guilt, and idealization. Also see Granger Westberg, *Good Grief* (Philadelphia: Fortress Press, 1962), whose stages are shock, emotion, depression and loneliness, physical distress, panic, guilt over the loss, hostility, and resentment. My point here is that the majority of these grief symptoms or stages are included in the Hebrew concept and term *aninut*.

28. TB *Sanhedrin* 46a; also see Maimonides, Laws of Mourning 1:9. The immediate context for this dictum comes from the law regarding individuals who suffered capital punishment for transgression of biblical law (which seldom happened, but is on the books). For these people, ritualized mourning was not observed but *aninut* was, for "*aninut* is only in the heart."

29. TB *Ethics of the Fathers* (*Pirke Avot*) 4:23; also see *Avot D'Rabbi Nathan* (a text related to *Ethics of the Fathers*) 29:1.

30. Rashi on *Ethics of the Fathers* (*Pirke Avot*) 4:23.

31. Maimonides on *Ethics of the Fathers* (*Pirke Avot*) 4:23.

32. R. Yonah on *Ethics of the Fathers* (*Pirke Avot*) 4:23. This explanation very closely matches the remainder of the quote and context from *Ethics of the Fathers*, which reads, "Rabbi Simon Ben Elazer says, 'Do not pacify your friend in his hour of anger; and do not comfort . . . do not question him at the hour he makes a vow; and do not try to see him in the hour of his disgrace.'"

33. Binyan Yehoshua on *Ethics of the Fathers* (*Pirke Avot*) 4:23, quoting R. Obadiah of Bartinora's (fifteenth-century Italy/Eretz Israel) commentary.

34. Aaron Levine, 254, puts it this way: "For then he has pain in the condolences, for he sees that the friend cannot share the sorrow with him."

35. TB *Brakhot* 17a, in the name of Rav Ashi.

36. See Lamm, 22-23.

37. See Aaron Levine, 244, who offers both of these reasons.

38. Proverbs 17:5.

39. Gersonides (Ralbag) (fourteenth-century Provence).

40. *Hokhmat Adam* 153:1.

41. TB *Brakhot* 17-18.

42. The sections of the service beginning with the important line "Hear O Israel, the Lord Our God is One" (Deuteronomy 6:4).

43. Proverbs 19:17. "Poor" here is understood by the rabbis to mean deceased, as it was in the first citation from Proverbs. The JPS Bible renders this, "He that is gracious to the poor lendeth unto the Lord." There may be a play on words here, for the Hebrew root for escorting the deceased is the same as the root for lend—*l-v-h*. One could sermonically connect these two themes, but this is beyond our scope.

44. Proverbs 14:31. Note that needy again refers to the deceased. Note also that this is the second half of the *lo'eg larash* verse.

45. Moshe Halevi Spero, "Reflections on the Inevitability of Death," *Judaism* 123:31:3 (Summer 1982): 342.

46. *Shiurei Harav* (Public Lectures of Rabbi Joseph B. Soloveitchik), ed. Joseph Epstein (New York: Yeshiva University, 1974), 18, and reprinted as "The Halakhah of the First Day" in Riemer, *Jewish Reflections*, 76-83. Rabbi Soloveitchik, who died in 1993, is still considered the preeminent thinker, mentor, and theologian of American modern Orthodox Jewry.

47. Soloveitchik, 19. Based on the text from Deuteronomy 16:3, "So that you may remember the day of your departure from the land of Egypt as long as you live."

48. This is in contrast to some beliefs or their practitioners that attempt to cover up the deep theological difficulties that arise when a loved one dies. (Conversation with Dr. Frank Stalfa, associate professor of Pastoral Theology, Lancaster Theological Seminary, August 8, 1990.)

49. Soloveitchik, 19.

50. Rabbinic sources for this idea are in JT *Brakhot*, chapter 3, and TB *Semahot*, chapter 10. Also see Audrey Gordon, "The Psychological Wisdom of the Law," in Riemer, *Jewish Reflections*, 97.

51. Gordon in Riemer, *Jewish Reflections*, ibid.

52. Confronting death, rather than denying it, is an important theme that colors a great deal of Jewish mourning tradition. Lamm, 65, uses this idea to elucidate the need for the mourners to actually participate in the *mitzvah* of burial. Facing the finality of death also partly explains why the Torah is against embalming, viewings, mausoleums, and metal caskets. All these, to some extent, retard the finality of death in an attempt to somehow preserve the body. Also, I have suggested to my own congregants that the notion of identifying with and facing the loss accounts for sitting closer to the ground during the *shivah* period. See chapters 9 and 10.

53. TB *Semahot*, chapter 10. The translation is mine. Spiro (see ahead) gives it a slightly different rendering but keeps the essence.

54. Spiro, 67–68. This might suggest that suffering or tragedy is generally considered a punishment, a theory we have rejected earlier in regard to illness. See ahead for my critique of Spiro.

55. 2 Samuel 19:1.

56. TB *Brakhot* 19a.

57. Rashi interprets the passage this way.

58. As I have often told my own congregants, "The Almighty does not clear His agenda with us."

59. Alfasi's code/commentary is written as a digest of conclusions of the talmudic discussions. He words our issue as follows: "If the deceased is not lying before them, they [the congregation] sit and read [the *Shema*] and he [the *onen*] sits in silence. They stand and pray (the *Amidah*) and he [the *onen*] stands and accepts upon himself the divine decree. And he says, 'You, O God, are righteous in all that befalls us. May it be Your will, O Lord our God, to repair our breaches and the breaches of your nation Israel in mercy.'" Alfasi's version is thematically related to the *Tziduk Hadin* prayer recited at the gravesite, which is discussed in chapter 9, and to the Meal of Condolence addition to the Grace After Meals, which is discussed in chapter 10.

60. *Shulhan Arukh, Yoreh De'ah* 366:2 in R. Isserles' addendum, which says: "A person should not say 'I have not been paid back for my [evil] deeds' or things such as this, because a person should never open his mouth to the Satan."

61. The idea of silence as a theme for the *onen* has a distinct biblical root. In Leviticus 10:4, Aaron's two sons die after coming too close to the

altar with a strange fire. The text tells us: *Va-yidom Aharon*, "And Aaron was silent." The choice of the Hebrew word *dom* for silent implies not a passive quiescent silence but rather a questioning, searching silence. The Kotzker Rebbe, noting the same Hebrew root for blood (*dam*), interprets the verse in Yiddish as *Ah Blutiger D'mama*, "a bloody silence." (My thanks go to Rabbi Jacob Goldberg for this quote.) It is no accident that the Talmud (TB *Moed Katan* 14-19) sees in the subsequent verses the sources for specific halakhic practices of mourning mentioned at the beginning of this chapter.

62. A few of the following issues are mentioned in Irion, *The Funeral and the Mourners*, 143-158, albeit from a Protestant perspective.

63. Lecture, Joel Morris, owner/partner, I. J. Morris Funeral Directors, Brooklyn, New York, given at the Elmont Jewish Center, November 1, 1993.

64. This is sometimes the source of controversy. An interesting example of a Conservative congregation that took on the local Jewish funeral director in an attempt to offer a more traditional funeral is found in Goodman. Fifteen years ago in the Orthodox community, an agreement was reached between the Rabbinical Council of America, the Union of Orthodox Jewish Congregations, and the Jewish Funeral Directors of America to educate and offer the public the basics of a Jewish funeral following halakhic guidelines.

65. There are sometimes conflicts between these two roles and the needs of the family. Occasionally, the family will reject elements of the traditional Jewish service or ritual. As an Orthodox rabbi, I usually make the attempt to resolve these without compromising the essence of *halakhah*. Most of the time I am successful. Occasionally, I have had to turn down funerals if the family was adamant and insisted on abandoning essential halakhic standards, such as the traditional washing and dressing, a closed all-wood casket, or below-ground burial. However, when it comes to personal observances such as *shivah* and the like, I cannot demand observance, for I am not a policeman, only a rabbi. Education and inspiration are ultimately the best ways of insuring observance of sanctified tradition and reaping its therapeutic benefits.

66. The rabbi here is not necessarily engaged in "comforting" the family, although families are often comforted by rabbinic presence. In fact, Maimonides in his Code (Laws of Knowledge 5:7) applies our aforementioned teaching from *Ethics of the Fathers*, "Do not comfort a person while his dead lies before him," specifically to rabbis and scholars!

67. This does not mean that all rabbis do it; see earlier in this chapter for my critique of rabbinic conduct in these areas and ahead in chapter 9 for my discussion of the eulogy.

68. Practical Rabbinics lecture, Rabbi Harold P. Smith, sometime in 1975, to the senior class of the Hebrew Theological College, Skokie, Illinois.

69. In Jewish Law (*Shulhan Arukh, Yoreh De'ah* 374:10), *aninut* also applies to a student (congregant?) when his/her rabbi or master teacher dies. While this is rarely, if ever, practiced today, the fact that this law is on the books underlies the importance of the rabbi's relationship as a member of the extended family in the way we have developed throughout this book.

CHAPTER 8

1. These include Genesis 37:29, 34—Reuben and Jacob over Joseph's apparent death; 44:13—Joseph's brothers over the finding of the royal goblet in Benjamin's sack; Numbers 14:6—Joshua and Caleb over the evil reports of the other spies; 2 Samuel 13:31—King David and his court over the death of his sons; Job 1:21 and 2:12-13—Job over his fate. (According to the Jerusalem Talmud, this scriptural source is a primary basis for the *mitzvah*, but this view is not accepted by many other authorities.) Also see Joshua 7:6; Judges 11:35; 1 Samuel 4:12; 2 Samuel 1:2, 2:3, 3:31, 15:32; 1 Kings 21:27; 2 Kings 2:12, 5:7, 6:30, 11:14, 18:37, 19:1, 12:1; Jeremiah, 36:24, 41:5; Esther 4:1; Ezra 9:3.

2. TB *Moed Katan* 24a. Also see Sifra on that verse. The reference to capital punishment is not meant to be taken as an actual legal threat or halakhic penalty but rather to underline the severity and importance of the obligation to tear.

3. Ritva (commentary on TB *Moed Katan* 24a), Raavad (R. Avraham ben David—twelfth-century Provence, cited in R. Asher's commentary on TB *Moed Katan* 24a), and others who see this as a direct biblical obligation deriving from this verse and talmudic comment.

4. Tosafot, Nahmanides, R. Asher (all in their commentaries on TB *Moed Katan* 24a) and others. According to this view, the biblical reference to *keriah* is simply "*asmakhta*," something upon which we can "hang" the obligation to tear, but not a true source in the Torah. Rather, the tradition of tearing upon news of death is of much later origin. Maimonides (Laws of Mourning 8:1) is not clear on this question. While he cites the biblical verse, his commentaries (such as the *Kesef Mishneh*—R. Yosef Caro, author of the *Shulhan Arukh* and the Radvaz) also interpret the biblical citation as "*asmakhta*." Among moderns, the *Arukh Hashulhan* (*Yoreh De'ah* 340:1) codifies it this way.

5. These are based in TB *Moed Katan* 25 and codified in *Shulhan Arukh, Yoreh De'ah* 340.

6. The original obligation for *keriah* over one's rabbi or teacher underscores this book's theme of rabbi as a member of the extended family. Earlier, we described this relationship as two-way. If so, though, why would a rabbi not tear when a member of the congregation dies? My own theory is that if we rabbis had to do this, we would have no more suits left!

7. See *Gesher Hahayyim* 4:1, and Aaron Levine, 178-179, both based on earlier sources.

8. Ibid.

9. Ibid.

10. In modern parlance we would term this a cathartic process.

11. *Gesher Hahayyim* 4:1; Aaron Levine, 178-179.

12. See Gordon in Riemer, *Jewish Reflections*, 99. This reason is the one I most often share with congregants when I help them perform *keriah* in times of grief.

13. Lamm, 38-39. Also see Spiro, 68-70.

14. See TB *Moed Katan* 22b.

15. Nimukei Yosef on TB *Moed Katan* 22b and others say that this was not a baring of the shoulders per se but a rolling up of the sleeve or perhaps a tearing off of sleeves in the spirit of *keriah* that was not done on that spot but elsewhere on the clothing.

16. "In order to despise one's self," TB *Moed Katan* 22b.

17. Unlike *keriah*; see later in this chapter.

18. Codified in comment of R. Isserles, *Shulhan Arukh, Yoreh De'ah* 340:17.

19. See comments of R. Elijah of Vilna ("the *G'ra*"), note 37 on *Shulhan Arukh, Yoreh De'ah* 340:17.

20. *Arukh Hashulhan* on *Shulhan Arukh, Yoreh De'ah* 340:17.

21. See further, where I discuss the difficulties in doing a proper *keriah* with some nonobservant people.

22. TB *Moed Katan* 22b, based on 2 Samuel 1. There is a dispute in halakhic practice as to how far this is carried out. *Arukh Hashulhan* and Lamm describe it as we do, in terms of the place of the tear near the heart. Many authorities (including Tuckaczinski) say that for a parent, one must make a cut in all the outer garments one wears. For other relatives, a cut in one garment suffices. Others (including Greenwald) say one just tears a garment one wears frequently, such as a vest, sweater, or shirt. Some, including the late Rabbi Eliezer Silver of Cincinnati, allowed the tearing of a necktie (or neck scarf for women), since in this country it is considered a garment and is usually worn "close to the heart" (Oral conversation with

Rabbi David Silver of Harrisburg, Pennsylvania, 1979). I have frequently recommended this method of *keriah* to nonobservant Jews who would otherwise prefer to tear the black ribbon offered by many of the funeral directors and much of the non-Orthodox rabbinate. See the end of this chapter for my critique on the use of the ribbon. If a woman tears a dress, the tear should be made in a spot that does not compromise her modesty.

23. See the reasons for *keriah* mentioned above.

24. We frequently use the English term "broken heart" to symbolize the rending of emotions when such a loss is incurred.

25. This is not to demean or underrate the sense of loss felt with the death of other relatives. In fact, my own pastoral and clinical experience has shown that the parental loss of a child is often much deeper and emotionally wracking than the loss of a parent.

26. See TB *Moed Katan* 20b in the name of R. Zera; commentaries of Alfasi, R. Nissim, Nahmanides, R. Asher, Tosafot; and codified in the *Shulhan Arukh, Yoreh De'ah* 340:18.

27. See the end of this chapter for an interesting case study involving this rule.

28. TB *Moed Katan* 20b, also commentaries of Alfasi and R. Nissim. However, Lehem Mishneh (R. Avraham di Boton—seventeenth- to eighteenth-century Greece), following Maimonides, Laws of Mourning 7:1, disagrees and holds that one cannot honor parents after the thirty-day *shloshim* period concludes. Apparently, Maimonides did not codify the obligation to tear for parents after *shloshim*.

29. The Talmud (TB *Kiddushin* 30a) states that the Decalogue's instruction to "honor your father and mother" specifically means providing their physical needs such as food, clothing, and so on. It does not necessarily mean that one is obligated to love them or share any emotional bond.

30. I have found that this is not always observed even in Orthodox circles, though some authorities protest this lack of practice (See Aaron Levine, 198). In funeral homes, the family usually goes into a nearby anteroom prior to the service and does the *keriah*, whether for parents or other relatives. When the funeral is a gravesite service, the tearing is done at the cemetery in the presence of the others.

31. TB *Moed Katan* 24a.

32. See commentary of Tosafot on TB *Moed Katan* 24a, who says this is highly subjective, and any time one feels this way can be considered *beshaat himum.*

33. Compare these with the Talmud's other times for tearing (TB *Moed Katan* 25-26 and codified in *Shulhan Arukh, Yoreh De'ah* 340). These

include being present at the death of any human being (see above at the beginning of this chapter), witnessing a Torah scroll's malicious desecration by fire, hearing very bad news, experiencing the death of one's teacher, and seeing "the cities of Judea in their destroyed state." All these, for a believing Jew, would elicit the same emotionally heated reactions of grief linked to *keriah*.

34. Based on the case of the sage Amemar, TB *Moed Katan* 20b-21a, who in turn based this on Job 1:20 ("And Job arose and tore his cloak . . ."), or possibly 2 Samuel 13:31, the requirement to tear standing is codified in *Shulhan Arukh, Yoreh De'ah* 340:1. In the Talmud's case, Amemar tore for the death of a grandson, not one of the required relatives. He tore while sitting, and then his son came into the room and Amemar tore once more. Then, recalling that both tears were done sitting, Amemar stood and tore a third time. Even though this shows that the tearing must be done while standing, Tosafot suggests that the additional tearing was done for a different reason—Amemar wishing to mourn together with his son over the grandson. We may refer to this as empathic mourning—sharing the sadness of the moment in a very graphic way, even though Amemar himself was not required to tear.

35. See, *Kol Bo*, 27, on both of these reasons.

36. See TB *Moed Katan* 25a, which teaches that the blessing is said when one witnesses a death and tears at that point. *Shulhan Arukh, Yoreh De'ah* 339:3 includes this blessing as part of the *Tziduk Hadin*, to be studied in chapter 9. While our practice is to recite *Tziduk Hadin* at the gravesite, the *Shulhan Arukh* rules to say it at the time one hears the news of death; according to this view this is also the time for *keriah*.

37. Thus Birnbaum's *Daily Prayerbook*, 777. Goldin's *Hamadrikh* (Rabbi's Guide, Orthodox), 109, renders it literally but accurately as "the Judge of truth." The *Rabbinical Assembly Manual* (Conservative), 101, inaccurately translates it as " righteous Judge."

38. TB *Brakhot* 60b.

39. See chapter 7 for Rabbi Soloveitchik's explanation of *aninut*.

40. See also Paul Irion's theological understanding of death as a part of "the normal human experience," 65.

41. I first heard this idea from Rabbi Jacob Goldberg in February 1989. While Rabbi Goldberg does not make this point about *Dayan Ha'emet* in his book *Pastoral Bereavement Counselling* (New York: Human Sciences Press, 1989), he does speak of the healing process after death in this fashion from a secular perspective.

42. See note 30 above.

43. Certainly a desirable role and one having precedent in Jewish mourning law—witness all the references we have cited earlier regarding people mourning for the loss of their rabbi or teacher!

44. *Shulhan Arukh, Yoreh De'ah* 340:18 and elsewhere; also *Kol Bo,* 363-365; *Gesher Hahayyim,* chapter 24, part two.

45. See further in chapter 10 for the guidelines of how to "sit" *shivah,* during the week-long mourning period following the interment.

46. Many years after this encounter, I discovered a direct reference that agreed with my conclusion. Aaron Levine, 183 n. 25, quotes a contemporary Israeli rabbi who writes: "Similarly . . . should not people tear over parents who were murdered in the Holocaust after many years when it is clarified that they were certainly killed and their [living] wives are permitted to remarry? If there are children, they should then tear over the [deceased] father at the time the mother is permitted to remarry."

47. My father is a Holocaust survivor, and I can truly affirm the constant *shaat himum* through my personal experience.

CHAPTER 9

1. Eisenstein, 102; *Encyclopaedia Judaica,* s.v. "*hesped.*"

2. TB *Ketubot* 26, and cited in Greenwald, *Kol Bo,* 96.

3. *Shulhan Arukh, Yoreh De'ah* 344:19-20.

4. Obviously, this is not always true in warmer climates. In Israel, most funeral services, including the eulogies, are actually done at the gravesite. Occasionally, this has also been the practice in some American communities such as my native St. Louis, Missouri.

5. Based on a lecture by Joel Morris of I. J. Morris Jewish Funeral Directors, Brooklyn, New York, at the Elmont (NY) Jewish Center, November 1, 1993, and oral conversation, April 28, 1994. Mr. Morris has suggested that the last few years have seen a reversal of these trends. Jewish families, like so many other American families, are smaller, more geographically detached, and sometimes more emotionally detached than in the past. Attendance at chapel services is down from what it used to be, and as a result, there is a growing return to gravesite services.

6. I currently live very close to one of the largest Jewish cemeteries in the New York area. I frequently get calls from funeral directors or the Hebrew Free Burial Society to perform funerals for indigent Jews with neither the resources nor family to arrange them. These are inevitably gravesite affairs, often with no one in attendance besides me, the staff person from the funeral home, and the grave diggers. I have never turned down these requests.

7. *Pirke Avot* 4:23.

8. See my critique of this in chapter 6.

9. See Lamm, 45-48, for a good translation and commentary on some of these.

10. There are numerous references to this Hebrew term throughout Scripture. For example, see Mandelkorn's concordance, 802.

11. Thus JPS for the references in Genesis 18 and 19, as well as Numbers 19:14, Deuteronomy 32:33, and numerous other places.

12. Exodus 3:16, for example, as well as literally hundreds of other examples throughout Scripture.

13. I have often used elements of this thought in my own eulogies.

14. Genesis 23:2. There are numerous other references to these terms as themes for the eulogy. Summaries of the themes can be found in Lamm, 50, and Aaron Levine, 330.

15. TB *Sanhedrin* 46b-47a.

16. In the talmudic period there were *sapdanim*, eulogizers whose role was specifically to orate at funerals as well as *mekonnenot*, women whose job was to publicly lament the loss and evoke tears. Apparently these were paid professionals or semiprofessionals, as recorded in TB *Moed Katan* 8a. These practices reflected the double themes of the eulogy. Today, rabbis definitely play the first role and, perhaps in a very subtle way, the second role as well.

17. This means that halakhically, the deceased could decline the eulogy if he or she explicitly specified so during his or her lifetime, and if not, we can compel the heir to pay the eulogy expenses. See Maimonides, Laws of Mourning 12:1; *Shulhan Arukh, Yoreh De'ah* 344:9,10; also *Kol Bo*, 96, and *Arukh Hashulhan, Yoreh De'ah* 344:7. Lamm, 51, points out that refusing the eulogy cannot simply be an assumption of the survivors but must have been clearly stated by the deceased. The possibility of the deceased's foregoing honor does not halakhically extend to the mourners' observance of the *shivah* or other postburial observances; these are generally observed regardless of the deceased's wishes. However, see Reuven Bulka and Jeffrey Woolf, "May Parents Forego the Eleven Months of Mourning Due Them?" *The Orthodox Roundtable, Nissan* (Spring) 1994. They suggest that if parents perceive that full observance of the yearlong restrictions would overburden their children, the parental wish to forego full yearlong mourning may be accepted. See the next chapter for details of postfuneral observances.

When a great leader or rabbinic scholar dies and has willed not to be eulogized, it is permissible to take the liberty of allowing the community an opportunity to mourn with a eulogy that includes elements of *bekhi* but not *hesped* (e.g., evocative language that moves the community, but without praise of the deceased). This is implied from the cases in the Talmud (TB *Sanhedrin* 46b–47a; also see TB *Moed Katan* 28b) regarding kings of Israel, whose eulogies concerned not just their own personal honor but the entire nation. See Aaron Levine, 335–336, and notes 31 and 32 above. *Kol Bo*, 96–97, cites numerous views that disagree with differentiation between a leader or scholar and a common person; in either case the desire not to be eulogized is respected.

18. He calls them "funeral sermons" and seems to be uncomfortable with referring to them as eulogies. See pages 101–106. Irion also considers his themes to be "criteria" for evaluating an effective funeral. While Judaism does not really need anyone's outside evaluation for effectiveness, it might be helpful to use Irion's efforts as points of reference.

19. Using tragedy as an entree to conversion is anathema to Judaism, not only because of the impropriety of the timing but because evangelism itself is foreign to Judaism. We do not seek converts. Judaism does stress that tragedy is a time of introspection, forcing us to evaluate our lives in the hope of improvement. See *Hamadrikh*'s anthology of homiletic funeral material, 216–224, some of which contains this theme. Also see Aaron Levine, 330, who connects the theme of *bekhi* to this idea.

20. Irion, of course, is speaking of death from the Christian perspective, and perhaps including some existential and psychological elements as well.

21. Professor Irion, in written communication to me (October 1991), suggests that he did not mean one should downplay the "obituary" aspects of the funeral sermon, that is, the deceased's life and activities, but rather "extensive praise of the person." A careful look at his work (104–105) shows that he focuses on using the remarks about the deceased to address the needs of the mourners. My suggestion here is that Jewish tradition requires words about the deceased for their own sake, as well as for the mourners' sakes.

22. See Tosafot "*Hespedah*" on TB *Sanhedrin* 46b, and also see Aaron Levine's footnote 30 on page 335, where he quotes a source that says, "A person is not permited to say, 'Do not eulogize me after my death,' because the eulogy is honor for the living."

23. *Gesher Hahayyim*, vol. 2, chapter 9, part 1. He defines "honor of the deceased" as assuming that the deceased is "listening in" on the eulogy.

24. See Marc Angel, *The Orphaned Adult* (New York: Human Sciences Press, 1987), passim, who frequently refers to the mourners' need for closure. The rabbinic prefuneral visit as well as the sensitive eulogy can help provide this.

25. It is unfortunate that Lamm, Weiss, Riemer, ArtScroll, and indeed nearly all the halakhic and reflective English works on bereavement ignore discussion of the eulogy's pastoral benefit.

26. See *Kol Bo*, 98, based on R. Asher's commentary to TB *Moed Katan*, 3:63, and other sources. Greenwald permits the eulogizer to moderately embellish the positive qualities of the deceased. He offers several explanations, but the most theologically intriguing reason for allowing this is because "Death atones for the sins of a person and the sins are thus reduced; all that remains are the positive qualities. . . ." Aaron Levine, 333, on the other hand, tends to be more restrictive about this. He quotes the above-mentioned sources but then quotes *Shulhan Arukh, Yoreh De'ah* 344:1, which says that "one should remember the good qualities (of the deceased) and add **a little, but should not exaggerate**. . . ." (Note that the boldface is in Levine's rendering!)

27. See my comments in chapter 6, where I "let the family write the eulogy for me."

28. Obviously, a rabbi must be sensitive to the issues of negative qualities or behavior when they have occurred. When this is the case, one must be especially careful not to turn the deceased into a person he or she was not, nor to embellish poor family relationships. I have occasionally found myself in situations where the person was a real scoundrel in the eyes of the family, and I had to either avoid referring to the relationships in my remarks or restrict myself to a "generic eulogy" where there just was not anything good to say about the deceased. Again, this underscores the importance of the prefuneral rabbinic contact with the family.

29. In addition, I always try to incorporate a Torah text or reference of some sort into my eulogies. I suppose this may make my words seem more like Irion's "funeral sermons," than what many people consider eulogies. Sometimes I will connect a comment from the Torah portion of the week to the deceased. Often I will use a reference to the Hebrew name of the deceased, whether in its literal meaning or its biblical or rabbinic antecedent, as a means of leading to my description of the life and qualities of the deceased. There are many other similar homiletical devices that rabbis use to develop effective and moving eulogies.

Irion tends to downplay "otherworldly oriented" funeral sermons (my term, but I think this is a correct reading of his work) in favor of a more pastoral approach that looks at the needs of the mourners. However, I have found that in my own experience, some of the best eulogies I have delivered were those that referred to otherworldly issues. I say best not only in the emotionally evocative sense but also in the pastoral sense, in the area of helping the mourners to begin their grieving and healing process. For example, I once delivered a eulogy for a prominent attorney and litigator, an active synagogue member, but also a rather contentious person, especially in the area of religious practice. I used the imagery of the *Bet Din Shel Maalah*, the Heavenly Court, that is frequently found in rabbinic literature. I pictured him missing his earthly court appointments because of a pressing call to the Heavenly Court. I described him arguing with the Almighty Himself and the divine response, "Come home, Brock. . . ." The family expressed deep gratitude for the way my eulogy helped them through a very difficult period.

For some interesting excerpts from eulogies of the talmudic period, see TB *Moed Katan* 25b. The Soncino translation of the text attempts to render these eulogies in rhyme, though they are not in rhyme in the original Hebrew-Aramaic. Note also that in the text, some of these eulogies were criticized by other rabbis of the Talmud for their poor imagery. This underlines Irion's point and ours that the speaker must be able to address the hearts of the mourners.

30. Rosh Hashanah, Yom Kippur, Sukkot, Shemini Atzeret, Pesah, and Shavuot.

31. These generally include any days that the supplicatory prayers of *Tahanun* are not said.

32. See Lamm, 51.

33. *Kol Bo*, 101, is quite emphatic that this cannot be done. Aaron Levine, 336, on the other hand, permits it. The question is whether certain prayers that are clearly not recited at night (such as the *tziduk hadin*—see further in this chapter for discussion of this prayer) as well as burial, which is not done at night, have the same status as the eulogy.

34. This is clearly defined in Jewish law as *me'abed atzmo ladaat*, one who knowingly destroys him or herself. A person in this category receives none of the traditional mourning practices that honor the deceased. This is because Judaism views life as sacrosanct; none of us have the right to play God, even with our own lives. In the modern application of traditional *halakhah*, however, we almost always give the deceased the benefit of the doubt. We presume that such persons were not in full control of their faculties when they took their life (mental illness, as we noted in Part I, has status in Jewish Law), or may have expressed regret for the act between the suicide attempt and actual death. As a result, in today's practice, we assume most suicides are not done "knowingly," and these persons are accorded full rites and honors. See Lamm, 215-220.

35. One who openly and freely renounces Judaism for another faith. See Lamm, 83, and Weiss, 82. In both this case and the classical case of

suicide, it may be permissible to offer remarks that deal strictly with the needs of the survivors. See further in this chapter regarding cremation.

36. Mourning is not observed if death has not been positively verified. See Aaron Levine, 336. This case came up recently in the Pan American flight that crashed in Lockerbie, Scotland. There were quite a few Jews on that flight, including some leaders of the Orthodox community, as well as two people connected with my own congregation. Eulogizing, mourning, and the various memorial services took place after it was fully ascertained that the death of all aboard had occurred. This point is directly related in *halakhah* to the point at which we would permit the surviving spouse to remarry under Jewish Law.

37. This is similar to *bikur holim* visits to non-Jews as outlined in chapter 4. *Kol Bo*, 98, and Aaron Levine, 336, clearly conclude the permissibility of eulogizing non-Jews, based on Tosefta Gittin, end of chapter 3. Levine musters an impressive list of historical occasions where great European rabbis eulogized deceased kings or queens. Others, such as Lamm, 55, limit participation in a non-Jewish funeral to accompanying the deceased to the cemetery and burial. In *Shulhan Arukh, Yoreh De'ah* 340:8, it is implied that we do not eulogize, while in 367:1 it is written that we do "bury their dead and comfort their mourners because of *darkei shalom*," though the references in both places are to idolators. *Arukh Hashulhan, Yoreh De'ah* 340:8 repeats the *Shulhan Arukh*'s list of cases for which we do not eulogize and omits non-Jews, showing that we do indeed eulogize them.

38. See chapter 6 regarding this source from TB *Moed Katan* 27b, from which we derive the notion of *bikur holim* societies.

39. The body is first washed of dirt and waste and then cleansed as a religious act. Afterward, the deceased is dressed in simple shrouds, regardless of the person's station in life, showing that all are equal. The body is then gently and carefully laid out in a simple wooden casket, with a handful of dirt from Israel. A *tallit*, the traditional fringed prayer shawl, is wrapped around males. All this is done by the members of the *hevrah kadisha*. Embalming and cosmetic tampering with the body are forbidden by *halakhah*, as they deny the finality of death and are considered a desecration of the divine vessel that once held the God-given soul.

In my current position, I occasionally have trouble from congregants who insist that their loved one be buried in a business suit or dress contrary to Jewish tradition. To counter this, I have to use every rabbinic role I have described—facilitator, teacher, healer of the soul, community representative, and member of the extended family—to convince these people of the halakhic, historic, and pastoral importance of this tradition.

40. These people are called *shomrim*, watchers or guards. The body is not to be left alone.

41. Only members of the Jewish faith should handle the body, both before and after it is in the casket. This includes the pallbearers. Some congregations have special committees whose members act as pallbearers and carriers for all funerals. In other cases, especially where few or no family members and friends attend the services, this is not possible, and we are forced to allow the funeral home or cemetery staff to carry and lower the casket.

42. *Hevrah Kadisha* participation is traditionally limited to the most pious members of the community—and those emotionally able to handle work with the deceased. Participation is considered a distinct honor within traditional Jewry. Nearly anyone can qualify for the other honors if they are of the Jewish faith, physically able to do so, and are not a *kohen*, a descendant of the Aaronic priestly family who by biblical law could not be in contact with a corpse.

For many years the trend in the general Jewish community was to let the funeral director handle all these functions, in contradiction to Jewish Law. Today the growing trend is to return to the traditional ways. This is not only true in the Orthodox community, which has fought to maintain these practices for a long time. Even the non-Orthodox world is taking these traditions quite seriously, for they represent the personal touch, dignity, and simplicity in the face of one of the most difficult aspects of life. See, for example, Arnold Goodman's *A Plain Pine Box*. Rabbi Goodman is a major leader in the Conservative movement.

43. This, however is not an absolute prohibition, and the presence of these would not invalidate anything else at the funeral. See Lamm, 18, who quotes the classic sources that suggest that while two thousand years ago flowers were used to offset the odor of the body, they were banned during the talmudic period because they became a distinctly "non-Jewish custom." See Irion, 111-112, who also criticizes floral displays and suggests, as we do, that charitable contributions are a better tribute to the deceased.

The question of flowers has only come up once in my career, in the case of a most prominent individual, where it was quite difficult to discourage the family from using flowers. In that case, I allowed the flowers to be displayed in front, but at a distance from the casket.

44. Irion, 106-108, in his analysis of music in the American Protestant tradition, discourages much of Christian funeral music as "obnoxious on . . . theological, aesthetic or artistic grounds." He suggests that if music is used, it be restricted to great hymns of the Church that specifi-

cally address the mourners' needs and perhaps were favorites of the deceased. He further suggests that congregational singing enhances the feeling of group solidarity, symbolizes the sharing of sorrow, and enables the community to make a contribution to the service. These issues are easily addressed in a Jewish service with a proper eulogy as outlined earlier and with the community's participation in the service and burial (see the next section).

45. Genesis 23:4-20; the *Me'arat Hamakhpelah* or "Cave of the Patriarchs" burial spot of Abraham, Sarah, Isaac, Rebecca, Jacob, and Leah still exists today in the Judean town of Hebron. The building around it is sacred to both Jews and Moslems and is often the source of much controversy and the unfortunate scene of occasional violence.

46. Though the reference in Genesis is the earliest Jewish historical source for burial, the actual halakhic source for both the positive and negative *mitzvot* is Deuteronomy 21:23, "You shall not leave his body [all night] . . . you shall surely bury him. . . ." While the verse refers to a specific case of an executed criminal requiring burial, the Talmud (TB *Sanhedrin* 46a) understands this verse to mean that all individuals require burial in the ground after death. *Halakhah* precludes anything that would contravene this, such as above-ground interment in a mausoleum. All this is codified in Jewish Law; see Maimonides, Laws of Mourning, 12:1; *Shulhan Arukh, Yoreh De'ah* 362:1; *Arukh Hashulhan, Yoreh De'ah* 362:1.

47. Irion, 112-115, interprets the usage of burial vaults or ornate caskets in Western society as part of the syndrome of denial of death, though he attempts to explain their social significance. Jewish tradition prohibits the use of anything other than all-wooden boxes, which will become part of the process of natural deterioration that accompanies death.

48. The guidelines for pallbearers at the cemetery are the same as those listed above for the funeral chapel. In the New York area, the unions are quite strict about who may handle the casket. Anyone wishing to follow the Jewish tradition encouraging Jewish members of the party to carry the casket must sign a release at the cemetery allowing them to do so. This is something I always discuss with the family in advance.

49. Usually seven times, but sometimes three, or every six to eight feet, depending on local custom. These stops are not done on the "semi-joyous days" mentioned earlier in our section on eulogies. The basis for our custom may be TB *Baba Batra* 100b, describing the talmudic practice of *moshav umaamad*, sitting and standing seven times during the cemetery procession with words of eulogy in between. The Talmud connects this practice to the seven times the word "vanity" is mentioned in Ecclesiastes 1:2. See also Lamm, 61.

50. In fact, the Hebrew name given to the entire funeral service is *levayah*, which actually means "the escorting" or "accompanying."

51. This must be done with great care. I have seen well-meaning people attempt to do this and actually fall into the hole. Some prefer to defer the lowering to the experienced cemetery people.

If the entire service is done at the gravesite, the eulogy and associated prayers are recited at this point.

52. This is also an important *mitzvah*. I usually invite all present who are physically able to participate in the tradition, explaining that it is an honor to the deceased as well as a way of saying good-bye. Though I do not usually say this publicly, I also believe it is therapeutic for the members of the party to face the finality of the death and loss by actual participation in the burial. This fits in with Irion's comments on pages 109–110 regarding the Committal, the brief Protestant service at the grave. See also Lamm, 65.

53. I have officiated at the funerals of recent Jewish immigrants from the former Soviet Union where the dirt was thrown in by hand rather than with shovels.

54. TB *Sanhedrin* 46b.

55. The decomposition of the body is very distasteful to the survivors. This may roughly correspond to *yekara d'hayya*, the "honor of the living" factor described on the same page of the Talmud.

56. This roughly corresponds to the idea of *yekara d'shekhiba*, "honor to the deceased."

57. This is codified in all the classical source references mentioned in note 46 above.

58. *Kol Bo*, 173–174, uses this as the reason that, unlike other commandments from the Torah, no blessing is recited over this *mitzvah* because (quoting TB *Menahot* 42) "All *mitzvot* which are proper by non-Jews [as well as Jews] do not require a *brakhah*." In other words, burial falls into that category of Torah commandments that the rational and intelligent mind, whether Jewish or not, could comprehend.

59. While the family is expected to make the proper arrangements for burial and can offer honor to their departed by being at the grave, it is not an absolute requirement that they are present at the gravesite for the actual burial. If it is too difficult for some members to be near during the emotionally charged moments when the grave is being filled, they may remain in the car while this takes place and come up for the prayers afterward. However, they should not leave altogether until the burial and its accompanying prayers are concluded. I usually discuss this with the family in advance. See the next footnote for case in point.

60. There are times when this role can take on Herculean proportions. I recall when once one of the older members of my congregation died on Passover eve. As desired by Jewish tradition and family preference, I had to arrange the washing and preparations, the funeral, as well as the burial, and have it all completed before the onset of Passover the same night. It was done.

There are other times when this role backfires, even with the best of pastoral and halakhic intentions. I remember one of the earliest funerals in my career, that of a prominent small-town synagogue and community leader. I had begun to teach my congregants of the importance of participation at the gravesite, but this family elected not to be present during the actual shoveling. I, of course, told them I would honor their wishes. I would appropriately signal the funeral director to bring the immediate family out of their cars when the interment was finished and the final prayers were to be intoned. Lo and behold, one of my other congregants told the director to bring the bereaved family to the grave while we were still filling it with earth. (To this day, I do not know if this was inadvertent or intentional. I do know the two families never got along. . . .) We nearly had a fistfight right then and there. No one blamed me for the mishap, but it left a bad taste for years afterward.

61. I have often found that simply as a shoulder to lean on, my mere presence at the cemetery has been a great source of comfort to the family. I suppose this may be construed as the rabbi being part of the extended family and the rabbi as an exemplar in empathy.

62. TB *Sotah* 14 and *Midrash Genesis Rabbah* 8.

63. For arguments in favor of cremation from a liberal Christian perspective, see Paul Irion, *Cremation* (Philadelphia: Fortress Press, 1968), and summarized as chapter 19, "To Cremate or Not," in Earl Grollman's *Concerning Death* (Boston: Beacon Press, 1974). Obviously, Irion's approach is not relevant to those seriously concerned with the observance of Jewish tradition.

64. Lamm, 56-57. There are more lenient opinions in Jewish Law regarding the burial of cremated ashes. Rabbi Y. Y. Weinberg in Responsa *Seridei Eish* 2:124 mentions both views and their respective rationales. He concludes that even according to those who allow burial of such ashes in a Jewish cemetery, cremation is still absolutely forbidden. According to the lenient view, burial would take place in a separate section of the cemetery, and there should be no rabbinic involvement. It is also, according to Weinberg, forbidden to engage in the washing and dressing preparation of the body (*taharah*) if cremation is to take place.

65. See further in this chapter in the section on liturgy for this doctrine's role in the Burial *Kaddish*.

66. *Kol Bo*, 1:3:21, 53-54.

67. *Kol Bo,* 53-54 n. 38.

68. Said after study of Torah selections but not specifically for mourning purposes.

69. Sefardic communities refer to this as the *Ashkaba* or "prayer for the laying down [of the deceased]." Their wording is somewhat different, but the themes are similar.

When a chapel service is done, the *hazkarah* is also recited there as well. This memorial prayer is used any time one wishes to recall the deceased, such as cemetery visits, the Hebrew anniversary of the death (*Yahrzeit*), or the memorial service associated with the conclusion of major Jewish holidays (*Yizkor*). See the next chapter about these observances.

70. See Rabbinical Assembly *Manual*, 131, for an alternate to the *Hazkarah*, and Goldin's *Hamadrikh*, 131-132, for alternate psalms. On these days, the regular Mourner's *Kaddish* is recited at the gravesite following the burial.

71. See the next chapter on how major festivals affect the timing of the *shivah* period.

72. See *Encyclopaedia Judaica*, s.v. "*El Male Rahamim*" (the Hebrew title for this prayer), as well as Eisenstein, 16 and 96-97, who suggests that the prayer may even have roots in the rabbinic period.

73. As with all translations in this work, this is mine. Most of the other translations render this as "perfect rest."

74. The Hebrew term for God's immanent presence is *Shekhinah.* "Wings" is a form of imagery.

75. The printed versions usually use "eternal rest" or "eternity."

76. This is the traditional version. I usually leave this line out when rendering it in English unless I know they are truly offering charity. In Hebrew I will often substitute "for whose memory we pray." More often than not, the people consider the rabbinic honorarium to be the charity that they are offering, while I prefer to see the honorarium as a professional fee. This issue should be taken up in rabbinic circles.

77. Literally in "the Garden of Eden," a metaphor for heaven.

78. See G. Selikovitsch, *Maaneh Lashon* (Memorial Prayers) (New York: Hebrew Publishing, 1910), who translated this as "the mystery of. . . ."

79. Literally, "His wings."

80. See Rabbi Soloveitchik's comments cited in chapter 7.

81. For an attempt to use this thought as the basis for an entire belief system, see David Blumenthal, *God and Evil* (New York: Ktav, 1989).

82. See Rabbi Jacob Goldberg's comments cited in chapter 7.

83. Aaron Levine, 403, questions whether one can correctly use this

prayer about a person who was not a righteous Jew and may not be among the "Holy and the Pure." He produces a version of this prayer originally suggested by the late R. Yosef Henkin (twentieth-century American rabbinic scholar and leader) without this line. However, in footnote 36 on the same page, he shows rabbinic sources that say that this prayer has been and is to be used for all, "from small to great, common folk to priest. . . ."

84. Thus the *ArtScroll Prayerbook*. This might answer Levine's objection cited in the previous footnote.

85. The original custom, as mentioned in *Shulhan Arukh, Yoreh De'ah* 339:3, was to say *tziduk hadin* at the time of death. Like the *keriah*, this has shifted to the time of the funeral, though Aaron Levine, 432 n. 90, mentions that the custom in Israel was to say it at both times.

86. Other translations of this moving prayer can be found in Birnbaum's *Daily Prayerbook*, 735-736; *Hamadrikh*, 126-128; and Lamm, 62-63. Note that the Conservative Rabbinical Assembly *Manual*, 126-127, includes this prayer without English translation. I purposely rendered my translation as close to the Hebrew as possible to give the reader the meaning of the words.

87. Deuteronomy 32:4.

88. Isaac.

89. Jeremiah 32:19.

90. Psalm 92:16.

91. Job 1:21.

92. Psalm 78:38.

93. TB *Avodah Zarah* 18a. See also *Midrash Sifre* on Deuteronomy 32:4 and *Midrash Numbers Rabbah* 88:4, which echo this.

94. Eighth- to ninth-century Babylon. See *Encyclopaedia Judaica*, s.v. "Zidduk Ha-Din," and Eisenstein, 345-346.

95. Lamm, 63-64, offers the following as themes:

> God has ordained this dreadful end and His decree is justified . . . we know there can be no imperfection in Almighty God. . . . We pray that God be merciful to the survivors . . . even at . . . grief, the Jew must concern himself with unselfish thoughts and pray for all of humanity . . . we must remember that as God was beneficent to give us this dear one . . . He beckons that soul to return to Him.

Lamm, of course, correctly understands the substance of the *Tziduk Hadin*. Still, his language is not well suited for people at the gravesite, though it may be helpful for study at other times. My own pastoral experience is that when helping to begin the healing of people in deep pain, this thematic approach is better.

96. See chapter 1, where I cite Pruyser's *The Minister as a Diagnostician*, for his analysis of religious language as a means of gauging the personality of the individual. Some of Pruyser's types would be better equipped to handle this kind of grief.

97. I first heard this from Rabbi Jacob Goldberg in February 1989. See his similar thought regarding the blessing of *dayan ha'emet* before the *keriah* in chapter 8.

98. *Kaddish* is a prayer that has vast significance in Jewish liturgy, most of which is beyond the scope of this book. The regular *Kaddish* is an affirmation of God's glory and contains no mention of death. Nevertheless, it is said by the mourner for eleven months after the death of a parent and thirty days after the death of other close relatives. See Lamm, 149–175, for a wonderful and complete explanation of *Kaddish*. Here, we will only deal with the gravesite version and its impact on the mourner.

99. Some good sources on the *Kaddish* include B. S. Jacobson, *Meditations on the Siddur* (Tel Aviv: Sinai, 1978), 295–306; David De Sola Pool, *The Kaddish*, first published in 1909; Hayim Donin, *To Pray as a Jew* (New York: Basic Books, 1980), 216–226; Leo Jung, "The Meaning of the *Kaddish*," and Seymour Cohen, "*Kaddish* in Many Places," both in Riemer's *Jewish Reflections on Death*; Lamm; and Meir Zlotowitz, *The Kaddish*, from the ArtScroll Jewish Heritage Series (New York: Mesorah, 1983).

100. The only other time this *Kaddish* is used is upon the completion of a major work of Torah, such as a tractate of Talmud. Donin, 225, speculates that this was to emphasize the talmudic dictum that "all who study Torah will attain life in the World to Come" (TB *Avodah Zarah* 3b). The major theme of the first paragraph directly connects to themes of life and rebuilding.

101. I have italicized the special section reserved for the Burial *Kaddish*. All other *Kaddishes* read as follows: "Magnified and sanctified be His great name, in the world that He has created according to His will. May He reign in His majestic glory during your life and your days, and the life of the whole house of Israel, speedily and soon, and let us say, Amen!"

102. Some medieval Jewish philosophers, including Maimonides, do not identify the resurrection of the dead with the coming of the Messiah, the rebuilding of Jerusalem, and the era of messianic peace. While these will happen within the realm of human history, the Resurrection, for Maimonides, will occur at some later point, in God's good time. See his Code, Laws of Kings, at the end, and J. David Bleich, *With Perfect Faith* (New York: Ktav, 1983), 638–656. This *Kaddish*, however, makes mention of all these eschatological points.

103. See earlier in chapter 7 regarding *aninut*.

104. See Birnbaum's *Daily Prayerbook*, 153-155, and the chapter "Resurrection" in Bleich, 619-688.

105. While the application of this idea to the Burial *Kaddish* is mine, the original source for this thought is in Hershel J. Matt, "The Fading Image of God," *Judaism* 141 (Winter 1987): 82-83. Matt is a Conservative rabbi with a distinguished career in the pulpit and as a geriatric chaplain. His thesis emanates from his dealing with the deterioration and death of the elderly, which he confronted daily (hence the article title). He posits that the doctrine of resurrection is the only comfort and assurance we have when confronting God's image fading away at death. Though coming from a non-Orthodox source, this is one of the best arguments in favor of the traditional doctrine of the resurrection of the dead that I have seen.

106. It may also be possible that the community can play a role in confronting the finality of death. The older members of the Orthodox synagogue I served in Lancaster, Pennsylvania, tell me that once upon a time, the officers of the congregation would come up to the gravesite at some point in the burial, and in Yiddish officially "excuse the deceased from his or her obligations to the *shul*."

CHAPTER 10

1. As is so throughout the book, "mourners" refers to those persons obligated to mourn, including children, siblings, parents, and spouses of the deceased. Others may join in but are not obligated to do so.

2. The Hebrew word here is *HaMakom*, literally, "the Place," which is one of God's classical Hebrew names. This name signifies God's presence everywhere, and can be a comforting thought to a mourner feeling acute loneliness after burying a loved one.

3. This practice is of most ancient origin. The talmudic sources assume that it was already done during the Second Temple period. See, for example, TB *Sanhedrin* 19a, which discusses how the high priest in mourning had the people come to him while he was on duty in the Temple. Also see TJ *Brakhot* 3:2, Maimonides, Laws of Mourning 13:1-2, and *Tur Shulhan Arukh, Yoreh De'ah* 374. The Talmud mentions that originally, the mourners would stand, and the lines of comforters would come to them offering condolences in a sort of "reception line" (as we would put it today). This was changed at some point—though it is not clear when—to the aforementioned practice of the mourner passing between the lines. The Talmud suggests that there were problems in Jerusalem when two families began to argue with each other over who should offer condolences first, so the

rabbis changed it to having the mourners pass. But the next paragraph mentions how elsewhere the custom was changed back to its original practice. The early halakhic sources require a *minyan* for this; some modern sources still maintain this rule (*Gesher Hahayyim*, 152; Aaron Levine, 446), others do not (*Kol Bo*, 216; Aaron Levine, 446 n. 132; Lamm, 67; Weiss, 87; *Hamadrikh*, 134). In spite of the extensive sources cited for this practice, it is not even mentioned in Karo's *Shulhan Arukh, Yoreh De'ah*, or the premodern *Arukh Hashulhan*. Nevertheless, it is an excellent illustration of the juncture all agree is a transition point in the mourning observance.

4. The connection to Jewish history is a recurring theme in the liturgies of crisis points. See the comments in chapter 5 regarding the *Mi-Sheberakh* prayer for the sick, which express the same thought.

I recently heard a wonderful interpretation of this theme in Rabbi Soloveitchik's name. He explains that the invocation of "the other mourners for Zion and Jerusalem," a direct reference to the destruction of the Temple, is actually a wish of hope for the mourners. He associates this with a talmudic story (TB *Taanit* 29a) connected with the Babylonian burning of the First Temple. At that tragic time, the young priests climbed up to the top of the walls and threw the Temple keys into the air, saying, "Master of the Universe! Since we have not been true custodians, we return the keys to You!" At that moment, a heavenly hand, as it were, came out and took the keys. Rabbi Soloveitchik suggests that the reason God took back the keys was to eventually return them to us, part of the ultimate hope of the Temple's rebuilding. In the same way, the reference to mourning for the Temple's destruction suggests the theme of hope and rebuilding for the mourners as well. (Conversation with Rabbi Fabian Schonfeld, who heard it from Rabbi Soloveitchik, January 15, 1992.)

5. Lamm, 67, analyzes this as a different but related transition between two important ideas discussed in the previous chapter, "The theme changes from honoring the dead to comforting the survivors." I leave it to the reader to consider the relationship of these two themes to my ideas of rabbinic versus community pastoral empathy.

6. See *Shulhan Arukh, Yoreh De'ah* 366:4, commentary of Shakh 4; *Kol Bo*, 216; Aaron Levine, 447.

7. See the previous chapter for my comments on why this doctrine is invoked at the moments of burial.

8. See Numbers 19:9, 10, 17.

9. See *Shulhan Arukh, Yoreh De'ah* 366:4. This washing is done not only after a funeral but after any occasion one has contact with the deceased, such as being under the same roof as the corpse, or an itinerant visit to a cemetery.

10. Many Jewish cemeteries have places of hand-washing on their perimeter specifically for this purpose.

11. Aaron Levine, 448-449, offers several reasons based on earlier sources including:

1. To note that the person did not die through the transgression of the community. This is based on the *Eglah Arufah* passage in Deuteronomy 21:1-9 of an untraced murder, where the leaders of the community wash their hands and state, "Our hands have not shed this blood."

2. A reminder of the genesis of humankind that is created from (and biologically composed of) water.

3. The general idea of cleansing and purification through water.

4. Nahmanides' notion that water was also one of the elements involved in the biblical purification of the person after contact with the deceased.

5. Water as a symbol of the resurrection of the dead.

12. For sources see TB *Moed Katan* 27b, TB *Semahot* 5:23, Maimonides, Laws of Mourning 4:9, *Shulhan Arukh, Yoreh De'ah* 388:1.

13. The commentaries on the *Shulhan Arukh* point out that if the mourner is for some reason alone or has no one to prepare the meal, then it is better that they should prepare it themselves rather than go hungry.

14. 24:17 and 24:22. This is a most interesting and significant source for other practices of *shivah* that obviously go back as far as the prophetic period. The prophet is told by God that he will experience a tragedy (the death of his wife), and this will be a lesson to his people as an analogy of the impending destruction of the Temple by the Babylonians. Because of the nature of the impending national tragedy, the people should not mourn in the traditional manner, just as God tells His prophet not to mourn in the traditional manner. The entire verse reads, "Son of man, behold I take from you the desire of your eyes with a plague; [JPS translates this as stroke] do not eulogize and do not cry and do not bring on tears. Sigh in silence, do not make mourning; put on your glory, [*tefillin*—phylacteries—see the direct reference to this point in chapter 7 on *aninut* where *tefillin* are not worn] and put your shoes on your feet, [leather shoes are not worn during *shivah*] do not cover [your hair to] your lip [this is how the Metzudot commentary reads this part of the verse] *and do not eat the bread of others*." The inference is that these are all normally common practices during the mourning period. See further in this chapter as these observances are described.

15. Halakhically, a mourner may not fill his or her own needs for this

meal, yet a mourner may still reach out to another in the same state! See chapter 1 regarding Webster's definition of sympathy as one who shares the same feeling through having the same experience.

16. TB *Moed Katan* 27b.

17. The *b* and *v* are interchangeable in Hebrew.

18. Gordon in Riemer, *Jewish Reflections*, 100, refers to this as a "Meal of Recuperation."

19. While this paraphrases the talmudic source, the term "first meal" is a change from the Talmud's wording the "first day." Some of the early commentators such as Tosafot say that food must indeed be brought for the mourner the entire first day. However, the vast majority of codifiers, including R. Asher, Maimonides, Tur, and the *Shulhan Arukh* just quoted, require this only for the first meal.

20. *Shulhan Arukh, Yoreh De'ah* 378:1.

21. This is found in many works; see for example Birnbaum's *Daily Prayerbook*, 759–770.

22. Isaiah 66:13.

23. Heb. *mishpat*, often rendered as justice or judgment. See Tosafot on TB *Brakhot* 46b, who questions the theology of this point, though he leaves the phrase in the prayer. Tosafot writes, "There is death without sin and there is suffering without transgression." In other words, death and suffering are not necessarily meant as punishment.

24. Specifically the *Tziduk Hadin* and the burial *Kaddish*.

25. In this paragraph Rabbi Soloveitchik was specifically referring to the Burial *Kaddish*, which for him marks the transition into *shivah*. But his words are appropriate here because they underscore the changes that *shivah* brings.

26. Soloveitchik in Riemer, *Jewish Reflections*, 79–80.

27. In the cases where it is impossible to obtain the *minyan* at the home, it is permitted for the mourner to leave the house to attend daily synagogue services.

28. Based on Moses' instructions to Aaron following the death of his two sons in Leviticus 10:6. As pointed out earlier, this is one of the primary biblical sources for mourning *halakhah*. See TB *Moed Katan* 14b and 18a, *Shulhan Arukh, Yoreh De'ah* 380:1 and 390.

29. See 2 Samuel 14:2 and TB *Moed Katan* 15 where the biblical phrase "clothes of mourning" implies that fresh clothing is not worn. Also see *Shulhan Arukh, Yoreh De'ah* 389.

30. The ban on grooming extends to covering the mirrors, usually used for grooming purposes, in the *shivah* house. This is actually one of the more well known practices among nonobservant Jews. However, many do not understand the real reason behind this practice. I have often heard

that it is done so that "the dead do not look back at you through the mirror." I attempt to take my prefuneral visits as an opportunity to educate people as to the background behind our traditions.

31. TB *Moed Katan* 15 and *Shulhan Arukh, Yoreh De'ah* 381.

32. Nonleather footwear is permitted. See the earlier-cited passage from Ezekiel 24:17 and TB *Moed Katan* 15b and 20b and *Shulhan Arukh, Yoreh De'ah* 382.

33. Based on 2 Samuel 12:24, TB *Moed Katan* 23a, and *Shulhan Arukh, Yoreh De'ah* 383.

34. TB *Moed Katan* 23a and *Shulhan Arukh, Yoreh De'ah* 384.

35. Most of these restrictions are followed by the observant Jewish community on Tisha B'Av, the national day of mourning on which both the First and Second Temples were destroyed. In effect, Jews "sit *shivah*" for the loss of the national shrine, even after thousands of years, because losing the Temple is considered like losing a close relative. Since the prohibition of studying the Torah is maintained on this day, only aspects of the Torah that reflect the sadness of the moment, such as Lamentations, sections of the prophets and the Talmud that relate to the destruction of Jerusalem, and aspects of the laws of death and mourning can be studied on Tisha B'Av.

36. In earlier times there were two other practices that have been lost. One was the covering of the head and face, designed to bring on a humbled feeling on the part of the mourner and based on Ezekiel 24:17. It is unclear why this is no longer practiced. The other one is the overturning of the bed, which has several rabbinic sources, including TB *Moed Katan* 15b and others. Emmanuel Feldman, "Death as Estrangement: The Halakhah of Mourning," in Riemer, *Jewish Reflections*, 92 n.10, connects this with the idea of death affecting the divine image in man and suggests that the current practice of covering the mirrors is a substitute for this, since the mirrors are connected to the idea of image. For the purposes of this book, I have followed Lamm and my own interpretations regarding the covering of the mirrors. There are some who symbolically keep the tradition of overturning the bed by sleeping less comfortably than usual during *shivah* by using, for example, one less pillow if they normally use more than one. This is often followed during Tisha B'Av as well.

37. See Feldman in Riemer, *Jewish Reflections*, 84-94.

38. Ibid., 88. Feldman's analysis of the laws almost contradicts Soloveitchik, who suggests that the Torah is calling upon the mourner during *shivah* to transcend death and begin to return to life. I would suggest that Soloveitchik holds that the tradition pushes the mourner along the path toward healing and reclaiming wholeness. Feldman suggests that

the tradition allows the mourner space so that the healing can begin of its own accord. There is no disagreement between these two as to the substance and content of Jewish tradition for the week of *shivah*.

39. Based on 2 Samuel 13:31, where King David tore his clothing (*keriah*) and lay on the ground. Also see Job 2:13, where in his grief, Job's friends sat with him on the ground. Also see TB *Moed Katan* 15 and 21, also *Shulhan Arukh, Yoreh De'ah* 387.

40. The scriptural source is Ezekiel 24:17, "Sigh in silence." See TB *Moed Katan* 15 and *Shulhan Arukh, Yoreh De'ah* 385.

41. Rabbi Charles Spirn suggests that the visitor recount some good deed of the deceased as a merit to his or her memory (written communication, October 1991). I would add that this can also be quite therapeutic to the mourner in the pastoral/psychoemotive sense.

42. See chapter 1 citing this rabbinic source as a major basis of Jewish pastoral theology. There is also a distinct similarity, both theoretical and practical, between this aspect of comforting the bereaved and *bikur holim*.

43. Thus, the mourners may leave their homes and attend synagogue on the Sabbath, as well as wear normal shoes. The bans on shaving, grooming, and marital relations remain.

44. Major holidays are the biblical festivals of Rosh Hashanah, Yom Kippur, Passover, Sukkot, and Shavuot. The transcendent joy of these festivals cancels out the *shivah* restrictions. It does not, however, necessarily cancel out the mourners' emotional needs. Family, friends, community, and the rabbi need to be sensitive to this, especially in welcoming the mourner back into the synagogue service during the holiday, and after the festival as well.

45. Again, rabbi and community should assist the mourners over the holiday due to the unusual nature of the timing. I experienced this case when my grandmother died on the second day of Sukkot. The funeral was on the third day, one of the intermediate days, which is considered part of the festival but not a holiday, in the sense that work can be done and the routine is semiweekday. My mother's *shivah* did not begin until after Simchat Torah, a full week later. We were living out of town from my parents; while my family and I attended and I officiated at the service and burial, none of us could remain through the holiday week and the subsequent *shivah* period.

46. Irion, 159-164, in his section "Post-Funeral Calls," anticipates some of this. He sees the minister's role during this time as: (1) developing the growth of rapport; (2) assistance in the mourning process and reintegration; (3) release of emotional tension; and (4) helping the mourner

understand the Christian view of death and resurrection. From the Jewish perspective, the first three functions devolve on anyone who comes to visit and not just the rabbi. The next paragraph will show that rabbis, as specialists in empathy, can fill these and other needs with their special skills.

47. Sometimes, though, this role can be crucial and affect a rabbi's career. In one of my early rabbinic positions, the family was not sure that they wanted a *shivah minyan*. They had returned from an out-of-town funeral Thursday, and I was not able to visit them before the onset of the Sabbath due to other pressing synagogue business. The family was deeply hurt and angry with me, and the issue came back to haunt me at contract evaluation and negotiation time. The moral of the story: a rabbi should always try to be available when tragedy strikes and attempt to ascertain the family's needs as soon as possible.

48. I always give my own congregants a copy of Lamm's book to read during *shivah*.

49. This is the Jewish parallel to Irion's pastoral function of "helping the mourner understand the Christian view of death and resurrection" (163).

50. This corresponds to the account of *bikur holim* committee development in chapter 6.

51. See earlier in chapter 7 where the symptomatology of grief in relationship to *aninut* is described.

52. Soncino translates this, "Between his shoulders."

53. TB *Moed Katan* 27b.

54. Maimonides, Laws of Mourning, 6:1. The biblical basis for *shloshim* is from the mourning for the death of Moses at the very end of Deuteronomy. See TB *Semahot*, chapter 7.

55. There is some question about whether shaving is permitted during this period. While the halakhic sources usually followed in this country allow shaving immediately after *shivah* for other relatives, they rule that for parents one should wait to shave until the mourner cannot publicly sustain his appearance. ("Until his friends are repulsed by him . . ." is how the codes put it.) This is obviously a highly subjective point that only the individual can determine. Other sources are stricter.

56. *Gesher Hahayyim* 22:1; *Kol Bo*, chapter 5; Lamm, 145. There is far more detail about the specifics of these observances, as well as special cases, than can be covered in this book. For further information, readers are urged to consult the halakhic sources cited herein or to ask their local rabbi.

57. As in the case of *shivah*, a major festival cancels *shloshim* as well.

58. See the earlier discussion regarding *keriah* and *aninut* for the dif-

ferences in the bonds between the mourner and parents versus bonds with other relatives.

59. Actually the *Kaddish* is only recited for eleven months. This is due to the view that *Kaddish* helps the soul achieve a higher level of heavenly reward. As Birnbaum puts it (page 46), "Formerly the *Kaddish* was recited the whole year of mourning so as to rescue the soul of one's parents from the torture of *Gehinnom* where the wicked are said to spend no less than twelve months. In order not to count one's parents among the wicked, the period for reciting the *Kaddish* was later reduced to eleven months." This can be interpreted within the idea that the soul, upon death, returns to its Maker, which is God. The *Kaddish* allows the soul to continue to rise to higher spiritual levels during the eleven-month period. Perhaps this is the meaning of the Yiddish phrase often used, "*Zol zein an aliyeh fur di neshomeh*," may it be an ascent for the soul!

60. At my son's *bar mitzvah* several years ago, a cousin who had lost her mother played an invaluable role by taking an excellent video of the celebration. Others can help by serving food or cleaning up.

61. This restriction does not apply on the Sabbath because, as is true during *shivah*, there is no public mourning on the Sabbath.

62. I have discovered that the period immediately following the end of *shivah* can be particularly difficult for mourners, since the visitors who have emotionally and physically carried the mourner for the past week are now gone. From the human (as opposed to the strictly halakhic) perspective, the rabbinic presence during the "reentry phase" can be most valuable. I always attempt to call upon the family some time after the conclusion of *shivah*.

63. Jacob Goldberg, *Pastoral Bereavement Counselling* (New York: Human Sciences Press, 1989.) Rabbi Goldberg's actual program is now called the Mourner's After-Care Institute and has received funding from some of the New York area Jewish funeral directors. Currently it operates in the New York area and is expanding nationally. Rabbi Goldberg sees his program as a bereavement counterpart to Clinical Pastoral Education (CPE) training for hospital chaplains.

64. This should be viewed as a modified Rogerian approach because classic Rogerian therapy is usually unstructured, and Rabbi Goldberg's program, while allowing for freedom within the sessions to explore the mourner's feelings, does have a structure.

65. TB *Moed Katan* 27b.

66. Glen Davidson, *Understanding Mourning* (Minneapolis: Augsburg, 1984.) This conclusion was based on his clinical research and studies of grieving people.

67. Compare this list with our comments on *aninut* in chapter 7.

68. While this process does not exactly echo the halakhic paradigm of *shloshim* and twelve months, it certainly fits and can match the general Jewish process of gradual decreases in mourning.

69. Davidson, 68-70.

70. See earlier in this chapter.

71. Davidson, 80-84.

72. See *Encyclopaedia Judaica*, s.v. "*Hazkarat Neshamot*" ("Remembrance of the Souls") and Eisenstein, 96-97.

73. This service has a powerful draw within Western Jewry. Rabbis of all groupings know that turnout is far higher for this service than for other holiday services. Ironically, more people will come to a service honoring their dead then will attend a joyous Sabbath or holiday service affirming life. Many even leave after the completion of the *Yizkor* part of the service but before the entire holiday service is over.

74. Some study selections from the *Mishnah* that spell out the Hebrew name of the deceased.

75. Abraham's and Sarah's in Hebron (Genesis 23:1-20, 25:9-10), Rachel's in Bethlehem (Genesis 35:20), etc., and throughout Scripture.

76. Many Jews wait a full year before this. Some select a time convenient for the family if they are scattered and wait for improved weather in colder climates.

77. See *Hamadrikh*, 156-163, and Rabbinical Assembly *Manual*, 137-145.

CONCLUSION

1. See the reference in chapter 2 from Numbers 16:29 and TB *Nedarim* 39b about Moses' complaint to God during the Korah rebellion.

2. The fact that life will at some point inevitably be defeated by death is Rabbi Soloveitchik's reason why the Torah considers contact with the dead to be ritually defiling. This also connects with his thesis about the rules of *aninut*. See my description and explanation of this in chapter 7.

3. Abraham Besdin, *Man of Faith in the Modern World* (adapted from the lectures of Rabbi Joseph B. Soloveitchik) (New York: Ktav, 1989), 102.

4. See Marc Angel's analysis comparing the expected serenity of traditional death scenes with modern impersonal death scenes in *The Orphaned Adult* (New York: Human Sciences Press, 1987), 27-31, and his look at the inevitability of death, 43-55. Also see Moshe Halevi Spero, "Reflections on the Inevitability of Death," *Judaism* 123 (Summer 1982): 342.

5. See the description of *aninut* symptoms in chapter 7. I first experienced these feelings when my best friend, Rabbi Stanley F. Greenberg, of blessed memory, was killed in a tragic car accident in August 1979. When I counsel the bereaved, it is with sympathy as well as with empathy, as defined in chapter 1.

6. See, for example, Rabbi Aaron Soloveichik's moving account of his stroke and neurologist Dr. John McMahon's comments on the patient's feeling that the affected limbs were foreign to the body in "A Glimpse at Eternity from a Hospital Dungeon," *Tradition* 21:3 (Fall 1984): 1-7.

7. The fact that large numbers of Jews are ignorant of and do not observe their own tradition does not detract from the relevance and importance of the Torah. On the contrary, one of my reasons for this entire project is to educate Jews about the wisdom of the *halakhah*. Chaim Rozwaski ("On Jewish Mourning Psychology," *Judaism* 17:3 [Summer 1968]: 346) suggests that the deviations in the observance of Jewish tradition as well as the exaggeration of the rabbinic role in mourning do not stem from a "Christianization of American Jewish life," as some have suggested, but rather from human weakness found among both Jews and Christians.

8. See the analysis of why this is so in chapter 1.

9. Witness the fact that my chapters on *bikur holim* were based mostly on primary sources, such as the Talmud, *Midrash*, and Codes rather than current sources by authors in English. In fact, the only contemporary work on the *halakhah* of illness of which I am aware is the first third of Aaron Levine's book, from which we have drawn some material.

10. Joseph B. Soloveitchik, "The Community," *Tradition* 27:2 (Spring 1978): 7-24.

11. Conversation with Rabbi Harold Schulweis, Encino, California, August 20, 1991, and written communication, March 18, 1994.

12. See, for example, chapter 5, "Empathy: Where Religion and Psychotherapy Converge," in Robert Katz, *Pastoral Care and the Jewish Tradition* (Philadelphia: Fortress Press, 1985), 99-109, and also Israel Kestenbaum, "The Rabbi as Caregiver," *Tradition* 23:3 (Spring 1988): 32-40. Kestenbaum defines the famous biblical dictum, "Love your neighbor as yourself," as an example of empathic love. See also my curriculum on *gemilut hasadim* (practice of lovingkindness) published by the Union of Orthodox Jewish Congregations of America, Yeshiva University, and the National Jewish Outreach Program (New York, 1994). I hope that there will be more of these efforts as time goes on.

13. The notion of structure may be the hardest idea for Protestants to accept, since the genesis of Protestantism was a rebellion against structure, and its subsequent theology does not emphasize law, sacrament, or

extensive ritual. Still, I suggest that Protestants ought to consider continuing development of their own structures and traditions to guide the ill and the bereaved, especially beyond the actual funeral service. In my opinion, the needs are there regardless of one's religious or ethnic background. All people need a "path," which is what the word *halakhah* means. People in pain definitely require the guidance of a system to address their deep emotional and spiritual needs while sick or in mourning. And because the issues of life and death are most definitely religious ones, a religious system is best equipped to help people through these times.

    14. Merle Jordan, "The Protestant Way in Death and Mourning," in Earl Grollman, ed., *Concerning Death* (Boston: Beacon Press, 1974), 84.

    15. *Report and Recommendations to The Most Reverend John McGann, D.D.*, by The Most Reverend John C. Dunne, D.D., Chairperson, Commission on Pastoral Care, Diocese of Rockville Center, New York (December 1, 1992). I thank Chaplain Carol Breslin of Franklin Hospital Medical Center, Valley Stream, NY, for bringing this study to my attention.

    16. Ecclesiastes 7:2.

    17. TB *Moed Katan* 28b.

    18. TB *Shabbat* 133b.

APPENDIX 1

    1. Literally, "jumped upon him."

    2. Taz (Turei Zahav, R. David Halevi, seventeenth-century Poland) commentary quoting Bah commentary. The reason for this waiting period is not to shorten his *mazal*, placing upon him the label of "sick one."

    3. See chapter 3 for the various definitions of these terms.

    4. Taz: A *ben gilo* is one who was born at the same time. His visit takes away 1/60 of the illness and every visit as such takes away 1/60 of what is left.

    5. Shakh: This does not apply to the funeral of the one hated, since this is the end of all humans, but rather to the ill or mourner. We fear he may rejoice. . . . but all goes according to [the nature of the] hatred and what they despise.

    6. Shakh: On Sabbath add, "His mercies are great, so rest in peace."

    7. Gra: This is to help him order his affairs . . . but not to speak of life or death.

    8. Taz: For reasons of modesty and the possibility of sexual misconduct. It is less dignified for a woman in this case, and it is to protect her from him.

Shakh: He may force himself on her, but we do not fear this if he is sick.

9. Shakh: Because comforting the bereaved is a kindness to both the living and the dead. Bah disagrees and says this only applies when the two acts cannot be done together. But if they can be done together, *bikur holim* comes first, in order to ask mercy or sweep and sprinkle, since these cause the patient to live.

Glossary

Aninut   The stage the Jewish mourner enters upon hearing the news of death of a close relative; lasts until the completion of the burial.

Ben Gilo   A person connected to another through some kind of a relationship.

Bet Din   Rabbinic court.

Bikur Holim   Visiting the sick.

Brakhah   A blessing, either in the general sense or the liturgical sense.

Dal   Detached, hanging, open, weak, drawn out, lessened, loosened, or lowered.

Darkei Shalom   Peaceful and mutual relationships within society.

Gadol   Great.

Gemara   See **Talmud**.

Gemilut Hasadim   Acts of loving-kindness.

Hakham   Wise man.

Halakhah   The corpus and specifics of Jewish Law.

Hazkarah   Memorial prayer for the deceased.

Hesped   Lamenting or mourning the deceased, also referring to the eulogy itself.

Hevrah   Committee, group, or association within the Jewish community organized for specific religious purposes (such as *bikur holim* or preparing the deceased for burial).

Kaddish   Prayer of acclamation of God's greatness, said by, among others, mourners for the period after death of a loved one.

Katan   Small.

Keriah   The tearing of a garment by the mourner.

Kibed   To honor or to sprinkle and clean.

Kohen   Priest, a descendant of the priestly tribe of Aaron.

Lo'eg larash   Literally, mocking the poor, but referring to mocking the deceased by eating or drinking, for example, in the presence of a corpse.

Mazal   Fortune or luck.

Melekh   King.

Menahem   Comforter.

Mezuman   The requisite three that can say Grace After Meals as a group.

Mi-Sheberakh   A genre of prayer for specific occasions such as on behalf of the ill.

Midrash   Rabbinic homiletical and exegetical literature, commentary on the Torah.

Minyan   The requisite ten that are required for communal prayer.

Mishnah   See **Talmud**.

Mitzvot   The commandments of the Torah (sing. *mitzvah*).

Navi   Prophet.

Neder   Vow.

Onen   Mourner in the period between death of a loved one and burial.

Posek   Rabbinic decision-maker of Jewish Law.

Rahamim   Mercy.

Seudat Havraah   The meal of condolence, eaten by the mourners at home after the burial.

Shaat Himum   A time of great emotional heat, when tearing of the garments is done.

Shabbat   The Sabbath.

Shaliah   Representative.

Shekhinah   God's presence.

Shivah   The week of mourning following the burial; the home at which the mourners are observing this period is referred to as a *shivah* house.

Shloshim   The thirty-day mourning period following the burial.

Shofet   Judge.

Shulhan Arukh   Code of Jewish Law, compiled by R. Yoseph Caro of Safed and R. Moses Isslerles of Cracow (sixteenth century).

Taharah   Washing and dressing of the body prior to burial.

Tallit   The prayer shawl with the traditional fringes at each of the four corners.

Talmud   The written version of the Oral (or Rabbinic) Tradition; includes the *Mishnah* (from the early Tannaitic period—first and second centuries) and the *Gemara* (from the Amoraic period—third through sixth centuries), which was written in Tiberias (the Palestinian or Jerusalem Talmud) or in Babylon (the Babylonian Talmud).

Tefillin   Phylacteries.

Torah   Either the Five Books of Moses or the entire corpus of Jewish legal, ethical, and moral tradition.

Tzedakah   Giving of charity.

Tziduk Hadin   Prayer affirming the divine decree, usually recited at the gravesite.

Yahrzeit   Hebrew anniversary of the date of death.

Yekara d'hayya   Honor to the living.

Yekara d'shekhiba   Honor to the deceased.

Yeshivah   A school for intense talmudic study, sometimes leading to rabbinic ordination.

Yizkor   Memorial service associated with the conclusion of major Jewish holidays.

Bibliography

ENGLISH SOURCES

American Jewish Archives. Centennial of the Rabbinate Issue. Cincinnati, OH, 1980.

Andrews, Howard F. "Helping and Health: The Relationship between Volunteer Activity and Health-Related Outcomes." *Advances* 4:1 (1990): 25-34.

Angel, Marc. "Hospice." *Journal of Halakha and Contemporary Society* 12 (Fall 1986): 17-27.

———. *The Orphaned Adult.* New York: Human Sciences Press, 1987.

ArtScroll Prayerbook. Trans. Nosson Scherman. New York: Mesorah, 1984.

Berkovits, Eliezer. *Major Themes in Modern Philosophies of Judaism.* New York: Ktav, 1974.

Berlat, Norman. "A Jewish Concept of Grief and Bereavement." In *Proceedings, Conventions of College of Chaplains* (Workshop Papers Edition), 1973, 138-143; reprinted in *Forum,* 23:3 (April 1976): 81-84.

Bernstein, Louis. *Challenge and Mission.* New York: Sheingold, 1985.

Besdin, Abraham. *Man of Faith in the Modern World* (adapted from the lectures of Rabbi Joseph B. Soloveitchik). New York: Ktav, 1989.

———. *Reflections of the Rav.* Jerusalem: World Zionist Organization, 1979.

Bleich, J. David. "AIDS: A Jewish Perspective." *Tradition* 26:3 (Spring 1992): 49-80.

———. *With Perfect Faith.* New York: Ktav, 1983.

Blumenthal, David. *God and Evil*. New York: Ktav, 1989.

Bomzer, Herbert. *The Kollel in America*. New York: Sheingold, 1985.

Brody, Jane E. "Personal Health (Laughter as Potential Therapy for Patients)." *New York Times*, 7 April 1988.

Bulka, Reuven, and Woolf, Jeffrey. "May Parents Forego the Eleven Months of Mourning Due Them?" *The Orthodox Roundtable*, Nissan (Spring) 1994.

Carr, Arthur, et al. *Grief: Selected Readings*. New York: Health Sciences Publishing, 1975.

Carter, John, and Narramore, Bruce. *The Integration of Psychology and Religion*. Grand Rapids: Zondervan, 1979.

Catholic Encyclopedia, s.v. "pastoral counselling."

Cavanaugh, John R. *Fundamentals of Pastoral Counselling*. Milwaukee: Bruce, 1962.

Christian Counselling Institute. Lancaster, PA. Various publications and brochures.

Clebsch, William, and Jaekle, Charles. *Pastoral Care in Historical Perspective*. Northvale, NJ: Jason Aronson Inc., 1983.

Clinebell, Howard. *Basic Types of Pastoral Counselling*. Nashville: Abingdon, 1966.

Cohen, A., trans. and ed. *The Psalms*. London: Soncino Press, 1945.

Collins, Gary. *Christian Counselling: A Comprehensive Guide*. Waco: Word Books, 1980.

"Comic Relief." *Prevention* 40:3 (March 1988): 38-42.

Daily Prayerbook. Trans. Philip Birnbaum. New York: Hebrew Publishing, 1949.

Davidson, Glen. *Understanding Mourning*. Minneapolis: Augsburg, 1984.

De Sola Pool, David. *The Kaddish*. First published in 1909.

Dietrich, Glenn. Unpublished verbatim. Lancaster (PA) Theological Seminary Doctor of Ministry Program. July 1, 1981.

Donin, Hayim. *To Pray as a Jew*. New York: Basic Books, 1980.

——. *To Be a Jew*. New York: Basic Books, 1972.

Dresner, Samuel. *The Jewish Dietary Laws*. New York: Burning Bush Press, 1959.

Dunne, The Most Reverend John C. *Report and Recommendations to The Most Reverend John McGann*. Commission on Pastoral Care. Diocese of Rockville Center, NY. December 1, 1992.

Encyclopaedia Judaica. Jerusalem: Keter Publishing House, Ltd., 1972.

Epstein, Isidore, ed. *The Talmud* (English edition). London: Soncino, 1987.

Epstein, Isidore, ed. *Hebrew English Edition of the Talmud*. London: Soncino Press, 1984.

Feifel, Herman. *The Meaning of Death*. New York: McGraw-Hill, 1969.

Fein, Harriet. "The Rabbi as Pastoral Counsellor." In *Shivim: Essays in Honor of Ira Eisenstein*, ed. Ronald Brauner, 241–255. New York: Ktav, 1977.

Goldberg, Chaim Binyamin. *Mourning in Halachah*. New York: Mesorah (ArtScroll), 1991.

Goldberg, Jacob. *Pastoral Bereavement Counselling*. New York: Human Sciences Press, 1989.

Goldin, Hyman. *Hamadrikh: The Rabbi's Guide*. New York: Hebrew Publishing, 1956.

Goodman, Arnold. *A Plain Pine Box*. New York: Ktav, 1981.

Goodman, Joel. "Laughing Matters." *Journal of the American Medical Association* 267:13 (April 1, 1992): 1858.

Greenberg, Blu. *How to Run a Traditional Jewish Household*. Northvale, NJ: Jason Aronson Inc., 1989.

Grollman Earl, ed. *Concerning Death*. Boston: Beacon Press, 1974.

——. *Talking About Death*. Boston: Beacon Press, 1970.

Harlow, Jules. *A Rabbi's Manual*. New York: The Rabbinical Assembly, 1965.

Helmreich, William. *The World of the Yeshiva*. New York: Free Press, 1982.

Hertz, Joseph. *The Pentateuch*. London: Soncino Press, 1962.

Heschel, Abraham J. *The Prophets*. New York: Harper and Row, 1962.

Hiltner, Seward. *Pastoral Counselling*. Nashville: Abingdon, 1949.

——. *Preface to Pastoral Theology*. Nashville: Abingdon, 1958.

Irion, Paul. *The Funeral and the Mourners*. Nashville: Abingdon, 1979.

——. *Cremation*. Philadelphia: Fortress Press, 1968.

Jackson, Edgar. *You and Your Grief*. New York: Hawthorn, 1961.

Jacobson, B. S. *Meditations on the Siddur*. Tel Aviv: Sinai, 1978.

Jastrow, Marcus. *Dictionary of Talmud*. New York: Pardes, 1950.

Katz, Robert. *Pastoral Care and the Jewish Tradition*. Philadelphia: Fortress Press, 1985.

Kestenbaum, Israel. "The Rabbi as Caregiver." *Tradition* 23:3 (Spring 1988): 32–40.

Kook, Avraham I. *Lights of Penitence*. Trans. and ed. B. Z. Bokser. New York: Paulist Press, 1978.

Kübler-Ross, Elisabeth. *On Death and Dying*. New York: Macmillan, 1970.

Kushner, Harold. *When Bad Things Happen to Good People*. New York: Schocken, 1981; Avon, 1983.

Lamm, Maurice. *The Jewish Way in Death and Mourning*. New York: Jonathan David, 1969.

Leibowitz, Nehama. *Studies in Shemot*. Jerusalem: World Zionist Organization, 1976.

Levine, Joseph. "Visiting the Sick: The Delicate Mitzva." *Moment* 6:1 (December 1980): 20-24.

Lindemann, Erich. "Symptomatology and Management of Acute Grief." *American Journal of Psychiatry* 101 (September 1944): 141-148.

Mandelkorn, Shlomo. *Biblical Concordance.* Jerusalem: Schocken, 1978.

Matt, Hershel J. "The Fading Image of God." *Judaism* 141 (Winter 1987): 75-83.

Moyers, Bill. *Healing and the Mind.* New York: Doubleday, 1993.

Nouwen, Henri. *The Wounded Healer.* Garden City, NY: Image, 1979.

Oates, Wayne. *Pastoral Counselling.* Philadelphia: Westminster, 1974.

Ozarowski, Joseph S. *Gemilut Hasadim–Practice of Lovingkindness.* New York: Union of Orthodox Jewish Congregations of America, Rabbi Isaac Elchanan Theological Seminary, and National Jewish Outreach Program, 1994.

——. *Jewish Pastoral Theology and Care at Life's Crisis Points.* Ann Arbor, MI: UMI, 1992.

——. "Malpractice." *Journal of Halakha and Contemporary Society* 14 (Fall 1987): 111-127.

——. "Models and Dimensions of Christian Pastoral Theology, Care, and Counselling." Lancaster Theological Seminary, 1984-1985.

——. "A Psychological Look at the Jewish Mourning Laws." Unpublished paper for Honors Reading, Loyola University of Chicago, 1975.

——. "Results of Supervised Counselling Verbatims." Lancaster Theological Seminary, 1983-1984.

Peli, Pinchas. *Soloveitchik On Repentance.* New York: Paulist Press, 1984.

Pruyser, Paul. *The Minister as Diagnostician.* Philadelphia: Westminster, 1976.

The Psalms. Trans. and ed. A. Cohen. London: Soncino Press, 1945.

Riemer, Jack, ed. *Jewish Reflections on Death.* New York: Schocken, 1976.

——. "Word for the Week." *St. Louis Jewish Light,* 7 November, 1979, 19.

Rozwaski, Chaim. "On Jewish Mourning Psychology." *Judaism* 17:3 (Summer 1968): 335-346.

Schur, Tsvi G. *Illness and Crisis: Coping the Jewish Way.* New York: NCSY-Orthodox Union, 1987.

Selikovitsch, G. *Maaneh Lashon.* New York: Hebrew Publishing, 1910.

Shilo Dictionary. New York: Shilo, 1963.

Soloveichik, Aaron. "A Glimpse at Eternity from a Hospital Dungeon." *Tradition* 21:3 (Fall 1984): 1-7.

Soloveitchik, Joseph B. *Shiurei Harav.* Ed. Joseph Epstein. New York: Yeshiva University, 1974.

——. "The Community." *Tradition* 27:2 (Spring 1978): 7-24.

Spero, Moshe Halevi. "Reflections on the Inevitability of Death." *Judaism* 123 (Summer 1982): 342.

Spiro, Jack. *A Time To Mourn.* New York: Bloch, 1985.

Switzer, David K. *The Minister as Crisis Counselor.* Nashville: Abingdon Press, 1986.

Wakerman, Elyce. *Father Loss.* Garden City, NY: Doubleday, 1984.

Webster's Ninth Collegiate Dictionary (1988), s.v. "empathy."

Weiss, Abner. *Death and Bereavement–A Halakhic Guide.* New York: Ktav, 1991.

Westberg, Granger. *Good Grief.* Philadelphia: Fortress Press, 1962.

Wimberly, Edward. *Pastoral Counselling and Spiritual Values: A Black Point of View.* Nashville: Abingdon, 1982.

Wolowelsky, Joel. "Self-Confrontation and the Mourning Rituals." *Judaism* 129 (Winter 1984): 107–111.

Zlotowitz, Meir. *The Kaddish.* ArtScroll Jewish Heritage Series. New York: Mesorah, 1983.

HEBREW SOURCES

Note: I have translated all Hebrew texts myself, unless indicated otherwise within the text of the book.

Classical Sources (in chronological order)

Mikraot Gedolot edition of the Torah (The Five Books of Moses), including classical commentaries such as *Targum Onkelos* and *Targum Yonatan* (Aramaic translation/commentaries), Rashi, Tosafot, Nahmanides, Or Hahayyim, Ibn Ezra, Sforno, Rashbam, and Kli Yakar. New York: Friedman, 1971.

Mikraot Gedolot edition of the *Tanakh* (The Prophets and Writings), including classical commentaries such as Rashi, Radak, Metzudot, Gersonides. New York: Friedman, 1971.

The Babylonian Talmud, various selections plus classical talmudic commentaries including Rashi, Tosafot, R. Asher, R. Hannanel, Alfasi, Maharsha, R. Yonah, Meiri, R. Nissim, Ritva, R. Gershom, Maharal, Ramban, *Shitah Mekubetzet,* Nimukei Yosef, Maharitz Hayyot. Gateshead: Judaica Press; New York: Friedman-Otzar Sefarim, 1973.

The Jerusalem Talmud, various selections plus commentaries of Radbaz, Korban Ha'edah, and Pnei Moshe. Jerusalem: 1975.

Midrash Rabbah, including commentaries of Yefeh Anaf, Matnot Kehuna, R. Zev Einhorn, and R. David Luria. Vilna: Romm, n.d. Reprint, Jerusalem, 1961.

Midrash Tanhuma. Jerusalem: Eshkol, 1972.

Midrash Yalkut Shimoni. New York: Pardes/Title, 1944.

Sifre and *Sifra.* Jerusalem, 1983.

Maimonides, Moses. *Mishneh Torah/Yad Hahazakah* (Code of Jewish Law), with commentaries of Ravad, Lehem Mishneh, Kesef Mishneh, Magid Mishneh, Hagahot Maimoniyot. New York: Friedman, 1963.

Codes of S'mag and Behag.

Rabbenu Yaakov. *Tur Shulhan Arukh, Yoreh De'ah,* sections 335–403, with commentaries of Bah, Perisha, and Beit Yosef. Bnei Brak: Rubenstein, n.d.

Caro, Yosef, and Isserles, Moses. *Shulhan Arukh* (Code of Jewish Law), *Yoreh De'ah,* sections 335–403 plus commentaries of Shakh, Taz, Sema, Magen Avraham, R. Elijah of Vilna, Shiurei Brakhah, and Divrei Shaul. New York: Friedman, 1966.

Premodern and Modern Sources

Breisch, Yakov. *Responsa Helkat Yaakov.* Jerusalem, n.d.

Danzig, Abraham. *Hokhmat Adam.* Jerusalem: Levin-Epstein, n.d.

Eisenstein, Judah D. *Otzar Dinim Uminhagim (A Digest of Jewish Laws and Customs).* Tel Aviv, reprint, 1970.

Epstein, Yehiel. *Arukh Hashulhan.* New York: Friedman, n.d.

Feinstein, Moshe. *Responsa Igrot Moshe.* New York: Moriah, 1959.

Greenwald, Y. Y. *Kol Bo Al Aveilut.* New York: Feldheim, 1973.

Hachen, A. *Daat Mikra on Psalms.* Jerusalem: Mosad Harav Kook, 1979.

Hakohen, Yisrael Meir. *Mishnah Brurah.* Israel: Mishnah Brurah Press, 1961.

Levine, Aaron. *Zikhron Meir.* Toronto: Zikhron Meir, 1985.

Tukaczinski Y. M. *Gesher HaHayyim.* Jerusalem, 1960.

Waldenberg, Eliezer. *Responsa Tzitz Eliezer.* Jerusalem, n.d.

———. *Responsa Ramat Rahel.* Jerusalem, n.d.

Weinberg, Yehiel Y. *Responsa Seridei Eish.* Jerusalem: Mosad Harav Kook, 1977.

Weiss, Y. Y. *Responsa Minhat Yitzhak.* Jerusalem, n.d.

Index

ABOUT THE AUTHOR

Joseph S. Ozarowski studied at Yeshivat Sha'alvim in Israel and received his rabbinic ordination from Hebrew Theological College, Skokie, Illinois, and his doctorate from Lancaster Theological Seminary, Lancaster, Pennsylvania. He is the author of numerous articles and has served pulpits in Pennsylvania, California, and the Midwest. Ozarowski currently serves as rabbi of the Elmont Jewish Center, Elmont, New York. He is a national officer of the Rabbinical Council of America and has chaired the Pastoral Care Committee at Franklin Hospital Medical Center, Valley Stream, New York. Rabbi Dr. Ozarowski is married and has four children.